2011–2012
Progress
of the World's
Women

UN Women is the United Nations organization dedicated to gender equality and the empowerment of women. A global champion for women and girls, UN Women was established to accelerate progress on meeting their rights worldwide.

UN Women supports United Nations Member States as they set global standards for achieving gender equality, and works with governments and civil society to design laws, policies, programmes and services needed to implement these standards. It stands behind women's equal participation in all aspects of life, focusing on five priority areas: increasing women's leadership and participation; ending violence against women; engaging women in all aspects of peace and security processes; enhancing women's economic empowerment; and making gender equality central to national development planning and budgeting. UN Women also coordinates and promotes the United Nations system's work in advancing gender equality.

View the Report at:
http://progress.unwomen.org

© UN Women 2011

IN PURSUIT OF
JUSTICE

This book is a gift from
Norm & Sally Christensen
Humboldt Library Foundation
"Buy a Book" Campaign
www.humboldtlibraryfoundation.org

HUMBOLDT LIBRARY FOUNDATION
OPEN THE WORLD

UN WOMEN
United Nations Entity for Gender Equality
and the Empowerment of Women

Foreword from Ban Ki-moon

Secretary-General of the United Nations

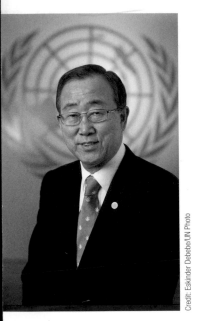

It is fitting that this edition of *Progress of the World's Women*, with its focus on justice, is being published in the first year of the life of UN Women. The international community set up this important new agency in affirmation of a simple fact: achieving women's equality is a fundamental human right and a social and economic imperative.

Justice is central to the effort to help women become equal partners in decision-making and development. Without justice, women are disenfranchised, disempowered and denied their rightful place. But with sound legal and justice systems, women can flourish and contribute to the advancement of society as a whole, including by helping to improve those very same systems for future generations – daughters and sons alike.

This edition of *Progress of the World's Women* examines the injustice that far too many women endure. It also highlights how essential it is to see women as far more than victims, but as agents of change. The report's comprehensive statistics, compelling stories and keen analysis combine to offer a sound basis for action. I commend it to all people who care about building a world of equality, opportunity and justice for all.

Ban Ki-moon

Foreword from Michelle Bachelet

Under-Secretary-General and Executive Director, UN Women

As the first major UN Women report, this edition of *Progress of the World's Women* reminds us of the remarkable advances that have been made over the past century in the quest for gender equality and women's empowerment. Even within one generation we have witnessed a transformation in women's legal rights, which means that today, 125 countries have outlawed domestic violence, 115 guarantee equal property rights and women's voice in decision-making is stronger than ever before. Today, 28 countries have reached or surpassed the 30 percent mark for women's representation in parliament, putting women in the driving seat to forge further change.

Progress of the World's Women 2011–2012: In Pursuit of Justice shows that where laws and justice systems work well, they can provide an essential mechanism for women to realize their human rights. However, it also underscores the fact that, despite widespread guarantees of equality, the reality for many millions of women is that justice remains out of reach.

The report highlights the practical barriers that women — particularly the poorest and most excluded — face in negotiating justice systems and the innovative approaches that governments and civil society are pioneering to overcome them. It explores the ways in which women are reconciling guarantees of their rights with the realities of living within plural legal systems. And it highlights the severe challenges that women face in accessing justice in the aftermath of conflict, as well as the enormous opportunities for change that can emerge in these most difficult times.

I am privileged to be the first Executive Director of UN Women, an agency that was created because of the growing recognition that women are central to development, peace and security goals and that equality for woman and girls lies at the heart of achieving the Millennium Development Goals. For UN Women to meet the expectations that spurred its creation it must inspire all of our partners — including governments, United Nations agencies and non-governmental organizations — with concrete and replicable examples of how change happens to expand women's access to justice.

This edition of *Progress of the World's Women* builds on the work of colleagues across the United Nations system in highlighting women's part in strengthening the rule of law and outlines a vision for the future in which women and men, worldwide, can work side-by-side to make gender equality and women's empowerment a reality.

Michelle Bachelet

Credit: Marco Castro/UN Photo

Contents: In Pursuit of Justice

Chapter 2: The Justice Chain

Chapter 3: Legal Pluralism and Justice for Women

Contents: In Pursuit of Justice

Part II: Gender Justice and the Millennium Development Goals

Ten Recommendations to Make Justice Systems Work for Women

Annexes

Introduction

In 1911, women were allowed to vote in just two countries of the world. Today, a century later, that right is virtually universal.[1] During this time, women have continuously expanded their political rights so that, at the time of writing, 28 countries have reached or exceeded the 30 percent critical mass mark for women in parliament and 19 women are currently serving as elected Heads of State or Government.[2] Alongside women's greater political influence, there has been a growing recognition of women's rights, not only political and civil, but also economic, social and cultural. To date, 186 Member States worldwide have ratified the Convention on the Elimination of All Forms of Discrimination against Women (CEDAW), which entered into force in 1981, signalling their commitment to fulfilling the human rights of women and girls and breaking down the barriers to achieving gender equality and justice.[3]

Greater economic empowerment for women has been achieved through progressive legislation that has prohibited discriminatory practices, guaranteed equal pay, provided for maternity and paternity leave, and put in place protection against sexual harassment in the workplace. Governments have turned their back on the idea that violence against women is a private affair, with laws in every region now outlawing this scourge in its many manifestations. Legislation prohibiting discrimination based on sex with respect to inheritance and citizenship, laws that guarantee equality within the family and policies to ensure that women and girls can access services including health and education have also contributed to significant advances in women's standard of living.

And yet, while examples of countries making immense strides in promoting gender equality abound, in many more, women continue to be deprived of economic resources and access to public services. All too often, women are denied control over their bodies, denied a voice in decision-making, and denied protection from violence. Some 600 million women, more than half the world's working women, are in vulnerable employment, trapped in insecure jobs, often outside the purview of labour legislation.[4] In the developing world, more than one third of women are married before the age of 18, missing out on education and exposed to the risks of early pregnancy.[5] Despite major progress on legal frameworks at national, regional and international levels, millions of women report experiencing violence in their lifetimes, usually at the hands of an intimate partner. Meanwhile, the systematic targeting of women for brutal sexual violence is a hallmark of modern conflicts.[6]

Pervasive discrimination against women creates major hurdles to achieving rights and hinders progress on all of the Millennium Development Goals – the benchmarks that the international community has set to eradicate extreme poverty – from improving maternal health, to achieving universal education and halting the spread of HIV and AIDS.

This volume of *Progress of the World's Women* starts with a paradox: the past century has seen a transformation in women's legal rights, with countries in every region expanding the scope of women's legal entitlements. Nevertheless, for most of the world's women the laws that exist on paper do not always translate into equality and justice. In many contexts, in rich and poor countries alike, the infrastructure of justice – the police, the courts and the judiciary – is failing women, which manifests itself in poor services and hostile attitudes from the very people whose duty it is to fulfil women's rights. As a result, although equality between women and men is guaranteed in the constitutions of 139 countries and territories, inadequate laws and loopholes in legislative frameworks, poor enforcement and vast implementation gaps make these guarantees hollow promises, having little impact on the day-to-day lives of women.[7]

The Convention on the Elimination of All Forms of Discrimination against Women (CEDAW)

CEDAW is an international treaty adopted by the United Nations General Assembly to protect and promote women's rights. Since entering into force in 1981, the legally binding treaty has been ratified by 186 United Nations Member States (see Annex 5).

The Convention lays out a clear definition of what constitutes discrimination against women and sets out a comprehensive agenda for achieving gender equality. It recognizes that as a result of historic discrimination, women do not start on an equal footing to men and therefore formally equal laws may produce unequal outcomes for women. Instead, the Convention is based on the concept of *substantive equality*, which focuses on the outcomes and impacts of laws and policies.

The key elements of CEDAW that establish the definition and implications of substantive equality are:

- Discrimination is defined as any act that has 'the effect or purpose' of impairing women's equal enjoyment of their rights (article 1).

- States must pursue a policy of eliminating discrimination by 'all appropriate means'. This includes not just repealing discriminatory laws, but also ensuring that no action or practice of the State – or of any private 'person, organization or enterprise' – discriminates against women (article 2).

- States shall take 'all appropriate measures' in 'all fields' to ensure women's full advancement and the equal enjoyment of their rights (article 3).

- 'Temporary special measures', such as quotas, shall not be considered a form of discrimination, because their ultimate goal is to achieve gender equality (article 4).

- States must take 'all appropriate measures' to change social and cultural patterns of conduct, and eliminate prejudices and customary practices based on stereotypes or ideas about the inferiority of women (article 5).[8]

The Convention requires governments to incorporate CEDAW's definition of substantive equality into their legal framework and carry out comprehensive reviews of legislation and constitutions, to ensure that the entire legal framework supports gender equality. For States parties to the Convention, removing discriminatory laws is just the first step. To achieve substantive equality, governments are also responsible for the impact of laws, which means tailoring legislation to respond to the realities of women's lives.

CEDAW calls on governments to legislate to regulate the private as well as the public domain, which includes extending protection to women against family violence. The Convention is clear that where plural legal systems exist, States remain responsible for the impacts of *all* laws and must maintain oversight to ensure that women are not discriminated against.

Countries that have ratified the Convention are committed to submitting national reports, at least every four years, on measures they have taken to comply with their treaty obligations. Furthermore, under CEDAW's Optional Protocol, ratified by 100 countries, the CEDAW Committee, the Convention's monitoring body, is given the authority to consider a State's compliance with the Convention. Under the inquiry procedure, the CEDAW Committee can initiate and conduct investigations on large-scale and widespread violations of women's rights occurring within the jurisdiction of a State party. Under the Protocol's communication procedure, individual citizens of a State party can make a complaint regarding violations of rights protected under the Convention directly to the Committee. The jurisprudence of the Committee has developed primarily through the decisions published in response to individual communications, in which the Committee makes a ruling on any violation of CEDAW and suggests protective, corrective and anti-discriminatory remedies that the State should provide in order to rectify it.

A number of cases taken under the communication procedure of the Optional Protocol have established States' duties to exercise 'due diligence' in the implementation of laws through providing gender-responsive governance and functioning justice systems that meet women's rights (see Balancing the Scales).

Well functioning legal and justice systems can provide a vital mechanism for women to achieve their rights. Laws and justice systems shape society, by providing accountability, by stopping the abuse of power and by creating new norms about what is acceptable. The courts have been a critical site of accountability for individual women to claim rights, and in rare cases, to affect wider change for all women through strategic litigation (see Balancing the Scales).

Laws and justice systems have been the focus of women's activism because women have recognized both their potential and their current failings. Where laws are missing or discriminatory and the infrastructure of justice is broken, access to justice must mean more than simply helping women to access existing justice systems. This edition of *Progress of the World's Women* underscores that laws and justice systems that are biased against women's interests and reinforce unequal power relations between women and men, must themselves be transformed in order to fulfil the potential they hold for accelerating progress towards gender equality.

What does justice mean for women?

Justice is an ideal that has resonated throughout history, across all societies and cultures. But what is justice? When it comes to defining justice, women have a range of perceptions, closely linked to the injustices they see and experience around them. Justice may be collectively desired, but it is individually experienced.

A woman in Kalangala in Uganda describes the barriers she faces in accessing justice.	*'Sometimes, we are seriously wronged by other people, usually men. Men beat us or abuse us sexually…If you try to pursue a case to the Kalangala Police Station, no single boat owner will allow you to use their boat or engine to go. They always protect their fellow rich and powerful. In any case, even this means raising money for fuel and hire of a boat and the engine. In the end, you simply give up and suffer quietly.'* [9]
A woman in Scotland in the United Kingdom of Great Britain and Northern Ireland (United Kingdom) describes her pursuit of a decent wage for her work as a teaching assistant. She is paid an annual salary of approximately US$15,600. Road workers, who are usually men, employed by the same local council earn $30,000.	*'What would I like to see happen, to change this whole unjust, unfair and unlawful situation? Well it all comes down to accountability. There seems to be none. There is no accountability for the employers who spend millions of pounds defending rightful equal pay claims. There is no accountability for employers to recognize the real skills that are required and used in low paid women's jobs such as mine, because of the mindset that I do this work because I am a woman and it is unskilled "woman's work". I love my job but it is not, nor should it be, a labour of love.'* [10]
A woman who survived the 1994 genocide in Rwanda describes her experience of seeking justice.	*'I'm all alone. My relatives were killed in a horrible fashion. But I survived, to answer the strange questions that were asked by the ICTR [International Criminal Tribunal for Rwanda]. If you say you were raped, that is something understandable. How many times do you need to say it?…When I returned, everyone knew I had testified. My fiancé refused to marry me once he knew I had been raped…Today I would not accept to testify, to be traumatized for a second time. No one apologized to me…My house was attacked. My fiancé has left me. In any case, I am already dead.'* [11]
A young woman, from South Shooneh, Jordan describes her perception of injustice.	*'Girls are always treated with injustice. They have marriage imposed on them by the age of 16. But men are allowed to get their education and can work any place they want. There are families here who will not even allow their daughters to go to the community centre.'* [12]

The views of these women show that when it comes to justice, women want a range of things: like the woman in Jordan, who perceives injustice as not being able to make choices about who to marry and about her own education and freedom of movement, they want to exercise autonomy over their lives, to have equal opportunities with their male peers. Like the woman in Scotland, who condemns what she sees as the illegitimate use of the justice system by her employers to deny her a decent wage, they want fair reward for the work that they do and for the justice system to implement the laws that are on the books. Like the woman in Uganda, who perceives that men act together in pursuit of their collective interests to deny her access to justice, they want an accessible and responsive justice system. Like the woman in Rwanda, whose experience of testifying in court reinforced the stigma and shame she faced, they want an end to impunity for the crimes they are subjected to and they want the process of seeking justice to be dignified and empowering.

These women may have differing views of what justice means, but they all have in common the view that currently the law and justice systems are not working for them. Governments and donors have invested millions in reforming legal frameworks, in building court rooms and training justice providers, to strengthen the rule of law. So why is it not working for women?

When it comes to justice, women have a range of perceptions, closely linked to the injustices they see and experience around them.

Does the rule of law rule women out?

The rule of law, a cornerstone of good governance and democracy, requires that laws are in place to hold everyone to account, from the individual up to the government. It requires that laws are 'publicly promulgated, equally enforced and independently adjudicated'.[13] The rule of law is about the existence of laws, but it is also about implementation, including in challenging plural legal contexts and in post-conflict societies. This requires good governance and a functioning justice system that carries out its duties fairly, without bias or discrimination. This is the ideal. However, for millions of women and girls, the reality is that the rule of law means little in practice.

While law is intended to be a neutral set of rules to govern society, in all countries of the world, laws tend to reflect and reinforce the privilege and the interests of the powerful, whether on the basis of economic class, ethnicity, race, religion or gender. Justice systems also reflect these power imbalances. In all societies, women are less powerful than men and the two areas in which women's rights are least protected, where the rule of law is weakest and men's privilege is often most entrenched, are first, women's rights in the private and domestic sphere, including their rights to live free from violence and to make decisions about their sexuality, on marriage, divorce and reproductive health; and second, women's economic rights, including the right to decent work and the right to inherit and control land and other productive resources.

There are challenges at every stage, starting with legal frameworks (see Chapter 1). In some cases, laws overtly discriminate against women, according them fewer rights than men. Examples of this include laws that limit women's rights within the family, or those that prohibit women from passing on their citizenship to their husband or children, impacting on their civil and political rights, and access to public services. In other cases, the protection of the rule of law is not extended to the private domain where millions of women work and where they are most likely to experience violence.

Effective implementation of laws and of constitutional guarantees is a key challenge for making the rule of law a reality for women. The justice chain, the series of steps that a woman has to take to access the formal justice system, or to claim her rights, often breaks

International law makes it clear that governments are responsible for ensuring women's access to justice and eliminating discrimination in all justice systems.

down due to lack of capacity in the justice system and discriminatory attitudes of service providers, including the police and judiciary (see Chapter 2). Services that do not take into account the barriers that women face, due to social norms, poverty or lack of awareness are a major problem in all regions. In the criminal justice system, high levels of under-reporting and attrition, whereby cases are dropped before they come before a court, are indicative of a system that is failing women.

The existence of legal pluralism can also present challenges to the realization of the ideals of the rule of law for women (see Chapter 3). In most countries of the world, there is more than one set of laws in place. There are often multiple strands of law based on custom, ethnic or religious identity incorporated into the state system, as well as a plethora of non-state justice systems, such as village courts, which are completely outside the purview of the state system. Family laws on marriage, divorce, custody and maintenance, as well as inheritance laws are particularly likely to be subject to plural legal provisions, which sometimes contain elements of discrimination against women. Cases of violence against women are

commonly adjudicated by non-state justice systems that lack adequate oversight or accountability mechanisms. International law makes it clear that governments are responsible for ensuring women's access to justice and eliminating discrimination in all justice systems.

The weakness of the rule of law in conflict and post-conflict settings impacts on everyone, but has particularly severe consequences for women (see Chapter 4). The sexual violence that is a hallmark of conflict often spills over into peacetime, precisely at the moment when domestic justice systems are at their weakest. There is now a growing body of international law to deal with violations of women's rights in conflict, but there is a significant implementation gap, with only a fraction of perpetrators indicted and convicted for their crimes. For the millions of women who have been raped during and after conflict, or who have been internally displaced, losing their land and livelihoods, justice remains out of reach.

So, given all these challenges, how can the law and justice systems be made to work for women to overcome the inequality, violence and lack of choices they face?

Making justice systems work for women

Part I of *Progress of the World's Women* **addresses how justice systems can be made to work for women. It shows how legal reform is changing the landscape for women's rights in all regions. It showcases the initiatives of governments and civil society to transform justice systems and create new models to meet women's rights. It also highlights how women – as legislators, as lawyers and judges, as paralegals and community activists – are at the forefront of this transformation.**

Women around the world have used strategic litigation to demand justice for individuals, but also to enhance the rights of all women. These cases have been used to change national laws, demand enforcement of existing laws, strike down discriminatory customary law and revolutionize the scope of international law. The report identifies some of the most important legal cases over the past 30 years that have changed the landscape for women's rights (see Balancing the Scales).

Chapter 1: Legal Frameworks examines the progress that has been made in reforming legislative and constitutional frameworks to advance gender equality and women's rights. In the past 50 years, constitutions in more than half of the countries of the world have been redrafted or amended, an opportunity that has been seized upon by women to write gender equality into the legal fabric of their countries.[14]

The chapter draws on CEDAW to lay out a three-part reform agenda for governments to implement, aimed at: ending explicit discrimination against women; extending the protection of the rule of law to the private domain; and taking responsibility for the law's impact on women.

Women's rights advocates have set their sights not only on formal equality before the law, but also on ensuring that laws are implemented and have a positive impact on the day-to-day reality of women's lives. Discriminatory provisions, from restrictions on women's employment to their rights within marriage have been challenged and overturned.

The chapter highlights some of the main routes to reform, including through strategic litigation, women's campaigns for legal reform and the efforts of women legislators. In a number of countries, steep increases in women's representation in parliament have been accompanied by wide-ranging legal reforms that have advanced women's rights.

Chapter 2: The Justice Chain looks at the implementation of laws and focuses primarily on the formal justice system. With growing momentum around laws and policies to guarantee women's rights, there has also been increasing attention on the implementation gap.

The chapter shows that making justice systems responsive to women requires changes in the mandates, procedures and organizational cultures of the police, the courts and other service providers. Because of the particular barriers that women face, specialized, tailored and integrated services are needed. Women must also be aware of their rights and have the knowledge required to navigate the justice chain.

While there are no instant solutions, ensuring that women are present in justice services can help to enhance accountability and create a system that is responsive to women. Reporting of sexual assault increases if there are women in the police, pointing to the need to ensure that women are part of front line justice service delivery.

Chapter 3: Legal Pluralism and Justice for Women explores how to make justice systems work for women when, as is the case in most countries, there is more than one set of laws in place. Even in countries with a well-functioning formal system, only a small fraction of grievances are taken to a formal court.[15] This means that the overwhelming majority of women, as well as men, access justice through systems that are not entirely or not at all within the purview of the State.

This chapter highlights the responsibility of governments to address barriers to justice posed by the existence of plural legal systems. It also points to the many examples where governments are working with civil society to implement successful interventions in legally plural contexts to increase women's access to justice, empowering women to retain the cultural identities they choose and to demand the human rights they value and need.

These programmes include training of paralegals to help women to navigate justice systems; initiating dialogues on women's rights with customary leaders; and supporting women's engagement with indigenous courts.

Chapter 4: Justice for Women During and After Conflict shows how over the past two decades, international law has, for the first time, recognized both the gender specific impact of conflict and the central part women play in building peace and rebuilding post-conflict societies. Given that sexual violence is routinely used as a tactic of war, women's justice needs are most acute during and after conflict, just at the moment when the State is least able to deliver.

This chapter analyses what is required to ensure that justice for women is achieved in these challenging settings. It also investigates what justice for women means in post-conflict contexts. Women often prioritize reparative as well as retributive justice, so support for livelihoods, health care and education is needed alongside prosecutions of perpetrators of human rights abuses. The aftermath of conflict has often proved to be an important opportunity to 'rewrite the rules' as the State is rebuilt, ushering in progressive new constitutions and legal reform.[16]

Ensuring that women are present in justice services can help to enhance accountability and create a system that is responsive to women.

Addressing underlying gender inequalities through comprehensive reparations, ensuring women's voices are heard in truth commissions and harnessing the post- conflict moment to fundamentally reshape society in more gender equitable ways, holds the as yet unfulfilled promise of transformational change in women's lives.

Gender justice and the Millennium Development Goals

Part II of *Progress of the World's Women* analyses advances towards the Millennium Development Goals (MDGs) from a gender perspective.

The Millennium Declaration and the eight Goals agreed in 2000 collectively present a vision for a more just and equal world: a promise by 189 countries to achieve social justice for all.

All of the Goals – from reducing poverty and hunger, to achieving universal education and stopping the spread of HIV and AIDS – are interdependent and each one depends on making progress on gender equality and women's empowerment. Achieving these Goals is also an essential precondition for women to access justice. Without education, awareness of rights and decision-making power, women are often unable to claim their rights, obtain legal aid or go to court.

There has been important progress on some of the MDGs, with impressive gains in education, and reductions in poverty and child mortality. However, with the target date of 2015 in sight, it is increasingly clear that progress towards meeting many of the Goals is off-track. Inequality, including gender inequality, is holding back progress and there have been the fewest gains on those Goals that depend the most on women's empowerment, for instance maternal health. Women and girls, particularly those who live in rural areas or in the poorest households, are too often being left behind.

In the final four years of the MDGs framework, Part II makes the case for a stronger focus on gender equality across all the Goals as an integral part of progress overall and as an essential foundation for women's access to justice.

Funding for women's access to justice

Making justice systems work for women – whether through catalysing legal reform, or supporting legal aid, one-stop shops and training for judges – requires investment. Recognizing the importance of strengthening the rule of law, governments spend a significant amount on legal and judicial development and human rights. However, targeted funding for gender equality remains low.

Two major sources of funding for justice sector programming in middle and low income countries are the 24 donors that make up the Development Assistance Committee of the Organisation for Economic Cooperation and Development (OECD-DAC) and the World Bank. United Nations agencies are also significant funders of this work.

The OECD-DAC and the World Bank collect and publish data on their aid spending, including on gender equality. United Nations agencies are also starting to make available this data, but overall it is not yet possible to draw strong conclusions about their funding for gender equality and justice.

In 2009, the most recent year for which data are available, OECD-DAC donors allocated $4.2 billion to justice, with the United States of America (United States) and the European Union (EU) together accounting for 70 percent of this total. Iraq, Afghanistan, Mexico, the occupied Palestinian territory and Pakistan were the largest recipients of this aid.[17]

Out of the total of $4.2 billion, $206 million (5 percent) was allocated to programmes for which gender equality was a primary aim and $633 million (15 percent) was allocated to programmes for which gender equality was a secondary aim.[18] The EU allocated no funds to justice programmes in which gender equality was a primary aim in 2009.

Sweden, Canada, Denmark, Norway and Germany were the largest donors to justice programmes in which gender equality was a primary aim, supporting a range of activities including training for judges; legal aid for survivors of violence; women's participation in peacebuilding and reconciliation; reintegration of victims of trafficking; and awareness-raising campaigns to reduce early marriage. Guatemala, Burkina Faso, the Democratic Republic of the Congo, Afghanistan and Colombia received the most gender-focused justice aid in 2009.

Over the decade 2000 to 2010, according to the World Bank project database, the World Bank has allocated $874 billion to 6,382 grants and loans, of which $126 billion (14 percent) was allocated to public administration, law and justice.[19] Over this time, 21 projects totalling $1.2 billion included components on gender equality and the rule of law, supporting activities such as improving women-friendly court infrastructure; providing legal aid; recruitment and capacity building of paralegals; and policy advocacy for legal reforms.[20] The total allocated to the gender equality components of these projects amounted to just $7.3 million, a small fraction of the World Bank's expenditure on public administration, law and justice over the decade (see Figure below).

In December 2010, the World Bank concluded the process of replenishing the International Development Association (IDA) fund, with 51 donors pledging $49.3 billion to support the poorest countries between 2011 and 2014. In this round, four areas of special focus were agreed, of which gender equality was one.[21] This could present an important opportunity to ensure that women's access to justice receives a larger share of the World Bank's funding in the future.

World Bank funding for grants and loans, 2000–2010

Only a very small fraction of World Bank funding has been allocated to gender equality focused rule of law projects over the past decade.

Total amount the World Bank has allocated to 6,382 projects:
$874 billion

Total amount allocated to public administration, law and justice:
$126 billion (14%)

Total amount allocated to 21 rule of law and gender equality projects:
$1.2 billion (0.14%)

Total amount allocated to the gender equality components of these projects:
$7.3 million (0.001%)

Source: Minaya 2011.

Balancing the Scales:

Groundbreaking Legal Cases that have Changed Women's Lives

Women who refuse to stay silent in the face of injustice, who persist in spite of overwhelming obstacles to use all legal avenues available in pursuit of their cause, these women have changed the world.

Strategic litigation is the process of bringing a case to court with the goal of creating broader legal and social change. Alongside political lobbying and mobilizing social movements, it is a tactic that advocates have used to challenge gender discrimination and raise awareness of women's rights.

Where it is successful, strategic litigation can have groundbreaking results. By identifying gaps or changing laws that violate constitutional or human rights principles, such cases can motivate government action to provide for citizens, guarantee the equal rights of minorities or stop discrimination. The greatest impact is achieved when cases are part of wider campaigns for social change that provoke public debate and discussion in the media, to help ensure that progressive decisions are embraced by society as a whole.

The cases highlighted have increased women's access to justice in countries all over the world. Some have advanced the legal understanding of women's human rights under international law and confirmed that they are enforceable at the national level; some have enforced or clarified laws already on the books; some have challenged laws that should be repealed; and some have created new laws. All have led to positive changes in women's lives.

When a husband rapes his wife, it is a crime

Meera Dhungana on behalf of FWLD v HMG

In Nepal, married women subjected to rape by their husbands had no recourse to justice until 2002, when the Forum for Women, Law and Development (FWLD) brought a case to the Supreme Court. The case invalidated the provision of the criminal code that exempted husbands from being charged with the rape of their wives.[1]

In rejecting the Government's argument that outlawing marital rape would offend Hindu beliefs, the ruling also ended the conflict between the country's Muluki Ain civil code, based on Hindu religious principles, and the 1990 Constitution, which pledges to end all forms of gender discrimination. The Court stated:

'Sexual intercourse in conjugal life is a normal course of behaviour, which must be based on consent. No religion may ever take it [marital rape] as lawful because the aim of a good religion is not to hate or cause loss to anyone.'[2]

The Court ordered Parliament to amend the rape law, but the penalty for marital rape was set at only six months' imprisonment, significantly lower than for other types of sexual assault. FWLD went back to court, winning a decision that the difference in penalties was discriminatory and that the law must be amended.[3]

Cases such as these reflect sweeping changes to the assumption that a wife implicitly consents to all sexual activity. By April 2011, at least 52 States had explicitly outlawed marital rape in their criminal codes (see Annex 4).

Women have the right to be free from sexual harassment in the workplace

Vishaka v State of Rajasthan

When Bhanwari Devi was gang-raped by local men while doing her job as a social worker in a village in Rajasthan, India she not only initiated criminal proceedings, but she also sought a broader remedy for other working women. Supported by five women's organizations, including Vishaka, she took the case to the Indian Supreme Court, where in 1997 she eventually won watershed recognition of sexual harassment in the workplace, against which the Government had an obligation to provide legal protection.

Undeterred by the absence of existing sexual harassment laws, the Court's decision recognized the right to gender equality and to a safe working environment, free from sexual harassment or abuse, based on the Constitution and India's international obligations under CEDAW.[4] The Court used the case to produce the first enforceable civil law guidelines on the rights of working women to be free from violence and harassment in both public and private employment. This prompted the Government to introduce a long-awaited bill prohibiting sexual harassment in the workplace in 2007.[5]

The case has also inspired other reformers in the region. In 2009, the Supreme Court of Bangladesh, referring to the Vishaka case, recognized that the 'harrowing tales of repression and sexual abuse of women in their workplaces' were a result of the Government's failure to enact a sexual harassment law. The detailed guidelines on protection against sexual harassment set out in the case now have the force of law in Bangladesh until the Government enacts the relevant legislation.[6] Similarly, in Pakistan, advocates looked to the Vishaka guidelines in preparation for their successful push for legislation to protect women from harassment in the workplace.[7]

Salman Usmani

Bhanwari Devi in her house in a village near Jaipur, India in 2007.

It is not enough to have laws in place, they must be implemented

Şahide Goekce (deceased) v Austria and Fatma Yildirim (deceased) v Austria

Şahide Goekce and Fatma Yildirim were both murdered by their husbands following years of brutal abuse. Despite reporting the violence to the police and obtaining protection orders, lack of coordination among law enforcement and judicial officials resulted in repeated failure to detain the offenders and ensure the women's safety.[8]

Two non-governmental organizations (NGOs) took the cases to the CEDAW Committee under the Optional Protocol. The Committee's decisions on the cases in 2007 were of global significance because they made clear that the State's obligation to protect women from domestic violence extends beyond passing laws. The Committee found that Austria had failed to act with 'due diligence', by not ensuring that the law was implemented properly. In the Goekce case the Committee said:

'In order for the individual woman victim of domestic violence to enjoy the practical realization of the principle of equality of men and women and of her human rights and fundamental freedoms, the political will…must be supported by State actors, who adhere to the State party's due diligence obligations.'[9]

In response to the Committee's recommendations and the media attention that surrounded the case, the Austrian Government introduced and accelerated legal reforms to protect women from violence, including an amendment to the Code of Criminal Procedure, new protection measures and the creation of specialized domestic violence prosecutors. In order to support these reforms, the Government increased funding for implementation of the law by 60 percent in 2007.[10]

Maria da Penha Fernandes v Brazil

As she slept at her home in May 1983, Maria da Penha Fernandes was shot by her husband. Having suffered years of debilitating abuse, the mother of three children was left paralyzed from the waist down. Two weeks after her return from the hospital, her husband attempted to electrocute her. The case languished in the criminal justice system for years and Maria's husband remained free for nearly two decades. When he was finally sentenced in 2002, he served just two years in prison.

Maria da Penha, March 2011, Brazil.

In this landmark ruling, the Inter-American Court of Human Rights held the Government of Brazil responsible under international law for failing to take effective action to prosecute and convict perpetrators of domestic violence. It stated that:

'Failure to prosecute and convict the perpetrator…is an indication that the Brazilian State condones the violence suffered by Maria da Penha and this failure by the Brazilian courts to take action is exacerbating the direct consequences of the aggression by her ex-husband.'[11]

The case contributed to the growing international consensus that States have a legal obligation to take positive steps, measured by the standard of 'due diligence', to uphold women's human rights.

In 2006, the Government of Brazil enacted domestic violence legislation, symbolically named the Maria da Penha Law on domestic and family violence, mandating preventative measures, special courts and tough sentences.[12] Maria da Penha continues to campaign for justice for survivors of domestic abuse and is outspoken about the need for thorough implementation of the law.

Intersectional discrimination can be challenged

Lovelace v Canada

After getting a divorce, Sandra Lovelace, an Aboriginal Maliseet woman, wanted to return to live on her reservation. However, according to Canada's Indian Act, she could no longer claim this right because she had lost her legal 'Indian status' when she married a non-Aboriginal man.

In this groundbreaking 1981 decision, the United Nations Human Rights Committee decided that the Indian Act amounted to a violation of Canada's human rights obligations. The Committee found that the restrictions in the Act were neither reasonable nor necessary to preserve Maliseet identity and in fact interfered with Sandra Lovelace's right to enjoy her culture.[13]

The decision prompted international discussion about the 'intersectional' discrimination faced by groups such as indigenous women, who are discriminated against on the basis of their ethnicity, which is compounded by the discrimination that they experience on the basis of their gender. Sandra Lovelace used the Committee's decision to campaign for the law to be changed and in 1985, the Government of Canada responded by amending the Indian Act to eliminate gender discrimination in determining 'Indian status'.[14]

Inspired by the Lovelace case, advocates have continued to challenge laws that discriminate against Aboriginal women. Strategic litigation in Canada has continued over the right to 'Indian status' for children on the basis of the gender of their grandparents.[15] Sandra Lovelace continues to campaign for Aboriginal women's rights and in 2005 she became the first Aboriginal woman elected to the Canadian Senate, representing New Brunswick.

Newly elected Senator Sandra Lovelace in Canada's Fredricton Legislature in 2005.

Noel Chenier/ CP Photo/ New Brunswick Telegraph-Journal

Customary inheritance laws must comply with guarantees of equality

Bhe v Khayelitsha Magistrate

When the father of Nonkululeko and Anelisa Bhe died, under the rule of primogeniture in African customary law and the Black Administration Act, their house became the property of the eldest male relative of the father, in this case their grandfather. The girls' mother took action and in recognition of its wider significance, the South African Human Rights Commission and the Women's Legal Centre Trust joined the case to seek relief on behalf of all women and children in a similar situation.

The Constitutional Court of South Africa declared in 2004 that the rule of primogeniture and the customary law was unconstitutional, because it violated women's rights. The Court said:

> 'The principle of primogeniture…violates the right of women to human dignity…it implies that women are not fit or competent to own and administer property. Its effect is also to subject these women to a status of perpetual minority, placing them automatically under the control of male heirs, simply by virtue of their sex and gender.'[16]

The Court further found that the Black Administration Act was anachronistic and racially discriminatory, since it solidified 'official' customary law and created a parallel system of succession for Black Africans. The Court implicitly recognized that the discrimination that resulted was 'intersectional', since 'the impact of the provisions falls mainly on African women and children, regarded as arguably the most vulnerable groups in our society.'[17]

Campaigners are working to raise awareness of this decision to ensure that all widows and children, especially those in rural areas, can benefit from it.

Discriminatory citizenship laws are incompatible with constitutional guarantees of equality

Unity Dow v Attorney General of the Republic of Botswana

Despite being a citizen born and raised in Botswana, the law held that because Unity Dow had married a foreigner, their two children born in Botswana required residence permits to stay in the country, could only leave the country on their father's passport, would not be allowed to vote and would be denied the free university education available to citizens.

In challenging the Government, Unity Dow declared:

'The time that women were treated as chattels or were there to obey the whims and wishes of males is long past and it would be offensive to modern thinking and the spirit of the Constitution to find that the Constitution was framed deliberately to permit discrimination on the grounds of sex.'[18]

The landmark 1992 case extended legal protection for women by successfully arguing that the guarantee of equality under the Constitution invalidated the section of Botswana's Citizenship Act that prohibited women who married foreign men from passing the rights and privileges of citizenship on to their children.[19] Since this case, at least 19 countries in Africa have enacted reforms to provide for greater gender equality in their citizenship laws.[20]

Rosey Boehm Photography

Unity Dow, speaking at the 2nd UniSA Nelson Mandela Lecture in 2009.

Women have the right to an abortion in certain circumstances

Judgment of the Constitutional Court of Colombia

In 2006, Women's Link Worldwide launched a strategic litigation case on behalf of Martha Solay, who was two months pregnant when she was diagnosed with cancer. Colombia's laws prohibited doctors from performing an abortion to enable her to receive life-saving chemotherapy. The lawyers argued before the Constitutional Court that consistency between the international human rights treaties that Colombia had ratified, including CEDAW, and national law was compulsory, not optional.

In overturning one of the world's most restrictive abortion laws, the Court held that the criminal prohibition of abortion in all circumstances violates women's fundamental rights and it also affirmed that the procedure must be accessible in certain cases. The Court stated:

'Sexual and reproductive rights…emerge from the recognition that…gender equality…and the emancipation of women and girls are essential to society. Protecting sexual and reproductive rights is a direct path to promoting the dignity of all human beings and a step forward in humanity's advancement towards social justice.'[21]

In response to the decision, the Government amended the penal code, developed clear rules regarding the provision of abortion services, issued technical guidelines based on the recommendations of the World Health Organization and made abortion available through the public health system.[22]

Recently however, political support for the implementation of these laws has been questioned. In 2010, the United Nations Human Rights Committee expressed concern that 'health-service providers refuse to perform legal abortions and that the Procurator-General does not support enforcement of the relevant Constitutional Court ruling'.[23] The campaign for full implementation of the Court's ruling continues.

Sexual violence is a tactic of war and a war crime

Prosecutor v Tadić; Prosecutor v Furundžija; Prosecutor v Kunarac et al.; Prosecutor v Akayesu; Prosecutor v Delalic; and Prosecutor v Krstic

Although it has long been possible to prosecute rape in war under the general prohibition of 'inhumane acts' in the Geneva Conventions, the conflict in the former Yugoslavia galvanized the international community to develop specific international law on sexual violence against women in armed conflict.[24]

The Statutes of the International Criminal Tribunal for the former Yugoslavia and the International Criminal Tribunal for Rwanda included rape as a crime against humanity. The case law expanded the scope further, finding that rape and other gender-based crimes are tactics of war that can amount to genocide and torture and as such are regarded as significant violations of international criminal law.

The Akayesu case at the International Criminal Tribunal for Rwanda produced the first convictions on charges of rape and sexual violence at the Tribunals, confirming that rape can constitute an instrument of genocide and is a crime against humanity.[25] The indictment did not initially include charges of sexual violence, but after a witness on the stand spontaneously testified about the gang rape of her six-year-old daughter, members of the bench questioned the witnesses and encouraged prosecutors to amend the indictment to include charges of rape.[26]

Perhaps the most significant legacy of these cases was their influence on the codification of sexual violence in the Rome Statute, which established the International Criminal Court in 2002, the first such court with the authority to punish crimes in armed conflicts. The Tribunals' work also brought about wider international understanding of sexual and gender-based violence in war. The landmark Security Council resolution 1820 has since confirmed that sexual violence can amount to a war crime, a crime against humanity and an act of genocide.

The mothers of murdered young women in Ciudad Juárez, Mexico in 2004.

Reparations for violence against women must be 'transformative'

Gonzalez and others ('Cotton Field') v Mexico

Hundreds of women, mostly young and poor, have been murdered in Ciudad Juárez in Mexico over the past two decades. Many of the women were abducted and subjected to sexual violence and torture before being killed. Their bodies have later been found hidden in rubble or abandoned in deserted areas near the city. In November 2001, eight bodies were discovered in a cotton field.

In 2009, the 'Cotton Field' case at the Inter-American Court of Human Rights, established that violence against women in Ciudad Juárez was part of a pattern of systematic violence based on gender, age and social class. The Court stated:

'these crimes…have been influenced…by a culture of gender-based discrimination which…has had an impact on both the motives and the method of the crimes, as well as on the response of the authorities… the indifferent attitudes that have been documented in relation to the investigation of these crimes…appear to have permitted the perpetuation of the violence against women in Ciudad Juárez.'[27]

The enduring significance of this case may lie in its approach to reparations. As well as providing monetary compensation for the families, the Government of Mexico was called upon to provide symbolic redress and guarantees of non-repetition, including a commitment to investigate the murders and implement gender training for the police. The Court declared that the reparations should be 'oriented to identify and eliminate the structural factors of discrimination' and in doing so should aim at transforming the underlying gender inequalities that gave rise to the violence.[28]

Legal Frameworks

CASE STUDY: **Nepal**

Over the past two decades, legal reforms have transformed the landscape for gender equality in Nepal, ensuring greater economic security for women, protecting them from violence, safeguarding their sexual and reproductive rights and amplifying their voices in decision-making.

While Nepal's 1990 Constitution decreed that 'all citizens shall be equal before the law', discriminatory laws in relation to citizenship, property ownership and inheritance remained on the statute books. However, in 1991, Nepal ratified CEDAW, providing major impetus for the women's movement to demand further reform.

In 1993, gender equality advocates filed a petition at the Supreme Court challenging discriminatory inheritance laws.[1] The Court asked the Government to introduce a bill within a year to reform existing family laws relating to property, but it was not until 2002 that Parliament finally passed the Country Code (11th Amendment) Act. The new law provided for equal inheritance rights for unmarried daughters and sons, but gender equality advocates were not satisfied. Women's property rights remained dependent on marital status and they were required to return their inherited property if they got married.[2]

In 2006, as Nepal emerged from a decade of conflict, further change was underway. The Nepal Citizenship Act was passed, enabling children to claim citizenship through their mothers for the first time. Moreover, the Gender Equality Act gave married women the right to keep inherited property, entitled women to use property without the consent of male family members and expanded divorce rights. The Act also extended the law to protect women, criminalizing domestic and sexual

violence.[3] These provisions built on strategic litigation brought in 2002, which led to the explicit criminalization of marital rape for the first time (see Balancing the Scales).

In 2007, the Ministry of Finance introduced gender-responsive budgeting, developing indicators to track the Government's expenditure on gender equality. As a result, spending categorized as directly responsive to women went up from 11 percent in 2007 to 17 percent in 2010, an increase of more than 50 percent.[4] Furthermore, in 2008, a 10 percent tax exemption was introduced for land registered in a woman's name to drive implementation of laws on property and inheritance. The exemption, aimed at incentivizing families to share their property with their daughters, sisters and wives was subsequently increased to 25 percent in cities and 30 percent in rural areas.[5] The impact of these measures has been significant: while in the 2001 census, 11 percent of households reported that some land was owned by women, according to data from 50 land revenue offices throughout Nepal, this figure had increased to 35 percent of households by 2009.[6]

The rights of women regarding their sexual and reproductive health have also been expanded. In 2002, abortion under certain circumstances was legalized and by 2008, working with civil society partners, the Government had trained nearly 500 providers throughout the country.[7] In 2009, a fund was created to ensure that

rural and poor women could access these services, and to educate both providers and the public on the law.[8] The maternal mortality rate nearly halved between 2001 and 2006, in part attributed to the increased availability of safe abortion and reproductive health services.[9]

In the 2008 elections, as a result of a quota, women's representation in the Constituent Assembly reached 33 percent, helping to maintain a consistently high profile for gender equality issues.[10] Sapana Pradhan Malla has long been an instrumental part of the campaign to expand women's rights in Nepal, first as an activist and now as a member of the Constituent Assembly:

'Nepal has witnessed great change in the last 20 years and women have been central to this, both as campaigners and legislators. I am proud to say that we now have in place a raft of progressive laws that guarantee gender equality. Many challenges remain, however, and we will not be satisfied until we have translated the promises of equality in our laws into substantive equality for all the women and girls of our country.'[11]

'Nepal has witnessed great change in the last 20 years and women have been central to this, both as campaigners and legislators. I am proud to say that we now have in place a raft of progressive laws that guarantee gender equality.'

Sapana Pradhan Malla

Rally on International Women's Day 2011 in Kathmandu, Nepal.

Introduction

Women parliamentarians in Rwanda drove through reforms that transformed women's rights to property and inheritance, and gave them legal protection against violence. An Indian woman who was raped at work refused to stay silent and as a result, after much legal work, there are now mandatory guidelines in India for combating sexual harassment in the workplace (see Balancing the Scales). Lawyers in the United Kingdom overturned a 250 year-old legal principle that considered it impossible for a man to rape his wife. The Turkish women's movement, after years of campaigning, finally rid the country of a family code that discriminated against women.

These and many other campaigns reflect the growing understanding that fundamental to women's access to justice is a legal and constitutional framework that guarantees women's rights. As the example of Nepal shows, laws have the power to shape society, by creating new norms and by bringing about social change. The law can provide a vital mechanism for women to hold individuals and institutions to account and to prevent abuse of power, particularly within the family and the workplace. Without a solid legal foundation, attempts to make courts more accessible to women, make police less hostile to their complaints and bring in other necessary reforms to the administration of justice, are likely to founder.

There has been significant progress on legal reform in favour of women's rights in the past 30 years. Globally, 139 constitutions include guarantees of gender equality, 125 countries outlaw domestic violence, at least 117 countries have equal pay laws, 173 guarantee paid maternity leave, and 117 outlaw sexual harassment in the workplace. Women have equal rights to own property in 115 countries and in 93 have equal inheritance rights.[12]

Despite this progress, in many contexts the legal framework remains fundamentally biased against women. In some cases, laws simply discriminate against women, affording them fewer or lesser rights than men. In many others, laws are based on a male standard of justice that assumes that women and men confront the law on an equal footing, which they rarely do. Consequently, even laws that on paper are gender neutral can have a biased impact.[13]

The two areas in which women's rights are least protected, where the rule of law is weakest and men's privilege is most fiercely guarded are, first, women's rights in the private and domestic sphere, including their rights to live free from violence and to make decisions about their sexuality, on marriage, divorce and reproductive health; and, second, women's economic rights, including the right to decent work and the right to inherit and control land and other productive resources.

The architects of CEDAW recognized the bias inherent in the law, outlining a visionary agenda for the legal, political and social reform that is needed to achieve women's rights. The Convention is based on the principle of substantive equality, which requires governments to review new and existing legislation to assess its actual impact on women and put in place laws that produce equal outcomes. Legal reform is needed to meet three key objectives:

Ending explicit legal discrimination against women. The most common examples of legal discrimination remain within family laws, on issues related to marriage and divorce, where women are accorded fewer rights than men. In too many countries still, women are not allowed to pass their citizenship to their children or foreign-born spouses, do not have the same rights to property or inheritance as men, or are barred from working in certain industries.

Extending the protection of the rule of law. Historically, legal jurisdiction has been divided between public and private matters, leaving the private sphere of the family 'outside justice'. As a result, violence against women, much of which occurs within the private domain, has not been widely legislated against until recently. Women's work in the domestic domain, as family, home-based and domestic workers, still largely remains outside the scope of legal protection.

Ensuring government responsibility for the impact of the law. The duty of governments to take responsibility for the law's different impacts on women and men has two key aspects. First, it is important to look beyond the letter of the law to prioritize implementation. Second, CEDAW requires governments to address the actual impact of the law, or lack of laws, on women.

This chapter looks in turn at each of these areas of reform to examine where progress has been made and where there is more to be done. It also examines how change has happened, showing how constitutional reform has brought about positive change in Uganda (see Box 1.1); how campaigns by women's organizations have catalysed sweeping legal reform in Turkey (see Box 1.2); how women in parliament have been instrumental in passing new laws and changing attitudes in Rwanda (see Box 1.5); and how strategic litigation has been used to hold governments and institutions to account for meeting women's rights (see Boxes 1.3 and 1.6).

Box 1.1 Women writing rights into the constitution

In the past 50 years, more than half the world's constitutions have been reformed or redrafted, an opportunity that has been seized upon by women to write gender equality into the legal fabric of their countries.[14]

Constitutions are the supreme law of the land, lying at the foundation of the institutional structure and the legal system, defining the relationship between both the State and its citizens, as well as between citizens.

Constitutions are powerful because, while legislation may be made and withdrawn according to the will of the political forces in power at any one time, constitutions are usually only amended, reformed or repealed at most once in a generation. Once gender equality guarantees and rights are entrenched in this way, they are less vulnerable to being rolled back when political will or leadership changes.

As with any legal mechanism, the true measure of the benefit of constitutional protection is whether it translates into real change in women's lives. Constitutional guarantees of equality can be used to amend or strike down legislation and other laws that discriminate

against women (see Balancing the Scales). Canada, Colombia, India and South Africa are among the countries that have set up special commissions to monitor the implementation of the gender equality provisions of their Constitutions.

Uganda passed a new Constitution in 1995, which guarantees gender equality and prohibits laws, customs and traditions that undermine women's empowerment. In 2005, the Equal Opportunities Commission was established to monitor implementation.

Since then, the Constitution has been used to introduce legal reform to advance women's rights. In 2009, The Ugandan National Assembly finally adopted a law criminalizing domestic violence and prohibiting female genital mutilation. A draft bill on marriage and divorce is currently before Parliament, which would significantly reform Ugandan family law to prohibit polygamy, guarantee women's right to choose their spouse and the right to divorce on equal terms to men.[15]

Women in parliaments and legal reform

Increases in women's representation in parliaments worldwide have often been followed by legal reform to expand women's rights and access to justice.

The former Yugoslav Republic of Macedonia 33%

Election Law (2002): 30 percent quota for the under-represented sex on candidate lists for elections to Parliament. Quotas introduced for local elections (2004).

CEDAW Optional Protocol was signed (2000) and ratified (2003). The National Commission to Combat Human Trafficking and Illegal Migration was created (2001); trafficking was added to the Criminal Code (2002). The Family Law was amended (2008) to include protection orders to prevent domestic violence. The Law on Equal Opportunities for Men and Women (2009) was amended to include direct and indirect forms of gender-based discrimination.

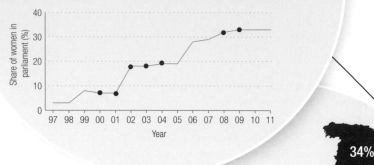

Costa Rica 39%

Reform to Electoral Code: Minimum 40 percent quota for women's participation (1996).

The Responsible Paternity Act (2001) promotes shared upbringing of children. The Law on Protection of Adolescent Mothers supports women with free health and education services (2002). The Law to Prevent Violence against Women (2008) introduced an integrated national monitoring system and services for survivors. Reform of the Labour Code (2009) specified terms of employment for domestic workers. Laura Chinchilla Miranda was elected first female president of Costa Rica (2010).

Spain 34%

Amendment to the Electoral Law (2007): Party electoral lists for lower house candidates must have a minimum of 40 percent and a maximum of 60 percent of both sexes.

The law on gender-based violence established the State Observatory on Violence against Women and specialized courts (2004). The first woman was chosen to preside over the Constitutional Court (2004). The law mandated affirmative action measures for employment and working conditions (2007). The share of women ministers reached 53 percent (2010).

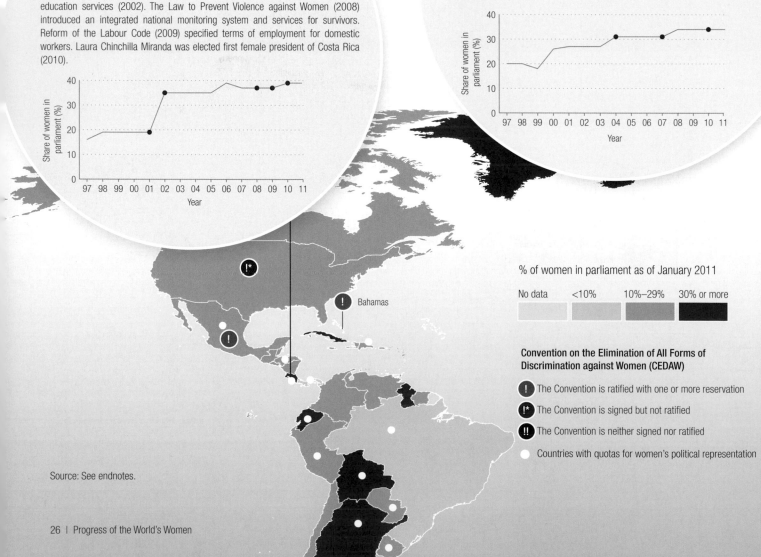

% of women in parliament as of January 2011

No data	<10%	10%–29%	30% or more

Convention on the Elimination of All Forms of Discrimination against Women (CEDAW)

! The Convention is ratified with one or more reservation

!* The Convention is signed but not ratified

!! The Convention is neither signed nor ratified

○ Countries with quotas for women's political representation

Bahamas

Source: See endnotes.

Rwanda

51%

Constitution (2003): Women must be in at least 30 percent of posts in decision-making at all levels. The Electoral Law (2006) granted women 30 percent of seats in local councils.

The Succession Act (1999) established gender equality in inheritance and property ownership. The National Land Policy (2004) and Land Law (2005) provided equality in statutory and customary land ownership. The Law on Prevention and Punishment of Gender-Based Violence was passed (2008); marital rape was criminalized (2009). 51 percent of parliamentarians are women; half of Supreme Court judges are women, including the President of the Court (2011).

United Republic of Tanzania

31%

Constitution amended (2000): Women to have no less than 20 percent (but no more than 30 percent) of seats in Parliament. At the local level, 25 percent of seats are reserved for women.

A gender unit was established in the Commission for Human Rights and Good Governance (2004). An amendment to the Land Act granted equal rights and access to land, loans and credit for women (2004). The Tanzania Police Female Network was established to protect women and children from violence (2007).

Nepal

33%

Under the 2007 Interim Constitution, women must be at least 33 percent of candidates for the Constituent Assembly. The Local Self Government Act (1999) mandates that 40 percent of candidates for municipal councils must be women.

The Gender Equality Act expanded women's inheritance and property rights (2006). The Finance Ministry adopted gender-responsive budgeting for all Government expenditure (2007). The Domestic Violence Crime and Punishment Act was passed (2009). A fund was created to ensure that rural and poor women can access abortion services (2009).

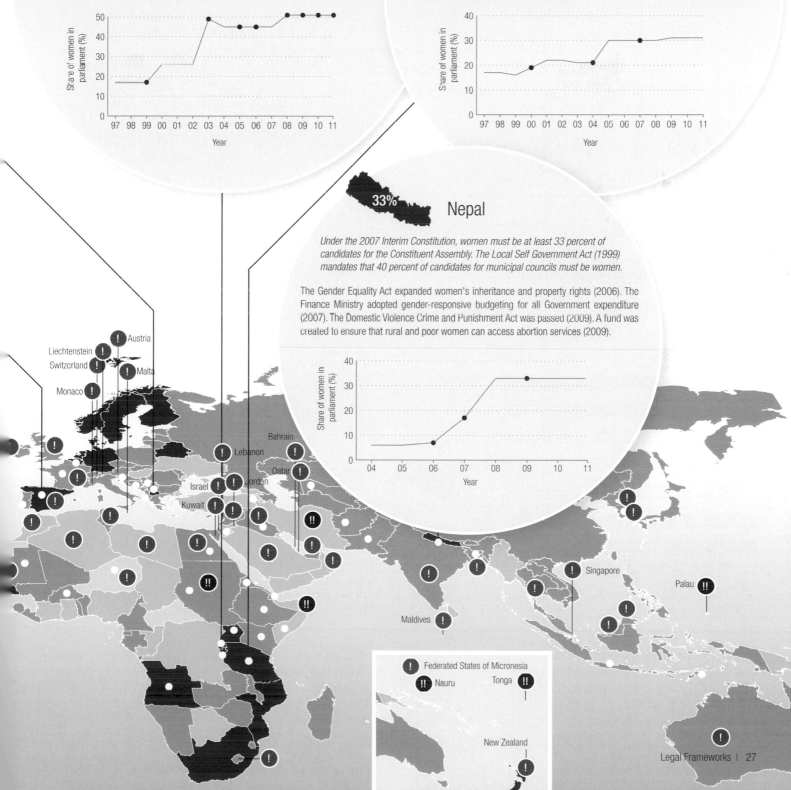

Ending explicit legal discrimination against women

There are a number of areas in which overt discrimination against women is enshrined in laws, restricting women's civil, political, economic and social rights. Reforming laws that explicitly discriminate against women is one important step in addressing gender-based bias in the rule of law.

In 49 countries, there are limitations on the industries in which women can work (see Figure 1.1). The most common restrictions are on jobs that involve heavy lifting or arduous work; jobs that threaten a woman's mental and physical health; and work in mines, quarries or underground. In 11 countries, female employment is restricted in jobs that are 'against women's morals'.[16]

These laws were originally conceived to protect women, but are now considered paternalistic and a limitation on women's economic opportunities. In 13 countries across six regions, laws specify that women must retire at a younger age than men.[17] Since women typically live longer but have lower savings than men, these laws can cause or exacerbate women's poverty in old age. In two rulings in 2008 and 2009, the European Court of Justice found that different pensionable ages for male and female civil servants in Greece and Italy violated the principles of equal pay. Both Governments responded by reforming their pension laws to eliminate this discrimination by 2013.[18]

FIGURE 1.1: Legal restrictions on women's right to work

In over one third of countries assessed, women are prohibited from working in some of the same industries as men.

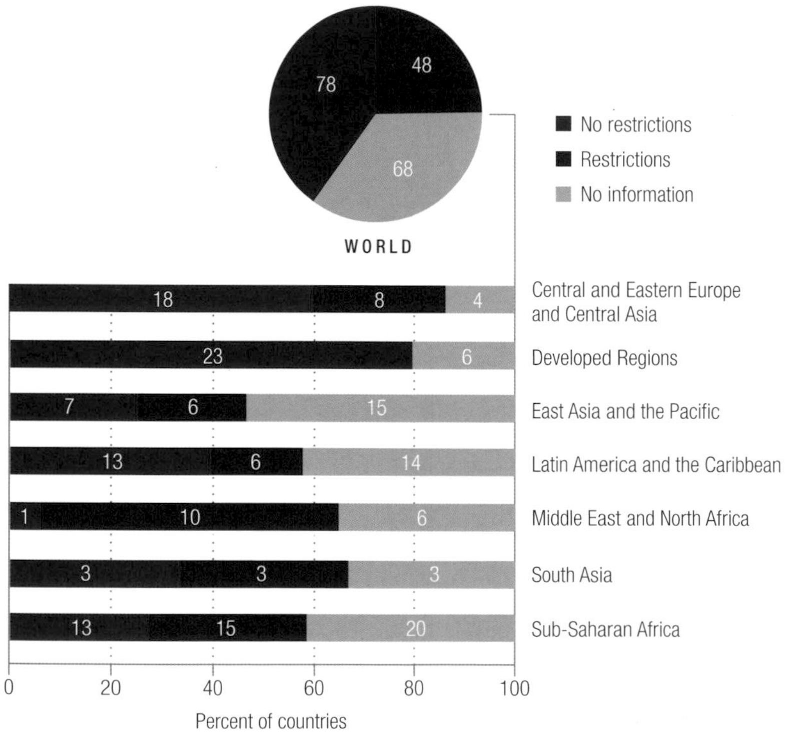

- No restrictions
- Restrictions
- No information

WORLD: 78, 48, 68

Region	No restrictions	Restrictions	No information
Central and Eastern Europe and Central Asia	18	8	4
Developed Regions	23		6
East Asia and the Pacific	7	6	15
Latin America and the Caribbean	13	6	14
Middle East and North Africa	1	10	6
South Asia	3	3	3
Sub-Saharan Africa	13	15	20

Percent of countries

Source: World Bank 2010f.

Note: Based on a World Bank assessment of labour laws using UN Women regional groupings.

Discriminatory laws on women's rights within the family also remain in place in many countries. These rights are guaranteed in several international treaties, including article 16 of CEDAW, which obliges States to take 'appropriate measures to eliminate discrimination against women in all matters relating to marriage and family relations'.[19] However, despite the almost universal ratification of CEDAW, 30 States have entered reservations to article 16 (see Figure 3.2 and Annex 5). In many cases, these reservations are in place because family laws are subject to plural legal provisions that can be discriminatory, the implications of which are discussed in Chapter 3.

There has been important progress in the reform of family laws. Acting on a case brought by the Ugandan Association of Women Lawyers, a court ruled that a law that made it harder for a woman to initiate a divorce than for a man was unconstitutional.[20] Partly as a result of this case, a new family law is currently being considered by the Ugandan Parliament, which will legally guarantee women's rights to divorce on equal terms to men (see Box 1.1). In Turkey, years of campaigning to reform the discriminatory family code was finally successful in 2001 (see Box 1.2).

FIGURE 1.2: Laws on age of marriage and incidence of early marriage

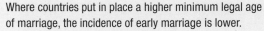

Where countries put in place a higher minimum legal age of marriage, the incidence of early marriage is lower.

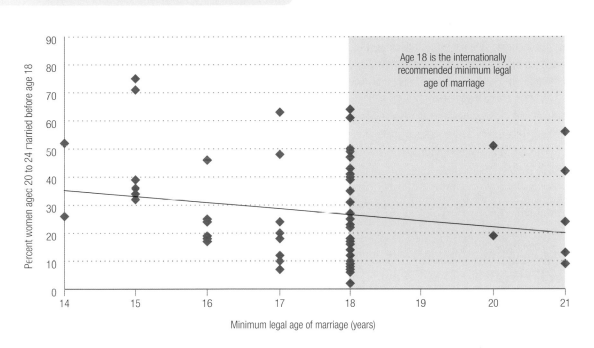

Source: UN Women analysis using prevalence of child marriage data from UNICEF 2011 and statutory legal age of marriage data from UN Statistics Division 2010b.

In 50 countries, the minimum legal age of marriage is lower for females, exposing girls to the risks of early marriage.[21] In the developing world, more than one third of women aged 20 to 24 report that they were married or in a union by the age of 18.[22] Early marriage curtails girls' opportunities for education and exposes them to the risks of early pregnancy and childbirth, the leading causes of death for girls aged 15 to 19 in developing countries.[23]

Tunisia was one of the first countries in the Middle East and North Africa to take steps to eliminate early marriage. The 1956 Tunisian Code of Personal Status set the minimum age of marriage at 15 years for girls, which was raised to 17 in 1964. In 1960, nearly half of Tunisian women were married before the age of 20, but by 2004, only 3 percent of girls between the ages of 15 and 19 years were married, divorced or widowed. In 2007, the age of marriage for women and men was finally equalized at 18 years.[24] In other countries too, where there are laws setting the minimum age of marriage at 18, there are lower rates of early marriage (see Figure 1.2).

In many countries, constitutions or other laws allow only men to transfer their nationality to their foreign spouses, or to have their children granted citizenship rights. In some cases, the law deprives women of their citizenship once they marry foreign nationals. These restrictions can limit women's exercise of other fundamental rights, to permanent residence, freedom of movement, the right to vote and to stand for office, as well as to access public services. Moreover, they can result in women and their children becoming stateless, without the legal protections provided by nationality from any State.

In most countries in the Middle East and North Africa, women do not enjoy fully equal citizenship and nationality rights. However, since 2002, Egypt, the Libyan Arab Jamahiriya and Morocco have introduced reforms to give women greater rights to transmit citizenship to children, while Algeria, Iraq, Qatar and Tunisia have taken steps to amend laws that discriminate against women in relation to passing citizenship to both children and spouses.[25]

Discriminatory laws on citizenship have also been subject to legal challenges, leading to important change. In the landmark citizenship case, *Unity Dow v Attorney General of the Republic of Botswana*, Unity Dow argued that the guarantee of equality under the Constitution of Botswana included an implicit prohibition of sex discrimination.[26] Having clarified the protection afforded by the Constitution, the Supreme Court struck down the section of Botswana's Citizenship Act that prohibited women who married foreign men from passing the rights and privileges of citizenship on to their children (see Balancing the Scales). Since this case, at least 19 countries in Africa have enacted reforms to provide for greater gender equality in their citizenship laws. Women now have equal rights to pass citizenship to children in

more than 80 percent of countries in Africa. However, further reform is needed, since in fewer than half of countries in Africa do women have the right to pass their citizenship to spouses.[27]

In recent years, the principle of non-discrimination, enshrined in numerous instruments of international law has been invoked to challenge laws that discriminate on the basis of sexual orientation. In the landmark *Toonen v Australia* case in 1994, the Human Rights Committee affirmed that article 26 of the International Covenant on Civil and Political Rights which guarantees 'equal and effective protection against discrimination on any ground such as…sex…or other status' prohibits discrimination on the grounds of sexual orientation.[28] Furthermore, international laws on gender equality clearly state that governments must promote and protect the rights of *all* women. The CEDAW Committee has recognized that discrimination on the basis of sexual orientation can exacerbate the discrimination that women may face on the basis of their gender, confirming that 'States parties must legally recognize and prohibit such intersecting forms of discrimination'.[29] The Committee has also urged States to reform laws that criminalize lesbian women and abolish penalties against them.[30]

FIGURE 1.3: Laws prohibiting consensual homosexual acts between adults, by region

Same-sex activity between consenting adults is criminalized in 40 percent of the countries surveyed.

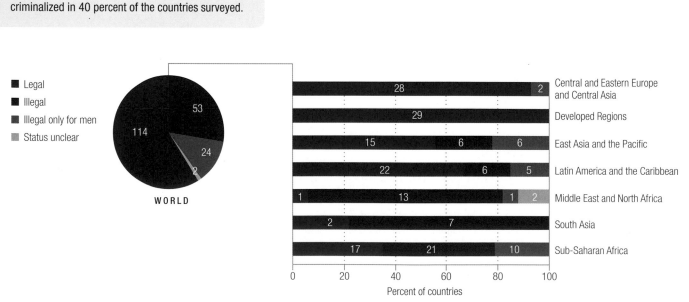

Source: Bruce-Jones and Itaborahy 2011.

In spite of these international commitments, in 53 countries, consensual homosexual acts between adult women are illegal (see Figure 1.3). Such laws and policies deny lesbian, transgender and bisexual women the protection of the law and limit their access to services. The Special Rapporteur on violence against women has expressed concern that 'women who...live out their sexuality in ways other than heterosexuality, are often subjected to violence and degrading treatment'.[31] The United Nations Special Rapporteur on the right to health recently urged the repeal of laws that discriminate in respect of sexual orientation and gender identity in order 'to meet core obligations of the right to health and create an environment enabling full enjoyment of that right'.[32]

Since 2000, a number of countries have decriminalized homosexuality, including Armenia, Fiji, Nepal and Nicaragua. Six countries prohibit discrimination on the basis of sexual orientation in their Constitutions: the Plurinational State of Bolivia, Ecuador, Portugal, South Africa, Sweden and Switzerland.[33]

Box 1.2 Turkish women's campaign for reform

Over the past decade, Turkey has witnessed major legislative reform on women's rights, in large part driven by advocacy and lobbying by the women's movement. The new civil code, passed in 2001 is based on the principle of equal rights and responsibilities within the household.

The campaign for these landmark legal achievements was long and hard fought. Once the Government of Turkey had ratified CEDAW in 1985, the women's movement seized the opportunity to lobby for reform of the civil code. Hopes were dashed when a series of petitions for change failed to obtain parliamentary approval. Throughout the 1990s, feminist advocates built the movement, highlighting how the civil code violated Turkey's own constitutional guarantee of gender equality, as well as its commitments under CEDAW.

By April 2000, a coalition government had prepared a draft civil code, integrating women's demands for full gender equality, but it was blocked by an alliance of conservative parliamentarians. The most controversial aspect of the women's demands was related to matrimonial property. Opponents claimed that the proposal that property acquired during the marriage should be divided equally was against Turkish traditions, would destroy the family, increase divorce rates and ultimately destroy Turkish society.

The women's movement responded by bringing together a broad coalition of more than 120 NGOs from all over the country. Women's rights organizations, representing different sectors of society and from different ideological viewpoints, came together to campaign on a common platform. One of the coalition's most successful tactics was to gain the support of the media, sparking public debate about the role of women in society and raising awareness of women's rights.

The new code equalized the legal minimum age of marriage and gave the same inheritance rights to all children, whether born within or outside of marriage. Under its provisions, property acquired during marriage must be shared equally.

After the passage of the civil code in 2001 and buoyed by their success, the coalition of NGOs next turned their attention to the penal code. Under the old code, crimes such as rape, abduction or sexual abuse against women were categorized as 'crimes against society'. The women's movement launched a bold campaign, which culminated in a new penal code in 2004, which included the criminalization of marital rape and sexual harassment in the workplace, the revision of all articles discriminating between single and married women and the strengthening of provisions on sexual abuse of children. Furthermore, the code banned courts from handing down lenient sentences for the perpetrators of so-called 'honour' killings or to rapists who marry their victims.[34]

Extending the protection of the rule of law

Going beyond removing laws that explicitly discriminate against women, the second key area of reform is measures to extend the reach of law to cover issues of critical importance to women. The rule of law has traditionally only covered the public sphere. This has meant that what happens within the private domain, particularly within the family and in the home, including the majority of gender-based violence and much of women's work, has been hidden and beyond the scope of the law.

Violence against women and girls

Violence against women and girls is both an extreme manifestation of gender inequality and discrimination, and a deadly tool used to maintain women's subordinate status. No woman or girl is entirely free of the risks or reach of this global pandemic. As the United Nations Secretary-General has stated: 'Violence against women and girls makes its hideous imprint on every continent, country and culture'.[35] Historically, governments' ambivalence towards regulating gender relations in the private domain and intimate relationships has been exemplified by the lack of domestic violence legislation, the reluctance to recognize marital rape as a criminal offence and the exemption of 'crimes of honour' from prosecution. This has contributed to a widespread perception that abuse of women in this sphere is acceptable (see Figure 1.4).

FIGURE 1.4: Perceptions of domestic violence

In 17 out of 41 countries, a quarter or more people think that it is justifiable for a man to beat his wife.

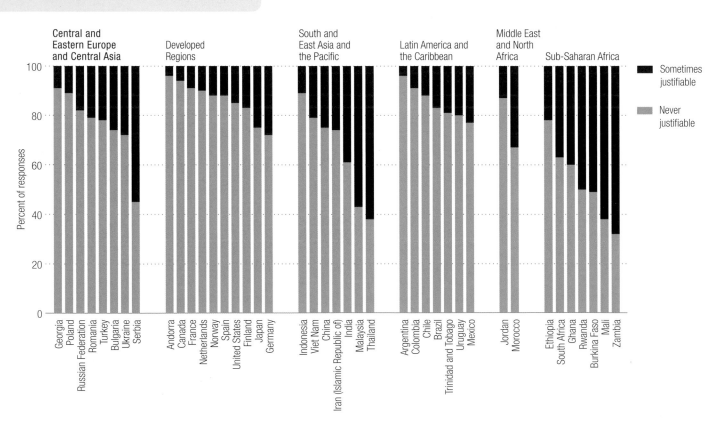

Source: World Values Survey Association 2010.

Note: The World Values Survey asks respondents to rate on a scale from 1 to 10 the degree to which they think it is justifiable for a man to beat his wife. The data refer to the proportion who responded that it is never justifiable (scale = 1) and those who responded that it is somewhat or always justifiable (responses 2 to 10).

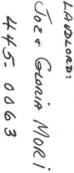
...enact and implement legislation ...ainst women and girls is well established in numerous international and regional conventions, declarations and treaties.[36] In recent years, governments have made very significant progress in this area. As of April 2011, 125 countries have passed legislation on domestic violence, including almost all countries in Latin America and the Caribbean. Two thirds of all countries have also taken steps to make workplaces and public spaces safer for women, by passing laws to prohibit sexual harassment (see Figure 1.5).

It is more challenging to assess progress on laws on sexual violence. While almost all countries criminalize rape, penal codes often define sexual violence very narrowly, with many still framing the problem in terms of indecency or immorality, or as a crime against the family or society, rather than a violation of an individual's bodily integrity. While a number of countries, including Turkey and Uruguay have taken the important step of abolishing laws that exempt perpetrators of sexual violence if they marry their victims, these provisions still exist in many others.

With regard to domestic violence, the courts at national and regional levels have played a key role in propelling legal changes. In 1992, the House of Lords in the United Kingdom finally struck down the 250 year-old common law principle that a marriage contract automatically implied each partner's full consent to all sexual activity. This principle had effectively meant that the law against rape did not necessarily protect a woman if she was married to the perpetrator.[37] The House of Lords decision signified a larger trend globally towards recognizing spousal rape as a crime: as of April 2011, 52 countries have amended their legislation to explicitly make marital rape a criminal offence (see Balancing the Scales and Annex 4). With momentum growing for laws to address violence against women, global consensus on guiding principles that shape effective laws is also emerging (see Box 1.3).

FIGURE 1.5: Laws on violence against women

Two thirds of countries have laws in place against domestic violence, but many countries still do not explicitly criminalize rape within marriage.

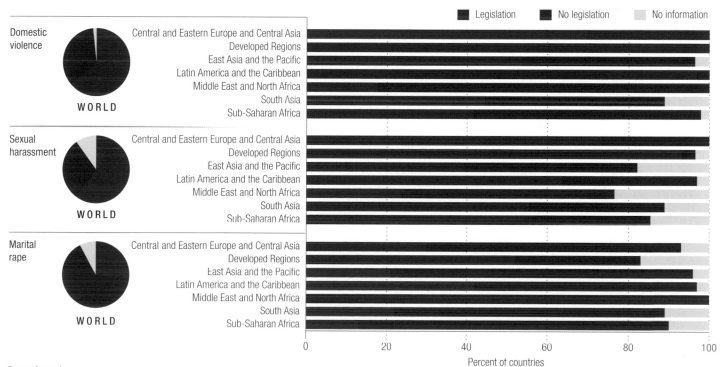

Source: Annex 4

Note: The data refer to the existence of laws specifically prohibiting each form of violence. See Annex 4 for details.

Box 1.3 Legislating to end violence against women and girls

As an increasing number of States take legislative action to address violence against women and girls, a body of best practice has developed to guide and shape effective laws, to ensure governments, their agencies and public services deliver protection and remedies to survivors.[38]

A comprehensive approach that involves the constitutional, civil, criminal and administrative law of the nation is essential. Legislation must recognize all forms of violence against women and girls and extend protection in all contexts: in the home, at work and in public spaces. Although violence against women is a criminal matter, there is significant overlap with other branches of the law. Family courts often deal with domestic violence and dowry violence cases, which may include significant civil components, including protection orders, divorce and custody issues. Courts adjudicating immigration matters often handle trafficking cases. A comprehensive approach also requires coverage for all women and girls, recognizing that

FIGURE 1.6:

Prevalence, laws and perceptions of domestic violence

Where there are laws in place on domestic violence, prevalence is lower and fewer people think that violence against women is justifiable.

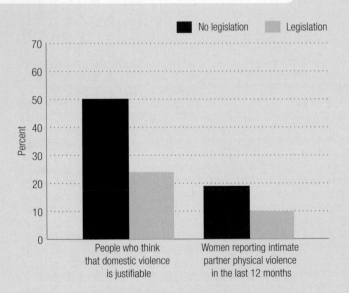

Source: UN Women analysis, using legislation and prevalence data in Annex 4 and perception data from World Values Survey Association 2010.

the gender discrimination they face may intersect with other forms of discrimination on the basis of ethnicity, class, disability, age and sexual orientation, among others.

Another important step is to ensure that no custom, tradition or religious tenet may be used to justify violence against women and girls. This is especially relevant to ensuring that harmful cultural practices, such as forced or child marriage and female genital mutilation are covered in national legislation. Among positive recent developments is the stipulation in the Protocol to the African Charter on Human and Peoples' Rights on the Rights of Women in Africa (the Maputo Protocol), that 'States parties shall prohibit and condemn all forms of harmful practices which negatively affect the human rights of women and which are contrary to recognized international standards'. This includes the prohibition, 'through legislative measures backed by sanctions, of all forms of female genital mutilation'.[39]

Full and sustained funding is essential to ensuring adequate implementation of legislation. A general budgetary obligation is an effective way to ensure that the goals of the law are achieved. The national budget of the Republic of Korea allocates funds to implement the Acts on Domestic Violence and Sexual Violence.[40] Spain's 2004 Act on Integrated Protection Measures on Gender Violence includes dedicated funding for education and public awareness.[41]

Regularly collecting data on the prevalence and impact of violence against women and girls helps to drive implementation of laws. After passing a new law on domestic violence in 2005, the Government of Cambodia conducted a baseline survey on prevalence and attitudes towards violence against women. In 2009, a follow-up survey was carried out. Among its findings were that while in 2005, 64 percent of respondents knew a husband who physically abused his wife, by 2009, that figure had dropped to 53 percent.[42] This pattern is reflected in other countries too. Where laws are in place on domestic violence, prevalence is lower and fewer people think that such abuse is acceptable (see Figure 1.6).

Although it remains a huge challenge, passing and implementing laws to protect women from violence plays a central role in changing attitudes and practices.

Women workers in informal and vulnerable employment

Although in most countries governments have taken steps to regulate formal employment, with laws on acceptable working conditions and pay, this protection typically does not cover the informal economy. The rule of law is seen as a key precondition for economic prosperity and development, yet in practice it does not apply to the majority of work that women do.

Globally, 53 percent of working women are employed in vulnerable jobs, as own-account workers or as unpaid workers in family businesses or farms. In South Asia and sub-Saharan Africa, more than 80 percent of women workers are in this kind of employment.[43] Millions work in the informal economy as home-based workers and paid domestic workers.

Extending the protection of the rule of law to informal and vulnerable work is vitally important to reducing poverty and inequality, as well as to ensuring women's rights. This is particularly critical in today's global economy, as labour markets have been de-regulated and standards relaxed, with the result that more and more jobs have been informalized, with workers losing legal and social protection.

Recent years have seen large numbers of women in developing countries employed in assembly manufacturing in Export Processing Zones (EPZs), areas in which labour and environmental standards may be relaxed or eliminated in order to attract foreign investors, often as part of free trade agreements (see Figure 1.7). Even where labour laws extend to these zones, they are often unenforced, leaving women exposed to low wages and poor conditions. Not deterred by limited union rights, workers have increasingly mobilized for improved conditions. In Honduras, for example, after a two-year campaign, a maquila union was able to secure a collective bargaining agreement for workers at the Yoo Yang garment factory in La Lima, with provisions for an expansion of medical benefits, increased maternity leave, education scholarships and other benefits.[44]

According to International Labour Organization (ILO) data from 18 countries, domestic work accounts for between 4 and 10 percent of the workforce in developing countries, and between 1 and 2.5 percent in developed countries. Between 74 and 94 percent of domestic workers in these countries are women.[45] The increased global mobility of labour and the feminization of migration have made domestic work a globalized profession, with women from poorer countries moving to richer ones in their millions to meet the growing demand for domestic services in recipient countries and to support their families back home. It is estimated that women account for nearly two thirds of Sri Lanka's one million international migrants, many of whom are employed in the Gulf States as domestic workers. These women contribute very significantly to the economies of their home countries, annually accounting for more than $1.7 billion in remittances.[46]

FIGURE 1.7: Employment in Export Processing Zones (EPZs), by sex

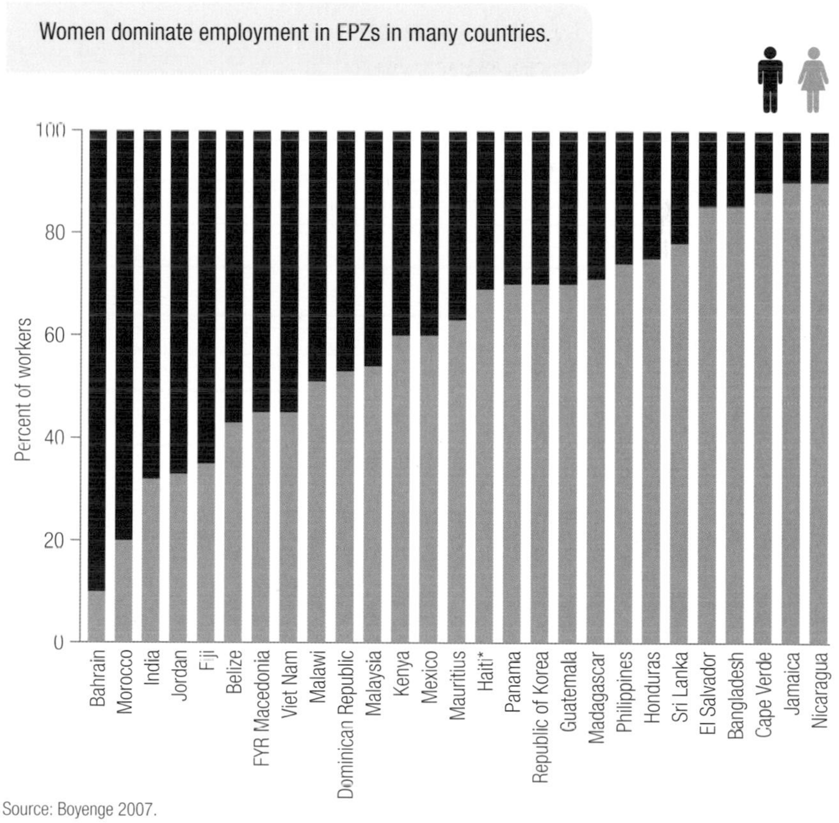

Women dominate employment in EPZs in many countries.

Source: Boyenge 2007.

Note: * In the apparel industry only.

Because it replaces the household and care services that women have traditionally provided unpaid, domestic work is typically undervalued, informal and undocumented. It is regarded as different to regular employment and therefore is often explicitly excluded from labour laws and social protection (see Figure 1.8). It has been widely documented that this lack of protection has left domestic workers vulnerable to exploitation and abuse by unscrupulous employers.[47]

Like domestic work, home-based work is generally assumed to be an extension of women's unpaid domestic responsibilities, so it is often not recognized or valued and is not regulated by the law. In South Asia alone, there are 50 million home-based workers, of whom four out of five are women.[48] Home work ranges from traditional crafts such as weaving or embroidery, and processing natural products like making rope or shelling cashew nuts, to industrial work, such as making leather shoes, garments or trimming rubber and plastic parts.[49] It is usually labour-intensive and done by hand. This work almost always takes place outside of formal systems of labour or social regulation, without basic rights to a minimum wage, social security or a pension.

FIGURE 1.8: Domestic workers and social security legislation, by region

In all regions, domestic workers lack basic protection and rights under the law.

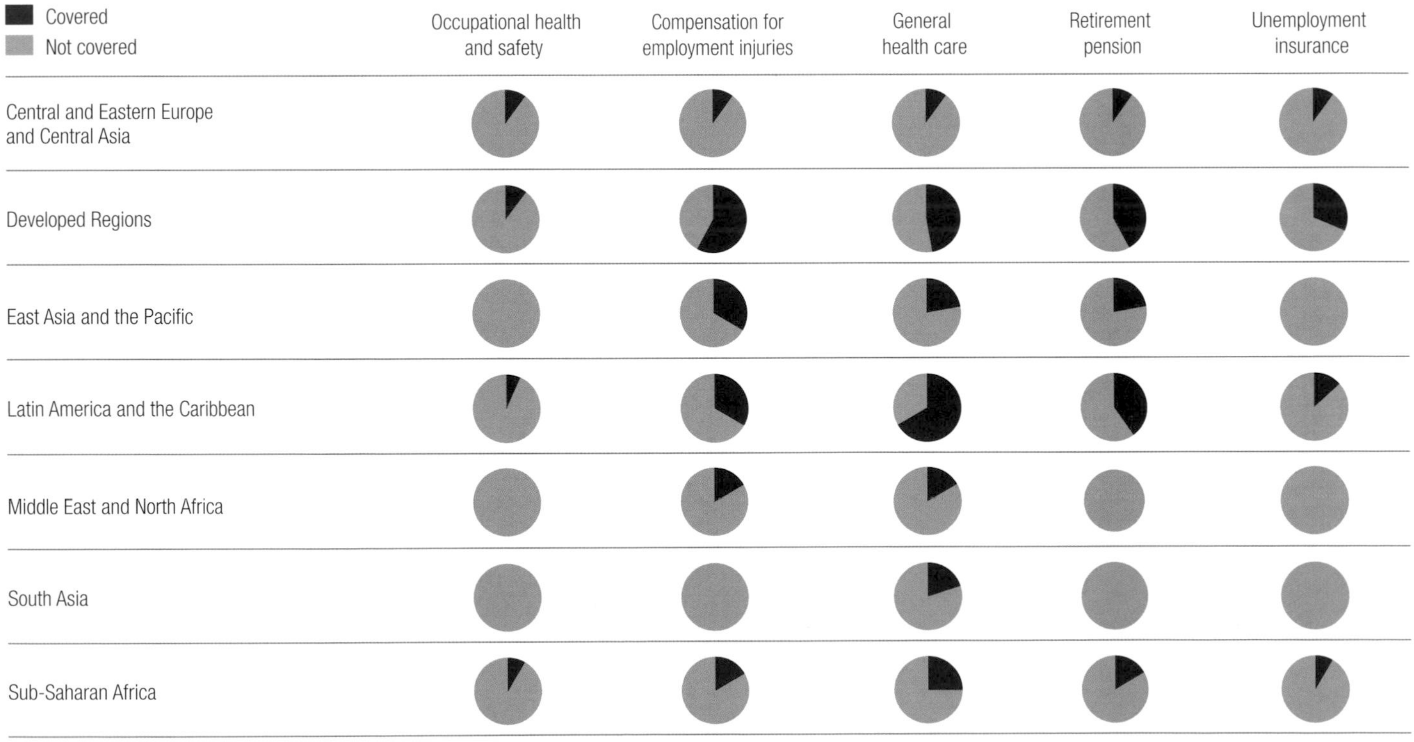

Source: Data adapted from Table V.2 in ILC 2010. Based on UN Women regional groupings.

Note: This analysis includes the explicit coverage of domestic workers by general social security legislation, as well as by ad hoc legislation regulating social security for domestic workers or by legislation on domestic work containing provisions on social security. It covers 10 countries in Central and Eastern Europe and Central Asia, 19 countries in Developed Regions, 9 countries in East Asia and the Pacific, 15 countries in Latin America and the Caribbean, 6 countries in the Middle East and North Africa, 5 countries in South Asia and 12 countries in sub-Saharan Africa. For country specific coverage and provisions, see Table V.2 notes in ILC 2010.

Over the past two decades, the ILO has adopted a number of standards to extend protection to women workers, including the Convention on Part-Time Work in 1994 and on Home Work in 1996. In 2011, the ILO is due to discuss a proposed new standard on domestic work at the 100th session of its International Labour Conference.[50] The steps that Member States are required to take to safeguard the rights of migrant domestic workers are also outlined in the CEDAW Committee's 2008 General Recommendation No. 26 on women migrant workers and the United Nations Committee on Migrant Workers Comment No. 1 adopted in January 2011.[51]

Several countries have legislated to protect domestic workers. For example, Jordan has amended its labour laws to include domestic workers, guaranteeing monthly payment of salaries, sick leave and a maximum 10-hour working day.[52] The law on domestic violence in Indonesia includes protection of domestic workers against violence within its scope.[53]

There is growing recognition that women's entitlement to social benefits should not depend on the type of work they do. In Brazil, the National Federation of Domestic Workers is lobbying to expand domestic workers' rights in the Constitution, obliging employers to provide both retirement and employment insurance, to observe strict limits on working hours, to pay for overtime and to provide social benefits on the same terms as other workers.[54]

Ensuring government responsibility for the impact of the law

The third set of reforms needed to address the bias against women in legal frameworks relates to the duty of governments to take responsibility for the law's impact. There are two key issues: first, it means taking a holistic approach to designing laws and policies to drive effective implementation, to ensure substantive equality and fair outcomes for women. Second, while claiming to guarantee equality for all, States need to take full responsibility for the result of their action, or inaction, in terms of the actual impact of legislation on women's lives.

Substantive equality for women in formal employment

In formal employment, there has been a very significant expansion of women's rights in recent years. At least 117 countries have passed equal pay laws, 173 guarantee paid maternity leave and 117 outlaw sexual harassment in the workplace.[55] In South Asia, in several landmark cases, the courts have called on governments to introduce sexual harassment legislation (see Balancing the Scales). In some countries, explicit discrimination remains, limiting the jobs that women are able to do (see Figure 1.1). However, others have adopted special measures to address historic discrimination against women in the workplace. For example, according to the law in Viet Nam, an employer must give preference to a woman who satisfies all recruitment criteria for a vacant position in an enterprise.[56]

Nevertheless, gaps in employment laws, lack of enforcement and inadequate policies, including on provision of childcare, continue to hold back women's employment prospects. Globally, the proportion of working age women in formal employment or seeking work stood at 53 percent in 2009, unchanged since 1991.[57] This impacts on women's livelihoods, but also has broader ramifications. It is estimated that limits on women's participation in the workforce across Asia-

Pacific cost the region an estimated $89 billion every year. These impacts are particularly seen in South Asia where the combination of gender gaps in education and employment accounts for annual per capita growth rates that are up to 1.6 percentage points lower than in East Asia.[58]

Despite decades of equal pay legislation, wage gaps remain wide and persistent across all regions and sectors. Based on available information from 83 countries, the ILO reports that women are generally paid between 10 and 30 percent less than men.[59] According to the International Trade Union Congress, the average gender pay gap is 29 percent in Argentina, 22 percent in Poland and 24 percent in the Republic of Korea.[60] These wage gaps reflect the fact that women doing the same or comparable jobs are paid less than men for the same work, but they are also indicative of the fact that women tend to be concentrated in low-paid work. Women have increasingly resorted to the courts to seek redress and establish that the failure

of employers to comply with equal pay laws amounts to sex discrimination (see Box 1.4).

While these cases show how employers in the public and private sector can be held to account, there is also recognition that substantive equality for women will only be achieved through a range of other laws and policies to make the workplace more accessible to women. Central to the success of these policies is taking into account the fact that in all countries, women are primarily responsible for household and child-rearing tasks – unpaid labour which impacts on their ability to access the labour market on equal terms to men. This limits their options to take advantage of formally equal opportunities, usually relegating women to part-time, temporary or casual work, which is less well paid and has fewer or no benefits.

There are a number of studies that show the link between the gender pay gap and the division of labour in the home. One such study in the United States found that

Box 1.4 Equal pay for work of equal value

Establishing the right to be paid the same as men is a struggle that women have taken through the courts.

In the largest class action gender discrimination case ever to go to trial in the United States, 12 female employees of the pharmaceutical company Novartis alleged they were discriminated against on pay and promotions.[61] The jury at the Court for the Southern District of New York found women were routinely paid $105 less per month than men with the same experience and that women were penalized for taking maternity leave. The jury unanimously awarded $250 million in punitive damages to the whole class of women affected by these policies and $3.4 million in compensatory damages to the 12 women who testified. In order to avoid an appeal and the possibility that 5,588 other eligible female employees could apply for compensatory damages, which it is estimated could have reached $1 billion, Novartis agreed to pay $175 million to settle the matter, including $22.5 million for improvements to policies and programmes that promote equality in the workplace.[62]

Legislation on equal pay has been in place in the United Kingdom since 1970. However, in 2010, the gender pay gap was 20 percent.[63] In 1997, 1,600 women health workers brought an equal pay case against the National Health Service (NHS) to an employment tribunal, in which they claimed that their jobs had been consistently undervalued compared to those of their male colleagues, for more than a decade.[64] Based on the principle of equal pay for work of equal value, the women argued that their predominantly caring roles should be equally rewarded to those of men, which tended to be more technical. In 2005, UNISON, the women's trade union, agreed with the NHS the largest ever equal pay award settlement for a total of approximately $480 million, including compensation for lower hourly rates, lower pension contributions and the non-payment of bonuses and attendance allowances, back-dated 14 years, all with compound interest. The women won between $56,000 and $320,000 each.[65] As part of the negotiations a new pay equity system, known as the 'Agenda for Change', was introduced by the NHS to put a stop to future pay discrimination.[66]

companies offer different remuneration to women and men based on expectations of their share of work in the household.[67] Another study of 15 developed countries found that where men do a greater share of housework, the gender pay gap is lower.[68] In a number of countries a 'motherhood penalty' has been identified whereby the gender pay gap is greater for women with children than those without.[69] Encouraging greater sharing of care responsibilities, for example through paid paternity leave, is therefore important. A review of legislation in 126 countries and territories indicates that 42 have laws in place to guarantee paid paternity leave.[70]

The Government of Sweden has had a policy of paid parental leave since 1974, with women and men equally entitled to take time off. However, in practice women took the majority of the allocated leave, so the policy was amended in 1995 and 2002 to encourage greater take-up among fathers through the introduction of 'daddy months', which are non-transferable. A study has found that for every month a father takes leave, a mother's earnings increase by an average of 6.7 percent, counteracting the 'motherhood penalty'.[71] Because of policies like this, as well as the provision of high-quality childcare, the gender pay gap in Sweden is 13 percent, significantly lower than other countries in Europe, such as Hungary (18 percent) and Spain (23 percent).[72]

Implementing laws on land rights

Control over land is the basis for the economic rights and livelihoods of millions of rural women. Legal recognition of women's rights to land has been growing. According to the World Bank, at least 115 countries specifically recognize women's property rights on equal terms to men.[73] While these laws are in place in almost all countries in Central and Eastern Europe and Central Asia, and Latin America and the Caribbean, in other regions, laws that explicitly discriminate against women remain (see Figure 1.9).

Furthermore, even in those countries with laws in place, women's actual control over land is limited (see Map 1.1). Property laws that guarantee equal rights may have unequal outcomes because they interact with discrimination built into other aspects of the legal

framework, particularly on divorce and inheritance. Furthermore, the factors that determine who controls land typically involve a complex interplay of different legal systems – state, customary and religious – and cultural norms (see Chapter 3). In some countries in sub-Saharan Africa and Asia, despite constitutional guarantees of women's land rights, customary law is recognized as taking precedence on issues of inheritance and marriage. This means that in the event of marital breakdown or widowhood, the control of marital property rests with husbands and their families. The HIV pandemic often makes women's position even more precarious, when widows are stigmatized as the 'carriers' of the infection, shunned by their husband's family and thrown off their land.[74]

FIGURE 1.9: Women's rights to property ownership and inheritance, by region

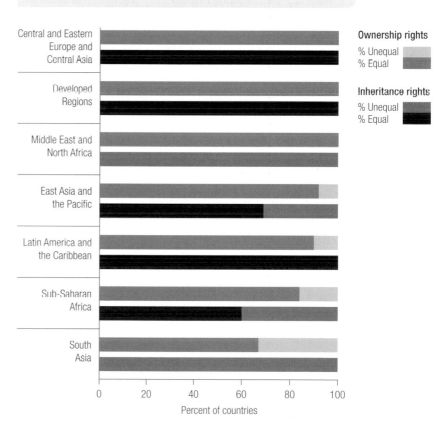

Women's property and inheritance rights vary widely between regions.

Central and Eastern Europe and Central Asia
Developed Regions
Middle East and North Africa
East Asia and the Pacific
Latin America and the Caribbean
Sub-Saharan Africa
South Asia

Ownership rights
% Unequal
% Equal

Inheritance rights
% Unequal
% Equal

0   20   40   60   80   100
Percent of countries

Source: UN Women calculated regional averages using women's right to ownership and inheritance data from World Bank 2010f.

Note: Based on a World Bank review of codified laws and regulations in 124 countries. Ownership and inheritance rights refer to both moveable and immoveable property. Customary practices are not taken into account.

Discriminatory legal codes and customary practices limit women's ability to control land.

Source: UN Women calculated unweighted regional averages using women's access to land data from OECD 2010c.

Note: Women's access to land measures women's rights and de facto access to agricultural land. The values are derived from assessments that take into account the legal situation in the country or territory, drawing on the constitution and other legal documents as a reference and an assessment of the extent to which these legal provisions are applied within the actual country or area context and whether other obstacles prevent women from access. Countries not included in the aggregation due to missing data are shown in grey. See UN Women regional groupings for the list of countries and territories included in each region.

Gender blind law reform and implementation sometimes exacerbate the problems for women. There are examples of land titling programmes in sub-Saharan Africa that have led to the transition from family holdings in customary tenure systems, under which women had some rights, to individually-owned parcels of land registered in the name of the male head of household. In Kenya, for example, only 5 percent of registered land titles are held in women's names. While there is no legal requirement that land be registered in the name of the male head of household, it is reported that this has become common practice among land registrars.[75]

Despite these hurdles, a number of governments have made women's land rights a reality, through comprehensive legal reform, but also through effective implementation of laws. In Rwanda, women parliamentarians have been instrumental in bringing about legal reform (see Box 1.5). In Nepal, tax exemptions were introduced to incentivize the transfer of land into women's ownership (see Case study: Nepal).

In 1994, the states of Karnataka and Maharashtra in India amended the Hindu Succession Act to give daughters the same inheritance rights as their brothers. Research on the impact of this reform found that, while gender inequality persists, the likelihood of women inheriting property has increased by 22 percentage points. Additional benefits have included girls marrying later and staying on longer at school. The research also found that the effects increased over time as awareness of the new law grew. In 2005, this reform was replicated at the national level.[76]

In Tajikistan, amendments to the 2004 land law included provisions for all citizens in rural areas to have equal rights to land shares. Previously, only full-time members of collective farms were eligible, which excluded part-time women members, women on maternity leave and those who performed non-agricultural work such as providing health or social services.[77] As a result of these reforms, as well as other measures, the proportion of women heading family farms in Tajikistan rose from 2 to 14 percent between 2002 and 2008.[78]

Box 1.5 Rwanda's women legislators lead the way

In Rwanda, the presence of women in parliament has been a pivotal factor in achieving progressive legal reform on land, marriage and inheritance.[79]

At 51 percent, the level of women's parliamentary representation in Rwanda is the highest in the world (see Display: Women in parliaments and legal reform).[80] The 2003 Constitution commits to 'a State governed by the rule of law, a pluralistic democratic government, equality of all Rwandans and between women and men reflected by ensuring that women are granted at least 30 percent of posts in decision-making organs'. A quota system was put in place and in the 2003 elections women exceeded this minimum target.

The Forum of Women Parliamentarians brought women together to develop strategies for change. Working with the Women's Ministry and women's civil society organizations, the Forum pushed through the 1999 Law on Matrimonial Regimes, Liberalities and Successions, which established women's right to inherit land for the first time. The legislation includes the principle that women may own and inherit property on an equal basis with their brothers, and requires that couples registering their marriage make a joint commitment to shared ownership of marital property. The 2004 National Land Policy and the 2005 Organic Land Law further entrenched women's land rights by introducing land titling, stipulating that women and men must have equal access.

Member of Parliament Patricia Hajabakiga described the efforts of women parliamentarians: 'We had a long, long sensitization campaign…this was a very big debate…we said "you are a man… you have children, you have a daughter who owns property with her husband. Would you like to see that daughter of yours, if her husband dies, everything is taken away?" When you personalize things, they tend to understand'.

The Forum recognized the need to get men on board as allies in bringing about change and shifting attitudes. When they organized a nationwide tour to monitor gender issues, they included their male colleagues. Senator Wellars Gasamagera commented on his role: 'I was in charge of delivering this particular message [on gender sensitivity] at the end of the meetings. Local leaders, local *male* leaders, were shaken up. Hearing the message from a man was an added value, [they were] more convinced, more able to take the message seriously'.

The Government has also put in place procedures to ensure that women are included in the land registration process. The National Land Centre has undertaken widespread training of local land committees across Rwanda, including making a video showing how women's rights should be recorded. Three NGOs, LandNet Rwanda, Imbaraga and Haguruka, have disseminated illustrated information booklets on the Organic Land Law and the Succession Law, explaining their content in simple terms for everyone to understand. NGOs also monitored the land registration trials and provided additional support and sensitization for officials.[81]

Research on the impact of the laws on women's land rights in Rwanda found that legal changes are affecting land inheritance patterns in practice. Although quantitative data are not yet available, many male family heads commented that under the new law they felt obliged to give their daughters land.[82]

The impact of laws on sexual and reproductive health and rights

Addressing sexual and reproductive health and rights is an integral part of efforts to advance gender equality and a foundation for women's autonomy.

At the International Conference on Population and Development held in Cairo, Egypt in 1994, the international community for the first time agreed on a broad definition of reproductive health and rights, recognizing that 'reproductive health is a state of complete physical, mental and social well-being in all matters relating to the reproductive system'.[83] Paragraph 96 of the Beijing Platform for Action further stated: 'The human rights of women include their right to have control over and decide freely and responsibly on matters related to their sexuality, including sexual and reproductive health, free of coercion, discrimination and violence.'[84]

According to CEDAW, States should ensure women's 'access to health care services, including those related to family planning'.[85]

Women's reproductive health and rights are increasingly recognized in laws and guaranteed in constitutions around the world. In 2010, a new Constitution was passed in Kenya, which includes broad guarantees of women's reproductive rights. It prohibits discrimination on the basis of sex, pregnancy and marital status and declares that every person has the right 'to the highest attainable standard of health, which includes the right to health care services, including reproductive health care'.[86]

Despite progress in some countries, in many more the failure to make reproductive health care available and accessible, and the criminalization of abortion, results in severe restrictions to women's rights and in some cases serious injury or death. Five countries outlaw abortion

FIGURE 1.10: Maternal mortality and unsafe abortion, by region

One in seven maternal deaths is caused by unsafe abortion.

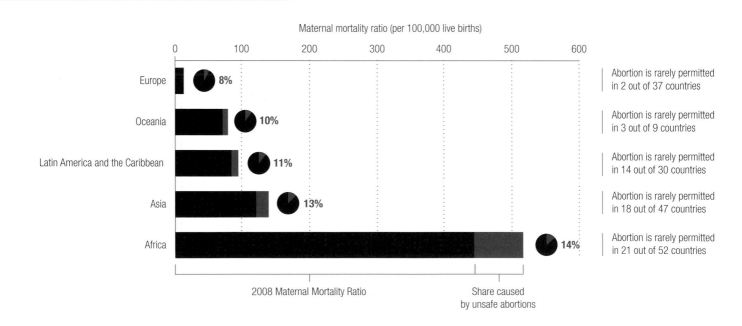

Source: Unsafe abortion data from WHO 2007. Maternal mortality data are UN Women calculated unweighted averages using data from WHO, UNICEF, UNFPA and the World Bank 2010. Abortion laws are from UN DESA 2011a.

Note: Maternal mortality ratio (MMR) refers to maternal deaths per 100,000 live births. In Annex 3, there are seven grounds upon which abortion is permitted. 'Abortion is rarely permitted' means that abortion is permitted on two or fewer grounds. When calculating regional maternal mortality ratios, to ensure consistency with WHO data, 17 countries for which data on abortion-related deaths are not available were excluded. Excluded countries include eight that rarely permit abortions.

under any circumstances, even when the mother's life is at risk and 61 countries only allow abortion under very rare circumstances (see Annex 3). As a result of such restrictions, approximately 20 million unsafe abortions are carried out annually, killing an estimated 68,000 women each year (see Figure 1.10).[87]

The principle of substantive equality means that States parties to CEDAW are responsible for addressing the unintended consequences of such laws. In its concluding observations on reports from States parties, the CEDAW Committee has raised concerns about the lack of access to safe abortion, particularly in cases of rape. It has asked

States parties to review legislation and to remove punitive provisions for women who have an abortion.[88] The criminalization of abortion has also been identified as a concern by the United Nations Human Rights Committee, the United Nations Committee on Economic, Social and Cultural Rights and the United Nations Committee on the Rights of the Child, with a number of States being asked to review or amend their legislation.[89] Using the body of international law on this issue, some landmark cases have been taken at national, regional and international levels to establish women's legal rights to reproductive health (see Box 1.6).

Box 1.6 Establishing women's legal right to reproductive health

Several landmark cases in Latin America and Europe have confirmed women's right to reproductive health, including safe abortion.

In Colombia, the Constitutional Court ruled that the criminal prohibition of abortion in all circumstances violates women's fundamental rights and affirmed that abortion must be accessible in certain cases (see Balancing the Scales). A decision by the European Court of Human Rights in December 2010 found that the Government of the Republic of Ireland must enable access to abortion when a woman's life is at risk. Although this right is guaranteed in the Constitution, doctors face criminal sanctions if such risk cannot be proven, which means in practice thousands of women are denied access to a legal abortion each year. In reaching its decision, the Court recognized that the restrictive nature of the legal regime in Ireland 'disproportionately harmed women', stigmatizing and financially burdening those who were forced to seek the procedure abroad.[90]

In Peru and Mexico abortion is legal when the mother's physical or mental health is threatened. In 2002, two teenage girls brought cases against their governments for failing to protect them from their doctors' decision arbitrarily to refuse them access to the abortions to which they were legally entitled. In both *K.L. v Peru*, decided by the United Nations Human Rights Committee in 2005 and *Paulina Ramirez v Mexico*, filed with the Inter-American Commission on Human Rights and settled in 2007, it was confirmed that governments are responsible for ensuring that women have access

to the reproductive health services provided under the law and would be in violation of this obligation if they permitted service providers to deny women their rights.[91] In response to the case, in 2009, the Government of Mexico put in place clear regulations regarding the implementation of the law.[92]

In 2005, a Roma woman from Hungary, who was sterilized while undergoing a caesarian section, brought a case under the CEDAW Optional Protocol.[93] The CEDAW Committee found that while on the operating table, the woman had been coerced into signing a note of consent, which used the Latin term for 'sterilization', which she did not understand. Noting the complainant's particularly vulnerable state, the Committee found that it was 'not plausible that...the author could make a well-considered and voluntary decision to be sterilized'. The Committee confirmed that forced sterilization breaches articles 12 and 16 of CEDAW, which guarantee women's rights to appropriate maternal health services and to decide freely and responsibly on the number and spacing of their children based on appropriate information.[94] In response, the Government of Hungary announced that it would provide financial compensation to the complainant and in 2008, the Public Health Act was amended to improve the provision of information and procedures to obtain consent in these cases.[95]

Another area of women's sexual and reproductive health and rights that is increasingly being subject to criminal law is HIV transmission.[96] Criminalization takes two forms: through the application of existing criminal law and through new laws that specifically criminalize HIV transmission. There are 63 countries that have HIV-specific criminal laws: 27 in Africa, 13 in Asia, 11 in Latin America and the Caribbean, nine in Europe, two in Oceania and one in North America. In 17 countries, these laws have been used to prosecute individuals for transmitting HIV.[97]

Since 2005, a 'model law' has been implemented in at least 15 sub-Saharan African countries which criminalizes transmission of the HIV virus 'through any means by a person with full knowledge of his/her HIV/AIDS status to another person'.[98] In some cases, these laws explicitly include mother-to-child transmission, a very punitive provision particularly in contexts where comprehensive HIV prevention and health care is not widely available.[99]

These laws are often justified on public health grounds and as a means of protecting women and men from infection, but they fail to take into account the discrimination and stigma with which women living with HIV must contend. In many instances, women will choose not to get tested for HIV, fearing the violence and shame they may face. This severely curtails their access to treatment and support. These laws exacerbate this problem, since an HIV-positive woman's best chance of avoiding criminal liability is to remain ignorant of her status by avoiding testing altogether.[100]

The United Nations Special Rapporteur on the right to health and the Joint United Nations Programme on HIV/AIDS (UNAIDS) have expressed concern about the impact of criminalization of HIV transmission on women, urging States to repeal such laws, which have had no demonstrable impact on reducing rates of HIV infection.[101]

Conclusion

In every region of the world, there has been significant progress on legal reform to expand the scope of women's rights. Where the law works for women, it can advance gender equality and improve women's access to justice. Women all over the world have used the courts to bring precedent-setting cases that have resulted in law reform to benefit millions of others.

Laws can play a positive role in shaping society, by creating new norms and by helping to bring about social change. For example, where laws are in place to prohibit domestic violence, prevalence is lower and fewer people think that violence against women is justified. In countries where there are laws specifying a minimum age of marriage, fewer women are married early. Moreover, social change makes legal reform possible. As they have entered the workforce in larger numbers, women have argued that they are entitled to the same pay and property rights as men.

Nevertheless, critical gaps in legal frameworks remain. The 1995 Beijing Platform for Action called for extensive legal reform to address gender discrimination. In 2000, the United Nations General Assembly reiterated this, asking governments to review legislation 'with a view to striving to remove discriminatory provisions as soon as possible, preferably by 2005'. Most recently in October 2010, the Human Rights Council passed a resolution, setting up an expert working group to identify best practices and make recommendations on the improvement of legislation and implementation of laws.[102] In ratifying CEDAW, governments have committed to addressing discriminatory laws, through three key areas of reform:

Ending explicit legal discrimination against women.

Repealing laws that codify lesser rights for women is an urgent priority in all regions. At least 19 countries in Africa have reformed citizenship laws to enable women and their families to gain permanent residence rights, have freedom of movement and access public services. Reform of family codes has challenged women's unequal status within the family.

Extending the protection of the rule of law.

More than two thirds of all countries now have domestic violence legislation in place, to ensure the rule of law protects women in the private domain. Strategic litigation has been used to establish that rape within marriage is a crime and to demand that governments legislate against sexual harassment in the workplace. However, the millions of women who work behind closed doors, including as domestic workers, are still largely excluded from labour legislation, exposed to poor pay and conditions, subject to abuse and denied access to social welfare benefits. Extending the protection of the rule of law to recognize these workers' rights is essential.

Ensuring government responsibility for the *impact* of the law.

While at least 115 countries recognize women's equal rights to property, discriminatory laws on inheritance and failures of implementation mean that women cannot claim what is rightfully theirs. Equal pay is unlikely to be achieved without action to redistribute women's unpaid care burdens. Taking responsibility for the law's impact also means paying attention to the unintended consequences of legislation and policy, including the toll on women's lives of the failure to fulfil their internationally recognized sexual and reproductive health and rights.

While acknowledging advances in legal reform, laws mean little unless they are implemented. Drafting laws to drive effective implementation, with clear mandates and procedures for service providers, in-built accountability mechanisms and adequate funding is critical. Chapter 2 builds on this to make the case that providing a functioning justice chain, with effective public services that meet women's rights, is key to advancing gender equality and women's access to justice.

The Justice Chain

CASE STUDY: **Bulgaria**

In March 2000, Valentina Nikolaeva Bevacqua left her marital home in Bulgaria with her young son, after years of suffering abuse at the hands of her husband and moved into her parents' apartment. She filed for divorce the same day and sought an interim custody order. Despite clear evidence of abuse, every stage of the justice chain failed her.

It took more than a year for the authorities to take appropriate action, placing Valentina and her son in serious danger. Her estranged husband battered her and forcibly took their son away for extended periods. With each new incident, she filed complaints with the prosecutor's office and approached forensic examiners to obtain medical documentation. On every occasion, the authorities demonstrated a lack of any sense of urgency in addressing the problem.

Valentina complained to the Ministry of the Interior that the police had done little to assist her to obtain custody of her son and had not taken necessary measures to protect him. She was told that there was nothing the police could do about a 'private dispute'. The courts did not address her requests for interim measures and enforced a two-month reconciliation period prior to the divorce proceeding. Valentina finally obtained a divorce and custody of her son in May 2001. When she went to her former home to collect her belongings, she was again attacked by her ex-husband. She lodged a complaint with the prosecution authorities, but they refused to initiate criminal proceedings against him.

That same year, supported by the legal NGOs, the Bulgarian Gender Research Foundation and Interights, Valentina and her son brought their case to the European Court of Human Rights (ECHR). She alleged that Bulgarian officials violated their right to respect for private and family life, including their physical and psychological integrity, under the European Convention on Human Rights.[1]

Previously, both the ECHR and European governments had interpreted the Convention to mean that family relationships and those between private individuals are matters beyond the purview of the State.[2] In this case, however, the Court reasoned that respecting private and family life may include 'a duty to maintain and apply in practice an adequate legal framework affording protection against acts of violence by private individuals'.[3] When the Court finally handed down the judgment in 2008, it found the State of Bulgaria in violation of the Convention for failing to implement these positive obligations.

This case and those that followed revolutionized the understanding of domestic violence, from a private act committed with widespread impunity, to a human rights violation that States have a responsibility to combat (see Balancing the Scales). In particular, it contributed to the emergence of a 'due diligence' standard to assess whether States have carried out their duty to provide a functioning justice chain to respond to domestic violence.

Pre-empting the ECHR's judgment, in 2005 the Government of Bulgaria passed comprehensive legislation, placing responsibility on the State to prevent domestic violence and assist victims. The law, which was drafted in close collaboration with the Bulgarian Gender Research Foundation, includes provisions to grant temporary custody of children and for emergency protection orders.[4] In 2007, guidelines for police officers were issued and a national database of domestic violence cases was established.[5] Women's organizations have been very active in lobbying for adequate funding for implementation of the law, spurred on by Valentina's case.[6]

'When a State makes little or no effort to stop a certain form of private violence, it tacitly condones that violence. This complicity transforms what would otherwise be wholly private conduct into a constructive act of the State.'

Bevacqua v Bulgaria, European Court of Human Rights, 2008

Photo: European Court of Human Rights

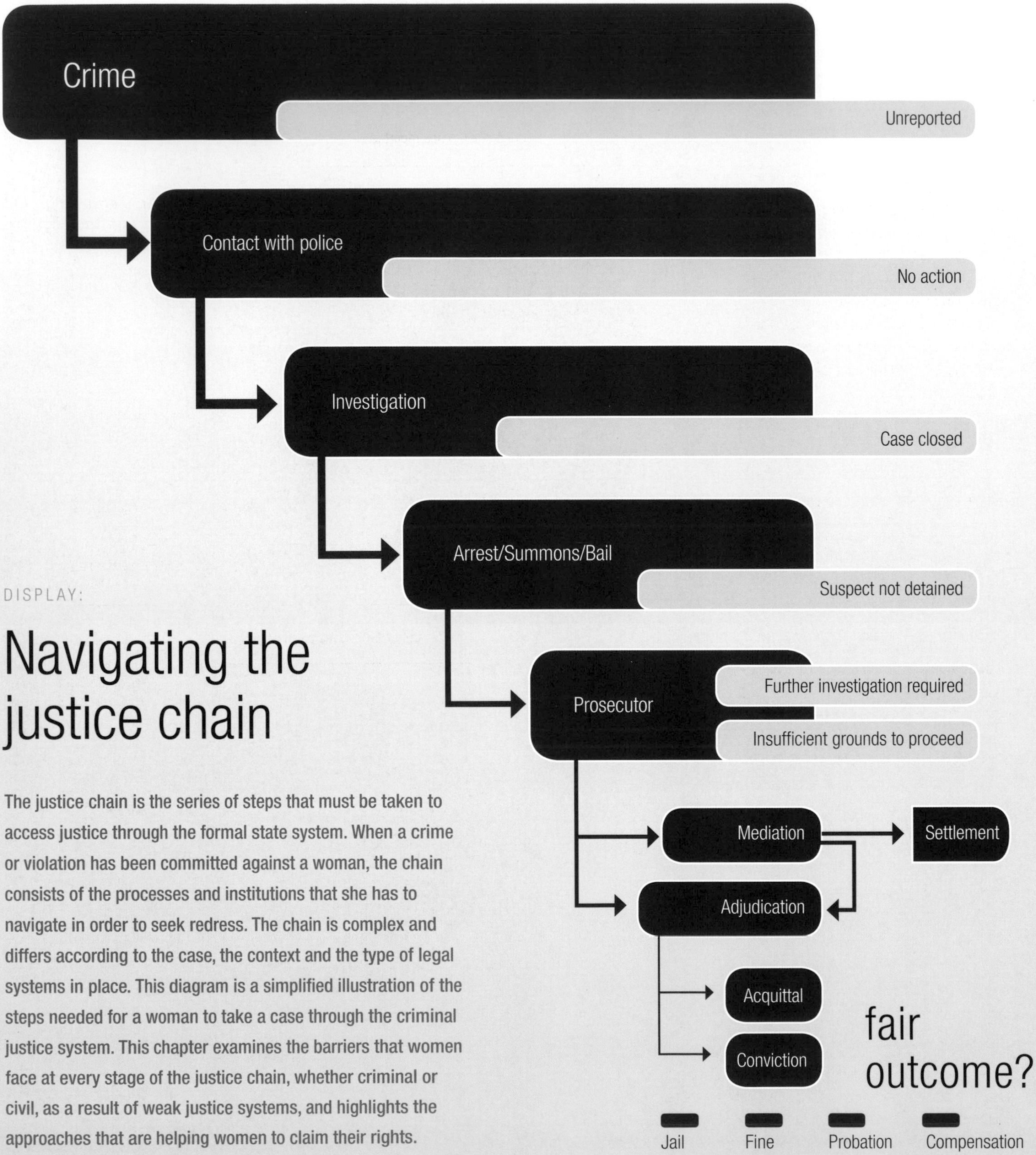

Crime

Unreported

Contact with police

No action

Investigation

Case closed

Arrest/Summons/Bail

Suspect not detained

Prosecutor

Further investigation required

Insufficient grounds to proceed

Mediation → **Settlement**

Adjudication

Acquittal

Conviction

fair outcome?

Jail   Fine   Probation   Compensation

Navigating the justice chain

The justice chain is the series of steps that must be taken to access justice through the formal state system. When a crime or violation has been committed against a woman, the chain consists of the processes and institutions that she has to navigate in order to seek redress. The chain is complex and differs according to the case, the context and the type of legal systems in place. This diagram is a simplified illustration of the steps needed for a woman to take a case through the criminal justice system. This chapter examines the barriers that women face at every stage of the justice chain, whether criminal or civil, as a result of weak justice systems, and highlights the approaches that are helping women to claim their rights.

Attrition in the justice chain in rape cases

All over the world, the justice chain is characterized by high levels of attrition, whereby most cases drop out of the justice system before they reach court and very few result in a conviction. Attrition is a particular problem in rape cases. The charts below show the findings of research in Gauteng Province, South Africa, illustrating the progression of rape cases through the system. Only 17 percent of reported rapes reached court and just 4 percent ended in a conviction for rape. These statistics are typical of rape case attrition in many other countries. In response, the Government of South Africa has invested in a network of one-stop shops, which have significantly increased conviction rates (see Box 2.3).

Attrition at the police investigation stage

Nearly half of cases were dropped at the police stage, usually because the perpetrator was not found. Descriptions of the perpetrator were absent from more than three quarters of victims' statements. In more than half the cases, an instruction to arrest the suspect had to be issued twice or more before the investigating officer complied with it.

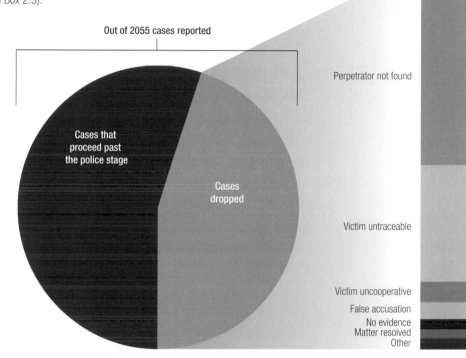

Out of 2055 cases reported

Cases that proceed past the police stage

Cases dropped

Perpetrator not found

Victim untraceable

Victim uncooperative

False accusation

No evidence

Matter resolved

Other

Attrition at the prosecution and court stages

Of those cases that proceeded to prosecution, one in five was dropped at this stage. Two thirds of cases went to court, but most were disposed of by the court before reaching trial. Of these, 63 percent were withdrawn by the victim or the victim was untraceable. In 14 percent of cases, evidence was lost or not obtained.

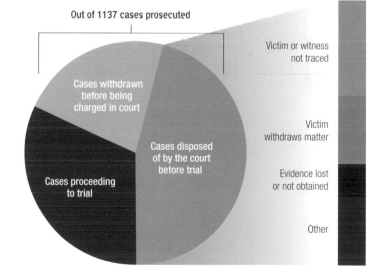

Out of 1137 cases prosecuted

Cases withdrawn before being charged in court

Cases disposed of by the court before trial

Cases proceeding to trial

Victim or witness not traced

Victim withdraws matter

Evidence lost or not obtained

Other

Trial stage

Some 17 percent of reported cases reached court. Cases were more likely to proceed to trial and result in a conviction if injuries were documented. Four percent of reported cases resulted in a conviction for rape, with a further 2 percent convicted for other offences. Out of 41 percent of convictions that were eligible for life imprisonment, only 4 percent (three people in total) received this sentence.

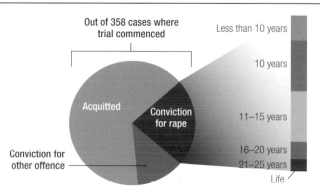

Out of 358 cases where trial commenced

Acquitted

Conviction for rape

Conviction for other offence

Less than 10 years

10 years

11–15 years

16–20 years

21–25 years

Life

Source: See endnotes.

Introduction

Valentina Nikolaeva Bevacqua showed extraordinary perseverance in her quest for justice, facing enormous obstacles from an unresponsive system and a dysfunctional justice chain. Millions of women like her face two major barriers when navigating the formal justice system. On the one hand, extensive social barriers discourage them from coming forward and pursuing cases. On the other hand, justice systems lack capacity, resulting in distant courtrooms, unaffordable costs and service providers who are not responsive to women's needs.

The rule of law requires not only that laws are passed, but that they are equally enforced and independently adjudicated, free from bias or discrimination.[7] Article 2 of CEDAW directs States 'to establish legal protection of the rights of women on an equal basis with men and to ensure through competent national tribunals and other public institutions the effective protection of women against any act of discrimination'.[8] Too often, however, States are not meeting their commitments and confidence in the justice system is often low. In 23 out of 52 countries, less than half of women and men surveyed said they have confidence in their country's justice system.[9]

Capacity gaps and the failure of justice services to be responsive to women's rights result in very high levels of under-reporting and attrition, which means that only a fraction of cases that are initiated in the formal system ever results in a court decision or a just outcome for a woman. Even where women access the justice system and obtain the right outcome, lack of enforcement means that, all too often, justice remains out of reach. High levels of under-reporting and attrition, and lack of enforcement indicate that justice systems are failing to respond to women's needs.[10]

FIGURE 2.1: Incidence and reporting of robbery and sexual assault

Women are much more likely to report robbery than sexual assault.

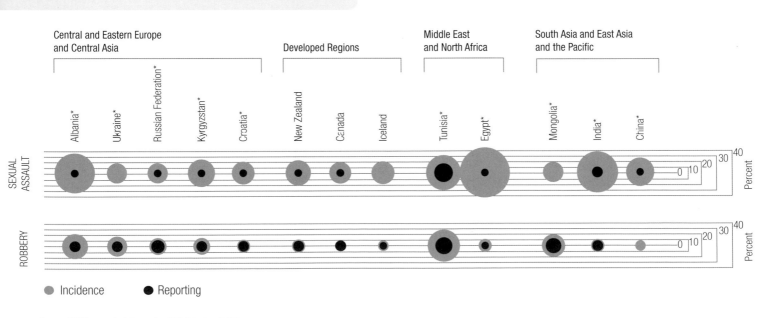

Source: UN Women calculations using ICVS (latest available).

Note: * indicates that the survey covers only a main city.

Data on sexual violence and robbery show the extent of the problems of under-reporting and attrition. Across 57 countries, on average 10 percent of women say they have experienced sexual assault, but of these only 11 percent reported it. This compares to a similar incidence of robbery, on average 8 percent, but a reporting rate of 38 percent. This pattern is evident in countries across all regions (see Figure 2.1). A 2009 study of European countries found that, on average, 14 percent of reported rapes ended in a conviction, with rates falling as low as 5 percent (see Figure 2.2).[11]

This chapter analyses the barriers that women face throughout the justice chain and examines what can be done to address these problems. There are an increasing number of innovative responses to overcome the barriers that women face. Governments are reforming justice services and creating new models that are specifically tailored to women's needs. Changes in the organizational mandates, procedures and cultures of justice sector service providers are helping to make them more responsive and accountable to women. Approaches that have made a difference include integrated and specialized services, boosting women's presence as justice providers and initiatives to increase accountability to women.

FIGURE 2.2: Rape case attrition in a sample of European countries

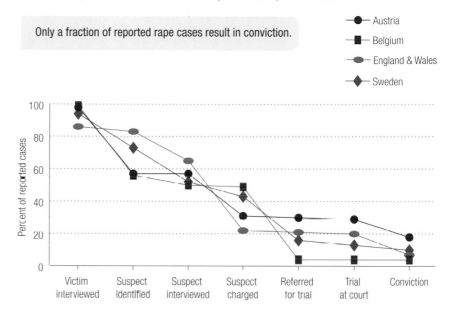

Only a fraction of reported rape cases result in conviction.

Source: Lovett and Kelly 2009.

Note: The data are from metropolitan or regional areas, and thus may not be representative of all rape cases in the country.

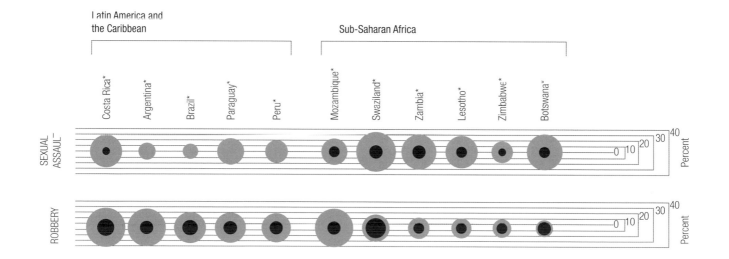

Barriers to women accessing justice

The justice chain is complex. In the criminal justice system, the chain includes the police, forensic services, prosecuting agencies, legal support and the courts. The chain also encompasses the route that women take to access justice in civil matters. In the formal justice system, employment matters as well as family laws, including those related to marriage, divorce, maintenance, custody and inheritance are dealt with through the civil justice system. As discussed in Chapter 3, in many countries the State recognizes multiple family laws – civil, customary and religious – which create parallel court systems that can complicate matters further.

While capacity gaps affect all justice service users, gender discrimination means that women typically have less time and money and lower levels of education, exacerbating the challenges.

Accessing the formal justice chain may involve engaging with various branches of the law or different legal systems that have different structures and procedures. For example, cases related to trafficking or migrant women may involve not only criminal charges, but also immigration proceedings, which are typically dealt with under administrative law. Civil and criminal issues often overlap, particularly in cases of domestic violence. The justice chain also interacts with a broader range of public services, such as providers of health care, social services and shelters for women, as well as local government institutions that are responsible for implementing laws at the local level.

For women facing this daunting array of institutions and processes, there are major disincentives to engaging with the formal justice system.

Social barriers

Lack of knowledge of their rights or the justice system, dependence on male relatives for assistance and resources, and the threat of sanction or stigma are some of the social barriers that women face in accessing the formal justice system.

In some communities, women are unable to approach justice systems without the assistance of a male relative and social norms hinder their ability to exercise autonomy outside the household. In Timor-Leste, a study found that 58 percent of Timorese – both women and men – disapproved of women speaking on their own behalf in local disputes.[12] Data from household surveys in 30 countries show that in 18 countries, more than half of married women have no say on everyday household decisions (see Figure 2.3).

Women's reliance on male relatives can be a particular barrier since in cases related to violence, family laws or inheritance, the case is likely to be taken against a family member, whom she may rely upon financially. Where women lack access to resources or independent income, the costs of pursuing cases in the absence of free legal aid can be prohibitive.

Social sanction for women who approach the formal justice system is especially acute in cases of sexual and domestic violence. Sexual violence is the only crime for which the victim is sometimes more stigmatized than the perpetrator, with women who report such crimes being shunned by their families and communities. In Canada, the most common reason for women survivors of domestic violence not wanting to call the police was 'fear of retaliation' by the abuser, family or community.[13]

For all these reasons, grievances are commonly resolved within families or communities, or through a customary or non-state justice process. In Lesotho, Mozambique and Viet Nam, more than three times as many women say they have contacted a traditional or community leader about a grievance than a government official in the past three years (see Figure 3.1). In a survey on the family courts in Morocco, 68 percent of women who had experienced domestic violence expressed a preference for resolving the problem within the family. Those women who did seek justice preferred to approach the family courts for a divorce rather than go to the police and initiate prosecution proceedings.[14]

Given these social pressures, it is not surprising that women are reluctant to access the formal justice chain. Institutional hurdles compound these pressures and pose additional barriers to women's access to justice.

FIGURE 2.3: Women's autonomy in the household

In 18 out of 30 countries, more than half of women report having no say in household decisions.

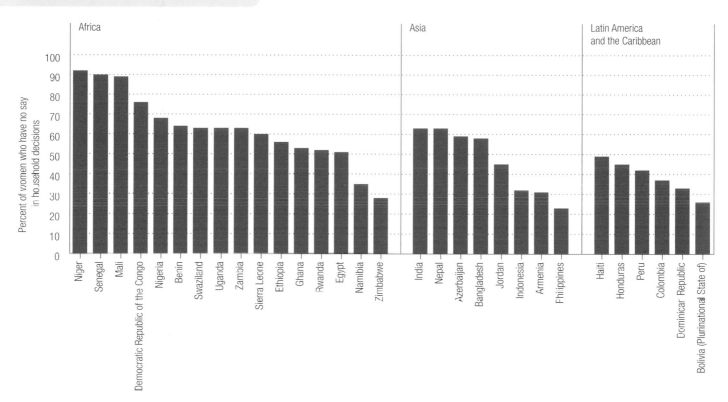

Source: UN Women calculations using MEASURE DHS latest available (2004–2009).

Note: Lack of autonomy is defined as having no say in any of these vital everyday decisions: own health care, large household purchases, purchases for daily needs, and visits to family or relatives. The data refer to women aged 15 to 49 who are married or in a union.

Institutional barriers

The institutional hurdles that women face arise from justice systems that lack capacity and do not respond to women's particular needs. Despite decades of donor-supported projects to build court rooms and train the police and judiciary, in many developing countries the reach of the formal system is very limited.

While capacity gaps affect all justice service users, gender discrimination means that women typically have less time and money and lower levels of education, exacerbating the challenges. In addition, excluded women, including those from ethnic, racial, religious or linguistic minorities; women living in poverty, or with HIV; disabled women; and migrant women face even greater barriers.

Many countries have critical shortages of trained police, legal and forensic staff. Only one doctor in Timor-Leste has reportedly been trained to collect evidence in rape cases, while in Sierra Leone, there are just 100 trained lawyers, 90 of whom are based in the capital Freetown, serving a population of more than 5 million people.[15] Lack of resources and basic equipment is also a problem. In Uganda, for example, women reporting domestic violence to the police are routinely asked to provide money for transport to arrest the suspect.[16] Capacity problems are especially marked in post-conflict settings or in the aftermath of crises, when levels of violence against women are exceptionally high.

Taking a case through the formal justice system entails high financial and psychological costs for women. In Kenya, a World Bank study found that a formal claim for land in an inheritance case can involve 17 different legal steps, costing up to $780 for lawyers' fees and

BARRIERS TO JUSTICE

Confidence
In 23 out of 52 countries, less than half of women and men say they have confidence in their country's justice system.

Autonomy
In 18 out of 30 countries, more than half of women have no say in household decisions.

Cost
A World Bank study found that in Kenya, a land claim in an inheritance case can cost up to $780.

Distance
In a study by UNDP and the Government of Indonesia only 38 percent of respondents said that courts were located within accessible distance of their home.

Language
In some parts of Latin America, most indigenous women do not speak Spanish or Portuguese and provision for translation in the justice system is limited or non-existent.

other administrative expenses.[17] In Nepal, gender equality advocates report that women claiming their inheritance rights sometimes have to provide DNA evidence to prove their family lineage, the cost of which is prohibitively high for most women.[18] A 2007 study by the Cambodian Ministry of Justice found that fees for forensic examinations – often crucial in rape cases – cost between $5 and $14, about two weeks' average income in rural areas.[19]

Another cost comes from corruption in the justice system, an endemic problem in countries where court staff are badly paid. The costs of corruption are borne disproportionately by women, who are more likely to face demands for bribes for services that should be free.[20]

Where the formal system encompasses more than one legal order, the costs of pursuing a case can escalate. For example, in Sri Lanka, Muslim Quazi courts have exclusive jurisdiction in financial matters relating to marriage but no power to enforce decisions. To secure the execution of Quazi court decisions, a woman has to turn to one of several different types of ordinary court, multiplying costs. For each additional step, the pressure to drop the case escalates.[21]

To take a case to court, women need legal advice and support. International treaties specify that legal aid should be available in any case where the interests of justice so require.[22] Not only is this far from the reality in many countries, but even where legal aid is provided, it is usually only for defendants in criminal cases. While this is vital, women also need access to legal advice and representation in civil cases and in cases where they are the complainant. Eligibility for free legal aid, where available, may be assessed against family income, without taking into account that women may not be able to access these resources in their own right.[23]

Courts are often distant and hard to reach for ordinary people, especially in rural areas. In a survey in Indonesia carried out by the United Nations Development Programme (UNDP) and the Government, only 38 percent of respondents felt that formal justice institutions were located within an accessible distance from their

homes.[24] The problems are compounded by frequent adjournments and delays. Courts are overloaded and have long case backlogs arising from a lack of qualified staff, limited budgets and inadequate infrastructure and logistical support.[25] In Nigeria's Delta state, court users reported having to come to court an average of nine times per case.[26] Lack of capacity also hampers enforcement of court decisions. For instance, the family section of the Tangier court in Morocco produces 20,000 judgments a year, but only has one bailiff, which means that divorced women are often left without the financial support they have been awarded.[27]

Court proceedings are often conducted in a language that large sections of the population do not understand. For example, in some parts of Latin America, most indigenous women do not speak the majority languages, Spanish or Portuguese, and provision for translation in the justice system is limited or non-existent.[28]

Police, court staff and other justice sector personnel typically reflect the discriminatory attitudes of wider society. In some cases, they may not be aware of the law and their obligation to serve women. In a study by the Population Council on police attitudes in two South Asian countries, between 74 and 94 percent of respondents agreed that a husband is allowed to rape his wife.[29] All too often, women seeking justice face hostility or contempt from the very people who are supposed to uphold their rights. In many countries, police turn away victims of domestic violence, which is widely regarded as a 'private' matter to be resolved within the family. Research carried out in 30 out of 34 provinces by the United Nations Assistance Mission in Afghanistan found that, in almost every case investigated, rape victims had themselves been charged with zina (extramarital sex), and this appeared to be 'standard practice'.[30]

The CEDAW Committee has recently expressed concern about bias in judicial decision-making, particularly highlighting the problems of 'rape myths', which are false and preconceived notions of how a rape survivor 'should' behave before, during and after an attack that unfairly influence trials (see Box 2.1).

As well as biased decision-making in courts, discrimination is also built into procedural aspects of the law that put women at a disadvantage in courtrooms. For example, in some countries, women's testimony carries half the weight of that of men.[31] In the United Kingdom, defendants in rape trials were allowed to introduce evidence of a woman's sexual history, which could be used to call into question the woman's credibility as a witness. The 'rape shield' law introduced by the Government in 1999 banned courts from using this evidence, but two years later, the House of Lords, in *R v A (No. 2)*, overturned this law, allowing judges to use their discretion.[32]

Excluded groups of women are sometimes at even greater disadvantage. In the United States, in rape cases involving African-American and Latina women, conviction rates are particularly low. The racial identity of the victim plays a significant role, with evidence that jurors are especially likely to question the credibility of these women.[33]

The combination of social barriers and institutional hurdles presents very significant problems for women accessing the justice chain. However, governments and civil society are demonstrating how gender-responsive justice services can meet women's needs and legal empowerment programmes can encourage them to access the formal justice system.

Box 2.1 Tackling 'rape myths' in the Philippines

A 2010 decision by the CEDAW Committee under the Optional Protocol highlights the problem of discriminatory attitudes among the judiciary.

The decision related to a complaint lodged by a rape survivor from the Philippines alleging that gender-based myths and misconceptions about rape were relied on by the judge in her case, leading to the acquittal of the alleged rapist. The complainant identified seven 'rape myths' related to her own behaviour and reaction to the attack, as well as to the characteristics of her attacker. These included the idea that rape victims are timid or easily cowed and that when a woman knows her attacker, consent is implied.

The Committee found that the woman had been 're-victimized' through her treatment by the court and stressed that 'stereotyping affects women's rights to a fair and just trial'. They further warned that 'the judiciary must take caution not to create inflexible standards of what women or girls should be, or what they should have done when confronted with a situation of rape, based merely on preconceived notions of what defines a rape victim or a victim of gender-based violence'.

The Committee recommended that the Government award compensation and put in place appropriate training for judges, lawyers, law enforcement officers and medical personnel, to avoid re-victimizing women and 'to ensure that personal mores and values do not affect decision-making'.[34]

As of April 2011, the Government had not yet formally responded to the Committee. However, even before the Optional Protocol case, the judiciary in the Philippines had already recognized the need to increase gender sensitivity in decision-making. As a result, the Philippine Judiciary Academy and the Ateneo Human Rights Center developed an interactive bench book, which tracks decisions on women's rights cases, making relevant jurisprudence and legal reasoning available to judges, and conducted a series of trainings for court personnel.[35]

Making the justice chain gender-responsive

There are four key areas where change is required in order to make the justice chain work for women. An overarching challenge is the need for institutional change at the level of organizational mandates, procedures and cultures to ensure justice services are accountable and accessible to women. In addition, one-stop shops and legal aid services; specialized courts; and gender-responsive policing and judicial decision-making are all proven to make a difference, especially to the poorest and most excluded women.

One promising approach to reducing attrition in the justice chain is to integrate services through one-stop shops.

Changing organizational mandates and procedures

National legal frameworks should provide for the development of standardized protocols, regulations to enforce laws and mechanisms to ensure coordination between different parts of the system. Adequate and sustained funding, as well as measures to monitor implementation are also needed.

Although there is further to go, laws on violence against women are beginning to establish the kind of clear mandates and procedures that are needed to drive implementation and improve women's access to justice. Recognizing that survivors of gender-based violence should not face court processes without support, at least 45 countries now provide free legal aid in such cases.[36]

In Austria, the law mandates psychosocial care for these women, as well as legal aid and support throughout the justice process.[37]

Laws can provide clear instructions to government ministries and public services in relation to training and monitoring. In Namibia, the domestic violence law requires the Inspector-General to issue specific directives on the duties of police officers, to keep statistics on reports of domestic violence and to submit regular reports to the relevant minister.[38] In Lesotho, the law on violence against women specifies that women must be provided with post-rape medical care free of charge.[39] In Kenya, the Ministry of Health has issued national guidelines calling for the provision of post-exposure prophylaxis to rape survivors to prevent HIV infection.[40]

Box 2.2 Realizing land rights in Kyrgyzstan

When the Government of Kyrgyzstan introduced agrarian reform in 1991, provisions for equal rights to land for women and men were part of its policy. However, a combination of procedural and social barriers precluded women from claiming their rights in practice.

Two thirds of the population in Kyrgyzstan rely on agriculture for their livelihoods. However, a land distribution survey conducted in 2002 found that of a total of 246,941 land holdings, only 12 percent belonged to women. Land management rights are typically registered with men and rural women often lack awareness of their rights. Women have to navigate complicated procedures to apply for land shares, especially in cases of divorce. Moreover, officials in rural areas do not always understand the procedures. Gender bias in the court system further hinders women's access to justice.[41]

To address this, UN Women has supported capacity building for local officials, as well as media campaigns to raise awareness about women's legal rights and the discrimination they face. In addition, legal clinics have been established in remote areas with local organizations to provide free legal aid and representation to thousands of women.

Between 2004 and 2009, project lawyers conducted over 9,000 individual and group legal consultations with nearly 17,000 people in rural areas, half of whom were women. Nearly 3,000 women attended 67 intensive legal training workshops. Using the legal advice provided to them, 1,200 women gained access to land that they had previously been prevented from owning, using or managing.[42]

Clear mandates and procedures for service providers and local government are also needed to implement land laws. Passing laws guaranteeing women's equal rights to control land and inherit property is a vital first step, but as illustrated in the case of Kyrgyzstan, comprehensive measures, including training and awareness raising for local officials are needed to ensure women can claim their rights (see Box 2.2).

One-stop shops and legal aid

Because of the institutional and social barriers that women face, they need specialized services – from legal aid to domestic violence courts – tailored to meet their needs. One promising approach is to integrate services, for example through one-stop shops. These help to reduce attrition by cutting down the number of steps that a woman has to take to access justice.

Several countries have had success in training health workers to provide integrated services for women in cases of sexual violence. Health workers can collect evidence, provide health care, including post exposure prophylaxis and emergency contraception, provide psychosocial support and refer women to other services. This approach is also cost-effective since it makes use of existing staff and facilities (see Box 2.3).

In the United States, sexual assault nurse examiners have been trained to thoroughly document evidence, which has led to increased prosecutions, especially in cases where the survivor knows the assailant and in cases involving children.[43] Furthermore, a study in the United States found that women supported by specialized advocates for survivors of rape, who helped them navigate police and health care systems, were more likely to make police reports, more likely to receive health care and less likely to report distress in their dealings with the different services.[44]

In India, the 2005 Protection of Women from Domestic Violence Act mandated the creation of a new cadre of protection officers.[45] These officers have the power to file domestic incident reports for women and facilitate access to courts and support services.[46] By 2008, protection officers had been appointed at the district level in all states and at the sub-district level in 10 states. Implementation has been

Box 2.3 Thuthuzela Care Centres in South Africa

Thuthuzela means 'comfort' in Xhosa. These Care Centres, introduced as part of the national anti-rape strategy, provide rape survivors with a range of integrated services.

The Centres are located in public hospitals and provide emergency medical care, counselling and court preparation in a joined-up and survivor-friendly manner. The goal of the one-stop shop Thuthuzela Care Centre (TCC) model is to address the medical and social needs of sexual assault survivors, reduce secondary victimization, improve conviction rates and reduce delays in cases. TCCs are staffed by specialized medical staff, social workers and police, who are on call 24 hours a day.

The victim assistance officer explains the procedures and helps the survivor understand the examination and complaint filing process. A case monitor works with the survivor to make sure her docket is kept in order and the site coordinator ensures all services are joined up to prevent secondary victimization.

It is estimated that the TCCs deal with about 20 percent of all victims of sexual offences in South Africa. The Soweto TCC, in Gauteng Province attends to approximately 165 survivors per month, including many children as young as two years old. The trial completion time for cases dealt with by the Centre has decreased to seven and a half months from the national average of around two years, and conviction rates have reached up to 89 percent.[47]

The TCC model has been heralded as a best practice model internationally, with countries including Ethiopia and Chile learning from South Africa's experience and adopting similar models.[48]

particularly effective in the state of Andhra Pradesh, as a result of strong inter-agency coordination between the police, legal aid groups, protection officers and other civil society service providers.[49]

In Guatemala, as part of the 1996 peace agreement and in recognition of the multiple forms of discrimination that indigenous women face, the Government committed to setting up an Indigenous Women's Legal Aid Office (Defensoría de la Mujer Indígena – DEMI). DEMI employs indigenous women lawyers and social workers, as well as developing policies and programmes to prevent violence and discrimination against indigenous women. Of the 2,600 cases taken up by DEMI in 2007, 85 percent involved family violence, 11 percent were rape cases and 4 percent concerned ethnic discrimination.[50]

Civil society also plays an important role in raising women's legal awareness and providing legal advice. The Bangladesh Rural Advancement Committee (BRAC) administers the largest NGO-led human rights and legal education programme in the world. It raises women's awareness of their constitutional rights as citizens, and of family, inheritance and land laws. With 541 clinics in 61 districts across Bangladesh, the programme has reached 3.5 million women. The clinics have enabled women to pursue inheritance claims and take action against illegal marriage, polygamy and the practice of dowry. The organization reports that nearly 140,000 complaints have been lodged since the programme started in 1986.[51]

The Fiji Women's Crisis Centre was established in 1984 to provide practical advice and support to women experiencing domestic violence. According to research by the Centre, two thirds of women in Fiji have been abused by their partners. But in Fiji, in common with many other countries, the majority of public funding for legal aid supports defendants in criminal cases, with little provision for survivors of violence or to deal with family law cases. This leaves many women without the support they need. In response, the Centre provides free

and confidential crisis counselling and legal advice, as well as referrals to courts, police stations, hospitals and other agencies. By 2010, they had provided assistance to nearly 20,000 clients.

The Centre also delivers awareness-raising programmes, including the Male Advocacy on Women's Human Rights Programme, which provides men with training and skills to challenge cultural and religious justifications for violence against women. Participants include police officers, village chiefs, church representatives, and youth and community workers. This programme has been expanded to New Caledonia, Papua New Guinea, Tonga and Vanuatu.[52]

Specialized courts

Specialized courts can improve the functioning of the justice chain for women. Mobile courts have been used in a number of settings to bring justice closer to

Box 2.4 Women's police stations and special courts in Brazil

The first women's police station (Delegacias Especiais de Atendimento à Mulher – DEAM) opened in São Paulo in 1985. Today there are 450 DEAMs throughout the country and they are credited with raising awareness of violence against women and increasing levels of reporting.

Since the passing of the Maria da Penha Law on domestic and family violence in 2006, the DEAMs have been granted a leading role in initiating legal proceedings in cases of violence against women. Police now have broader responsibilities for securing protective measures and providing other immediate assistance to survivors, undertaking inquiries and steering cases through the criminal justice system.

In a recent survey of women DEAM users, 70 percent of the respondents felt welcome, around three quarters were given guidance and information on the process and the majority received referrals to other agencies for support.

Recognizing the importance of this specialized service, activists and researchers monitoring the implementation of the Maria da Penha Law have identified a number of areas where improvements are needed, including developing and disseminating information about the Law to DEAMs and associated services; comprehensive training

for all staff; better incentives for staff, including opportunities for career progression; improved data collection to drive monitoring and accountability; and better coverage for young girls and teenagers – currently fewer than half of DEAMs have specific services for this group.

The Maria da Penha Law also reverses previous provisions that saw perpetrators being dealt with in fast-track courts, often avoiding criminal sanction. The new Special Courts for Domestic and Family Violence against Women are supported by a multi-disciplinary staff, including social workers and psychologists. They are mandated to work closely with police, as well as with other services and agencies, including shelters, health centres, training and employment facilities, and public defenders' offices. To date, however, only 147 of these courts have been set up, serving a population of nearly 200 million, indicating that greater investment is needed if they are to realize their potential to serve women.[53]

Women's representation in the judiciary is a matter of equality and fairness, but it is also important for maintaining public confidence in the justice system. There is evidence that women judges can create more conducive environments for women in courts and can make a difference to outcomes. One study in the United States found that women judges were 11 percent more likely to rule in favour of the plaintiff in employment discrimination cases. Another concluded that male judges on federal appellate panels were significantly more likely to support the plaintiff in sexual harassment or sex discrimination cases if there was also a woman judge on the panel.[61]

Networks such as the International Association of Women Judges and Sakshi, an Indian NGO, have provided judges, both women and men, with specialized training and space to discuss the challenges they face, which can help to build understanding of and commitment to gender equality.

In 1996, Sakshi conducted interviews with 109 judges from district courts, high courts and the Supreme Court, and with female lawyers and litigants to explore the impact of judicial perceptions and decision-making on women who come to court. Around half of the judges interviewed said that women who are abused by their spouses are partly to blame and 68 percent said provocative attire was an invitation to rape.

Sakshi developed an education programme to change internalized myths and gender stereotypes, which has since expanded to 16 countries in the Asia-Pacific region. Workshops bring together judges, NGOs, health care professionals and complainants, and judges are encouraged to explore the reasons behind their decisions, the social context and the barriers that women face. Visits for judges to domestic violence shelters and women's prisons are organized to generate greater understanding of the challenges confronted by survivors of gender-based violence. In order to assess the impact of its work, Sakshi monitors decisions in relevant cases. They have tracked dozens of major cases in the region, on rape, child sex abuse and sex discrimination in the workplace, including the landmark Vishaka case, in which positive decisions were made by judges who had participated in their workshops (see Balancing the Scales).[62]

FIGURE 2.6 Women's representation in supreme, constitutional and regional courts

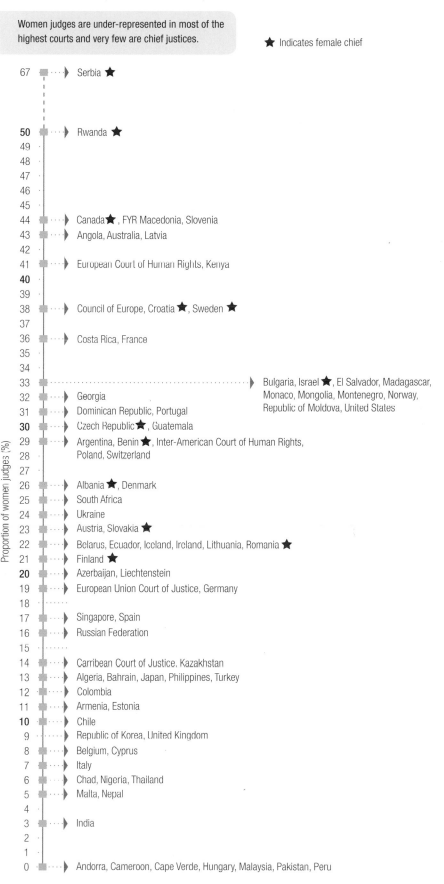

Women judges are under-represented in most of the highest courts and very few are chief justices.

★ Indicates female chief

Proportion of women judges (%)

- 67 — Serbia ★
- 50 — Rwanda ★
- 44 — Canada ★, FYR Macedonia, Slovenia
- 43 — Angola, Australia, Latvia
- 41 — European Court of Human Rights, Kenya
- 40
- 38 — Council of Europe, Croatia ★, Sweden ★
- 36 — Costa Rica, France
- 33 — Bulgaria, Israel ★, El Salvador, Madagascar, Monaco, Mongolia, Montenegro, Norway, Republic of Moldova, United States
- 32 — Georgia
- 31 — Dominican Republic, Portugal
- 30 — Czech Republic ★, Guatemala
- 29 — Argentina, Benin ★, Inter-American Court of Human Rights, Poland, Switzerland
- 26 — Albania ★, Denmark
- 25 — South Africa
- 24 — Ukraine
- 23 — Austria, Slovakia ★
- 22 — Belarus, Ecuador, Iceland, Ireland, Lithuania, Romania ★
- 21 — Finland ★
- 20 — Azerbaijan, Liechtenstein
- 19 — European Union Court of Justice, Germany
- 17 — Singapore, Spain
- 16 — Russian Federation
- 14 — Carribean Court of Justice, Kazakhstan
- 13 — Algeria, Bahrain, Japan, Philippines, Turkey
- 12 — Colombia
- 11 — Armenia, Estonia
- 10 — Chile
- 9 — Republic of Korea, United Kingdom
- 8 — Belgium, Cyprus
- 7 — Italy
- 6 — Chad, Nigeria, Thailand
- 5 — Malta, Nepal
- 3 — India
- 0 — Andorra, Cameroon, Cape Verde, Hungary, Malaysia, Pakistan, Peru

Source: Data collected from the individual courts' websites as of April 2011.

Note: In some countries there are multiple courts of last resort. Where possible, efforts were made to include information on all relevant courts, otherwise information on the constitutional court only is included.

Box 2.5 Women in prison

There are more than half a million women and girls in penal institutions around the world. Prisons are almost always designed for the majority male prison population and rarely meet women's needs. In 2010, the United Nations General Assembly adopted the 'Bangkok Rules', to provide guidance to Member States on the treatment of female prisoners.

In most countries, women make up between 2 and 9 percent of the prison population, with the highest rates of imprisonment in China, the Russian Federation, Thailand and the United States.[63] Female imprisonment rates are increasing rapidly. For example, in Australia between 1984 and 2003, the rate of imprisonment among women rose by 209 percent, compared to 75 percent for men. Steep increases are primarily due to greater use of imprisonment for offences once punished by non-custodial sentences.[64]

Most offences for which women are imprisoned are 'crimes of poverty' and are non-violent, property or drug-related. Globally, women are imprisoned for drug offences more than for any other crime, with women often used as couriers to smuggle drugs across borders.[65] Women are particularly vulnerable to being detained because they cannot pay fines for petty offences or pay bail. As a result, women are over-represented among those held in pre-trial detention.[66]

Women in prison share many common traits: they are typically young, have low levels of education and dependent children. In Brazil's largest women's prison, 87 percent of women prisoners are mothers. Many have histories of mental health problems, alcohol and substance abuse, and a high proportion have experienced violence. A study in Canada found that 82 percent of women in prison have a history of sexual or physical abuse.[67]

The 'Rules for the Treatment of Women Prisoners and Non-Custodial Measures for Women Offenders', or the 'Bangkok Rules', were initiated by the Government of Thailand and Her Royal Highness Princess Bajrakitiyabha Mahidol, who has long been a vocal advocate for the rights of women prisoners.[68] The rules build upon the 'Standard Minimum Rules for the Treatment of Prisoners', which were adopted by the United Nations Economic and Social Council in 1955.[69] The 70 rules include guidance for governments on health care, safety and sanitation standards; appropriate treatment of children of female inmates; and the use of non-custodial measures for women who commit minor offences.[70]

Meanwhile, some countries have responded to the needs of women prisoners by providing special facilities, including mother and baby units. One of the most child-centred systems is in Frondenberg in Germany, where mothers live with their children up to the age of six in self-contained apartments. The success of this approach is demonstrated by the fact that between 1997 and 2008, just eight women held in Frondenberg were transferred to a closed prison for breaching the terms of their sentence, and reconviction rates upon release are only 10 percent, much lower than recidivism rates among other groups of offenders.[71]

'Jurisprudence on the Ground' is a programme of the International Association of Women Judges. It brings together the Society for Women and AIDS in Africa – Tanzania (SWAA-T), which provides educational and medical services to rural women, and the Tanzania Women Judges' Association (TAWJA), which trains magistrates and judges on human rights laws. Working together, the two organizations share knowledge with judges and magistrates to tackle gender bias in the judicial system. They also train local women to understand their basic rights and support them to navigate the legal system. As part of this process, they have developed accessible public education materials in English and Swahili on women's rights, including practical information on which court to approach, what to expect as a witness and how to register a complaint if a court officer asks for a bribe. This programme has helped to improve accountability of judges to ordinary women. When judges are aware of the barriers that women face, attitudes change and they come up with simple but effective solutions, such as waiving court fees, providing forms free of charge or prioritizing sensitive cases.[72]

In the United States, accountability of the courts has been enhanced through court monitoring programmes. WATCH is one such programme based in the state of Minnesota. It was founded in 1992, after a young woman was sexually assaulted and murdered by a paroled prisoner with an extensive history of sex crimes. A group of concerned citizens decided that a strong public presence in the courtroom could help to hold the justice system accountable for protecting the public and ensuring victim safety. Trained volunteers have been a constant presence in the courts ever since, identifying problems such as high risk offenders being released without bail. WATCH provides feedback to judges, attorneys and other court personnel.[73]

Conclusion

Making the justice chain work for women is critical for their access to justice, but huge challenges exist at every stage. Landmark legal cases have established that governments' 'due diligence' obligations mean they are not only responsible for enacting legislation that guarantees women's rights, but also for ensuring that these laws are implemented through a functioning justice chain that is gender-responsive.

Social and institutional barriers deny women access to legal redress. Discriminatory attitudes among service providers are compounded by the lack of capacity of many justice systems. The high cost of litigation, language barriers and the geographical distance of many courts are just a few examples of the capacity deficits that prevent women from coming forward and pursuing their claims through formal legal channels. These problems result in very high levels of under-reporting and attrition, which means that only a fraction of cases that are initiated in the formal system ever results in a court decision or just outcome for women.

However, governments and civil society are responding by reforming justice services and creating new models that are specifically tailored to women's needs. Changes in the organizational mandates, procedures and cultures of justice sector service providers are helping to make them more responsive and accountable to women.

One-stop shops and legal aid.

In some countries free medical care and legal aid is guaranteed for survivors of violence against women to ensure that they enter the justice system supported and with sufficient knowledge of court processes. One-stop shops that integrate services, thereby reducing the number of steps that a woman must take to access justice, are proven to reduce attrition and increase conviction rates.

Investing in women service providers.

Women service providers can help to improve justice services and create greater accountability. A number of countries have put in place gender desks or created women's police stations. Data show that there is a correlation between women's representation in the police and reporting of sexual assault.

Specialized courts and gender-sensitive judicial decision-making.

Specialized courts, including mobile, domestic violence and family courts, can help to bring justice closer to women, ensure victim protection and safety by streamlining navigation of the system, and increase the expertise of judges and other personnel. Sensitizing judges, through targeted training and bringing them into contact with the women they serve, can help to eliminate biased decision-making and increase responsiveness to women.

While increasing the capacity of the formal justice system is a central part of improving women's access to justice, governments and policymakers are increasingly recognizing the reality of legal pluralism in most countries of the world. Making plural legal systems work for women is the focus of the next chapter.

Legal Pluralism and Justice for Women

CASE STUDY: Ecuador

For centuries, indigenous populations in Latin America have had their own forms of governance and justice systems. In recent decades, the legitimacy of these institutions has been recognized in laws and constitutions across the region. Indigenous women, who face triple discrimination on the basis of gender, ethnicity and poverty, have mobilized to open up spaces at both national and local levels to promote gender equality from within their own cultures and in keeping with their own justice systems.

When the Constituent Assembly was announced in 2007, the Kichwa Women's Network of Chimborazo developed an agenda for equality, focusing on ending gender-based violence and expanding women's participation in indigenous governance and decision-making. They joined forces with the National Council of Ecuadorian Women (Consejo Nacional de las Mujeres de Ecuador – CONAMU) and the Confederation of Indigenous Nationalities of Ecuador (Consejo de Cacionalidades Indígenas de Ecuador – CONAIE).[1]

The women took part in public consultations calling on the State to guarantee collective and indigenous cultural rights, including economic and land rights, the elimination of ethnic and gender-based discrimination, and respect for and protection of ancestral languages. At times, they struggled to have their agenda prioritized by either the indigenous movement or the women's council, but they persevered and their work paid off.

The Constitution of Ecuador, approved in 2008, is far-reaching in its recognition of both gender equality and indigenous rights. It prohibits gender discrimination and includes provisions for equal employment and property rights, sexual and reproductive rights, shared responsibility in the family and social security for home-makers. Articles 57 and 58 recognize and guarantee indigenous peoples' rights, enfranchising thousands of people living in the country's poorest regions. Most importantly for indigenous women, article 171 guarantees women's participation and decision-making in indigenous governance and justice systems.

At the local level, Kichwa women in Cotacachi in the highlands have been putting these principles into practice. Indigenous justice administration is based on written community regulations or statutes (reglamentos comunitarios). Traditionally, these regulations have not addressed issues of violence against women. So, the women have developed their own 'Regulations for Good Living' (Reglamentos de Buena Convivencia).

The regulations were drafted by the Integrated Centre for Women's Aid (Centro de Atencion Integral de la Mujer), with support from UN Women, CONAMU and the indigenous mayor. They aim to regulate family and community life and are in line with indigenous justice principles in relation to rehabilitation and reintegration. While the regulations leave the adjudication of serious crimes such as rape to state authorities, they condemn forms of physical, psychological and sexual violence, as well as restrictions on women's participation in public affairs and economic activities. Both men and women have been trained to promote the regulations in indigenous and state justice forums to increase women's access to justice and the realization of their rights.[2]

Indigenous women, who face triple discrimination on the basis of gender, ethnicity and poverty, have mobilized to ensure that their rights are protected at both national and local levels.

Indigenous women in Ecuador queue at a polling station during the constitutional reform referendum in 2007.

Introduction

A Muslim Kenyan woman who seeks financial support from her husband has a variety of options. She could request help from the head of the family, who is seen as responsible for the actions of family members. She might address the village chief, who is officially mandated to maintain peace and security in the community. She could turn to the local imam, who can act as a mediator. She has the option to file her case with a Kadhi court, which has formal jurisdiction over members of Muslim communities in family matters. Or she could go to a magistrate and seek redress under maintenance laws that apply to everyone in Kenya.

All States, religious or ethno-linguistic communities, and other groupings such as villages, neighbourhoods and families have their own systems for resolving problems, conflicts or grievances, known as 'legal orders'.[3] Within any given context there are often a variety of these orders in place in addition to the formal justice system, which may itself recognize multiple legal orders.

Legal pluralism has a long history and today exists in developed as well as developing countries. Even in countries with a well-functioning formal system, only a tiny fraction of grievances are taken to a formal court.[4] This means that the overwhelming majority of women and men access justice through systems that are not entirely or not at all within the purview of the State. In

fact, people commonly express a preference for resolving disputes through means other than the formal system (see Figure 3.1). However, this preference may reflect the lack of choices available to people, especially the poor and women, because of the social and institutional obstacles they face when approaching the formal state system (see Chapter 2).

Understanding the world as legally plural is an important starting point for looking at women's access to justice beyond the limited reach of the formal state system. Governments and international organizations have become more engaged with legal pluralism, in particular looking to justice institutions outside the formal system to provide faster, more efficient and more legitimate

FIGURE 3.1: Women's contact with community leaders and government officials

In many countries women are more likely to contact a community leader than a government official when they have a grievance.

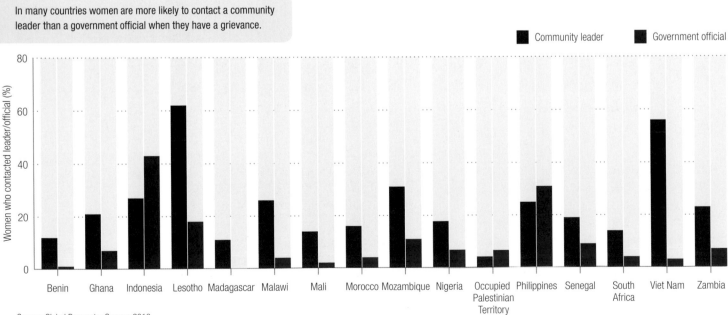

Source: Global Barometer Surveys 2010.

Note: The data refer to the percentage of respondents who said that in the previous three years they had at least once contacted a government official or traditional/community leader for personal, family or neighbourhood problems, or problems with government officials and policies.

solutions for poor people in situations where formal justice systems are weak.

This recognition of the reality of legal pluralism is welcome. However, it is also essential to recognize and address the particular barriers that plural legal systems can pose for women's rights and access to justice. International law recognizes the right of all communities to culture and in the case of indigenous populations, the right to determine their own systems of law and justice.[5] The State has responsibility for ensuring that compliance with human rights standards extends to all justice practices, including non-state legal systems that exist without formal state sanction.

The first part of this chapter briefly outlines three types of legal pluralism. It then focuses on three sets of challenges to women's rights that legal pluralism can pose: discriminatory elements of non-state laws and state-recognized identity-based laws; the practical barriers that existing legal pluralism can present for women's access to justice; and the challenges of reforming plural legal systems.

The second part of this chapter highlights many positive examples of initiatives undertaken by both governments and civil society that aim to improve women's access to justice in plural legal systems – empowering women to retain the cultural identities they choose and to demand the human rights they value and need. Women's organizations and other NGOs have often been leaders in successful interventions in legally plural environments. Depending upon context, these organizations are negotiating for progressive change within such systems, pressing for their dismantling altogether, or taking a combination of such reform approaches.

These initiatives show that it is possible to engage critically with plural legal systems while simultaneously supporting local cultures, traditions and practices. They also show how important it is that governments and international organizations support efforts to ensure that gender equality remains centre stage in any programmes related to legal plurality. Success should be measured in terms of whether the rights of women are upheld in all legal systems and justice processes, in line with international agreements, including CEDAW.

Understanding legal pluralism

Justice systems are often categorized as formal or informal, state or non-state. However, as the examples of the indigenous women in Ecuador and the Muslim woman in Kenya show, justice institutions cannot be neatly divided into these categories. In reality, different legal orders coexist and overlap, often in confusing and contradictory ways.

Broadly speaking, there are three types of legal pluralism. The first is where legal orders exist in parallel to the state system and are not formally recognized and are not state-sanctioned. Such non-state legal orders exist in every country. Examples include informal village jirgas (assemblies), a local conflict resolution mechanism made up of influential men in Afghanistan and Pakistan; street committees in Brazil that run conflict resolution forums; and customary water management bodies in the United Republic of Tanzania.[6]

The second kind of legal pluralism is where the state legal order is plural. Formal legal pluralism is common in many countries and takes various forms. For example, family and some property matters are governed by different laws for different religious or ethnic communities in many countries in the Middle East, South Asia and parts of South-East Asia.[7] In Indonesia, for example, there are six official religions and the State recognizes different provisions regulating marriage and divorce for each. In Lebanon, there are 18 different state-recognized family laws. In many countries in Africa, women married under the customary, religious, civil or common law system are subject to different state-recognized laws on inheritance and property rights.[8]

In many countries in Latin America, States also encompass multiple legal systems. In 1989, the ILO approved Convention 169 concerning Indigenous and Tribal Peoples in Independent Countries, the first comprehensive international treaty specifying the rights of indigenous peoples. It sets out States' obligations to recognize and respect indigenous peoples' forms of law, 'where these are not incompatible with fundamental rights defined by the national legal system and with internationally recognized human rights'.[9] Since then, 11 States in Latin America have recognized the right of indigenous communities to decide their own forms of law and conflict resolution, creating legal pluralism within the state system.[10] In 2007, the General Assembly adopted the United Nations Declaration on the Rights of Indigenous Peoples, which emphasizes their rights to maintain and strengthen their own institutions, cultures and traditions, and to pursue their development in keeping with their own needs and aspirations.[11]

The third kind of legal pluralism is where quasi-state legal orders are established or the State incorporates non-state legal orders. For example, through decentralization, many African States have incorporated customary chiefs or local power-holders as the lowest tier of the state legal system.[12] In some developed countries, the dispute resolution mechanisms of certain ethnic or religious communities have been recognized by the State. In the United Kingdom, for example, under the 1996 Arbitration Act, private religious arbitration on some disputes between spouses conducted by Jewish and Muslim organizations is recognized by the State.[13]

Increasingly common forms of quasi-state legal pluralism, in developed and developing countries, are new alternative dispute resolution mechanisms. These are established by the State to provide a means of resolving legal disputes and grievances without the use of the formal court system. In poor countries, the use of these mechanisms is justified on the basis that they provide a vital service where state capacity is weak or overburdened. But even in countries with relatively well-resourced justice systems, they are used to divert some cases out of the formal court system in order to reduce backlogs and costs to the State.

Legal pluralism can at times enhance choices and access for women seeking justice. However, there is growing evidence of the ways that it creates barriers to women's rights.

Women's access to justice and legal pluralism

The State's responsibility for ensuring compliance with human rights standards extends to all justice practices, including non-state legal systems that exist without formal state sanction, customary and religious systems that are incorporated into the state system, as well as quasi-state mechanisms such as alternative dispute resolution. But in practice, as with all justice systems, elements of discrimination and barriers to women's access to justice remain in many instances.

Legal pluralism can at times enhance choices and access for women seeking justice. However, there is growing evidence of the ways that it creates barriers to women's rights, which are explored below. First, non-state justice systems and plural formal laws based on specific interpretations of religious or ethnic identity sometimes contain provisions that discriminate against

women. In common with all justice systems, they tend to reflect the interests of the powerful, who have a greater say in shaping and defining laws and values. Second, the practical complexity of legal pluralism can create barriers for women's access to justice by, for example, enabling the powerful to 'forum shop' to gain legal advantage. Third, plural legal systems, defended on the basis of culture and religion can be resistant to reform in favour of women's rights.

Elements of discrimination within plural legal systems

There are three areas in which elements of discrimination against women exist within plural legal systems. First, plural family laws often contain unequal provisions for women and men. Second, customary and religious justice systems often do not have sanctions against gender-based violence. And third, these legal systems are sometimes procedurally biased against women.

Family laws – marriage, divorce, maintenance and custody – and property laws, which have a major impact on women's lives, are most likely to be subject to legal plurality. The family is central to community identity and as a result, the articles of CEDAW relating to family law are those on which States have most frequently imposed reservations citing cultural or religious factors, limiting or excluding the application of these provisions (see Figure 3.2). In many countries, these laws are influenced by interpretations of religion or culture that tend to restrict women's rights. Inequality between women and men in divorce, maintenance and custody rights has trapped women and their children in violent relationships or left them destitute. As the CEDAW Committee has noted: 'Inequality in the family is the most damaging of all forces in women's lives, underlying all other aspects of discrimination and disadvantage'.[14]

There are efforts both from within the international human rights system and civil society to challenge discriminatory family laws. While pressing for the removal of reservations to article 16 of CEDAW and the implementation of General Recommendation No. 21 on equality in marriage and family relations, the CEDAW Committee is also considering a new general recommendation on the economic consequences of marriage and divorce, to further extend international law in this critical area.[15]

The Equality without Reservations campaign brings together women's organizations from across the Middle East and North Africa region to call for the removal of reservations to CEDAW and ratification of the Optional Protocol.[16] Meanwhile, the global Musawah initiative

for equality and justice in the Muslim family is one of several civil society campaigns calling for reforms to discriminatory family laws and practices. It asserts that Islam mandates justice, equality, human dignity, love and compassion in relations in the family, principles that are also recognized as universal values and enshrined as rights in many national constitutions and international laws.[17] Civil society organizations have also played an important part in enabling women to access property and inheritance rights in legally plural contexts in all regions (see Figure 3.3).

The goal of many non-state justice systems is not individual redress but the restoration of peace and social harmony, which may mean that discrimination against women is perpetuated and that individual women are denied their rights. In addition, many customary and religious legal systems, whether recognized as part of the state system or operating beyond its control, do not include sanctions to outlaw violence against women. Such violence is usually considered a private matter and tacitly accepted as a natural feature of gender relations. As highlighted in the examples of Ecuador (see Case study: Ecuador) and Mexico (see Box 3.4), women in Latin America have been finding innovative ways of safeguarding their individual rights and tackling violence within indigenous justice frameworks that emphasize community harmony.

The seriousness of violence against women can also be downplayed where States use alternative dispute resolution mechanisms, introducing pluralism into the formal state system. These forums often deal with cases of violence against women on the basis that they are 'minor' matters. In some instances, they have been criticized for not providing 'due process', resulting in 'second class' justice for poor and excluded people who have less power to insist that their cases are dealt with through formal channels.[18]

In Brazil, Special Criminal Courts (Juizados Especiais Criminais) were set up as a form of alternative dispute resolution to provide mediated solutions for minor offences, but 60 to 80 percent of plaintiffs were women, mainly bringing complaints of bodily harm and threats. By dealing with these cases in these courts, most domestic violence cases were effectively decriminalized, with only a few of the most serious cases dealt with by the penal

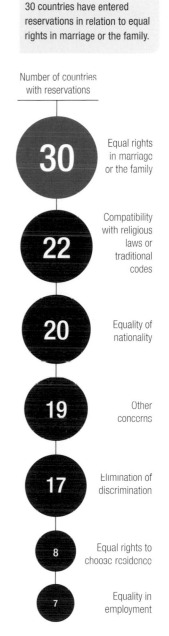

FIGURE 3.2:

Reservations to CEDAW

30 countries have entered reservations in relation to equal rights in marriage or the family.

Number of countries with reservations

30 Equal rights in marriage or the family

22 Compatibility with religious laws or traditional codes

20 Equality of nationality

19 Other concerns

17 Elimination of discrimination

8 Equal rights to choose residence

7 Equality in employment

Source: Annex 5.

Discriminatory legal codes and customary practices limit women's right to inherit. But, women across the world are finding innovative ways to demand their rights.

East Asia and the Pacific ■

88

In Cambodia, although the Constitution states that women and men are equal, Chbab Srey, the traditional code of conduct for women, reinforces unequal inheritance practices. The Women's Media Centre produced a television drama on women's rights to catalyse public debate. An evaluation found that 60 percent of survey participants had discussed the drama with friends, colleagues and relatives, and said they had a greater understanding of women's rights and inheritance.

Latin America and the Caribbean

In the Plurinational State of Bolivia, the 1996 land law recognizes women's equal rights to land, but customary inheritance practices mean that land often passes from father to son. In the community of Tarairí, a group of women organized with the help of the Guarani People Assembly leader, Alejandrina Avenante, to demand equal rights. Despite initial resistance from indigenous authorities, the women succeeded in reforming the customary practices that barred them from inheriting.

.95

1.0

Equal right to inherit

.80

---

system. It was reported that 90 percent of domestic violence cases ended at the first stage of conciliation, either because the woman was intimidated by the presence in court of her abuser, or because the judge pressed for the case to be closed. For those found guilty in these courts, sentences included small fines or the requirement to make a donation to charity.[19]

Recognizing the negative impact of the trivialization of these crimes, Brazil's 2006 Maria da Penha Law on domestic and family violence put a stop to this practice, banning compulsory mediation and introducing new courts on domestic and family violence, which can impose appropriate penal sentences and protection orders (see Balancing the Scales and Box 2.5).

Finally, in common with some state justice systems, non-state and parallel identity-based legal orders can be procedurally biased and are less likely to accept women as equal adjudicators, complainants, representatives or witnesses. This has been addressed in Malaysia, where

women have been permitted as judges in the civil courts for years, but in 2010, for the first time they were also allowed to sit as judges in the Syariah courts (state courts that deal with aspects of Islamic law).[20]

Practical barriers to women pursuing justice in plural legal systems

The existence of legal pluralism in itself can pose particular challenges to women seeking justice. It can create a complex web of overlapping systems, which in some instances mean that women fall through the 'cracks' and lose their protection or access to rights entirely. For example, in systems based on identity or religion, women who do not belong to one or other of the state-recognized identity groups or who marry across community lines may lack any redress. One approach is to provide civil remedies to which people belonging to any religion, or none, can appeal. In Israel, for example, the Government has provided the option for women to

.50

Middle East and North Africa

The Women's Democratic Association of Morocco and the Forum for Alternatives have supported the indigenous Soulaliyates women's right to collective lands, on equal terms to men. As a result of legal action, sit-ins and street demonstrations, the Ministry of the Interior formally recognized their rights in September 2009.

South Asia

In Sri Lanka, the EMACE Foundation provides free legal clinics in the capital Colombo. To reach women in rural areas, they also run a free 24-hour hotline, which fields on average 50 calls a month about property and inheritance rights.

.56

.37

Sub-Saharan Africa

Protecting women's inheritance rights in the context of HIV is vitally important. In Zambia, the Justice for Widows and Orphans Project (JWOP) assists women through training to write wills and providing legal aid. Based on local dispute resolution mechanisms, JWOP's legal tribunals focus on property and inheritance cases. While the tribunals' recommendations are not binding, they raise awareness of gender equality and support women in their pursuit of justice.

.60   .40   .20   0

Unequal right to inherit

Source: Inheritance data are UN Women calculated averages based on data from OECD 2010c. For the Plurinational State of Bolivia, Chávez 2008, for Cambodia, WID Tech 2003; for Sri Lanka, EMACE 2010; for Morocco, ADFM 2010; and for Zambia, Varga 2006 and Stefiszyn 2010.

Note: The values in the figure are based on the inheritance indicator in the OECD Gender, Institutions and Development Database (GID-DB) which measures whether women and men have equal rights as heirs. A score of 1 – equal inheritance rights and practices, and 0 – inheritance rights and/or practices favour male heirs. The measure takes into account the legal situation, drawing on the constitution and other legal documents as a reference and assesses the extent to which these legal provisions are applied in practice.

approach a civil court, rather than religious courts, in order to obtain maintenance.[21]

'Forum shopping' in legally plural contexts theoretically offers choice to litigants. In some countries, laws and constitutions permit the adjudication of personal and family matters under religious and customary laws. While both parties have to consent to have the case heard in a traditional forum, there are typically no mechanisms to monitor such consent.[22] Because they have less power, women are vulnerable to pressure from family and society, and where men have greater awareness, finances and flexibility, legal pluralism enables them to shop around for a favourable outcome while the options for justice for excluded women are very much more limited. In Sri Lanka, men who had married under the General Law but later sought a divorce could circumvent its restrictive divorce provisions by converting to Islam. Since the Muslim Marriages and Divorces Act permits polygamy, they were able to take another wife and leave their first wife in limbo. This matter was finally resolved in 1996, when the

Supreme Court in Sri Lanka ruled that the provisions of the General Law applied to all those who married under it, including those of Muslim faith.[23]

Other barriers to women's access to justice originate in confusion over jurisdictional boundaries. In the United States, for example, the interaction between federal, state and tribal jurisdictions meant that crimes committed by non-Native Americans on reservations often went unpunished.[24] High levels of rape of Native American women have been partly attributed to this jurisdictional confusion, whereby it was not clear which authority was responsible. To address this, in July 2010, the Tribal Law and Order Act was passed, with the aim of clarifying responsibilities and increasing coordination among the various law enforcement agencies.[25]

As noted in Chapter 2, under-resourced justice systems present barriers to justice for women and other excluded groups. Where there are a multiplicity of laws recognized by the State, the problems of weak infrastructure can

There are many examples of governments and women's organizations engaging with plural legal systems to bring about positive change.

be exacerbated, since the State has to resource several justice systems. In Indonesia, the Government has recognized that there is considerable unmet demand among women to access the religious courts and has invested in them in order to improve the service that women receive (see Box 3.2).

Challenges in reforming plural legal systems

Plural legal systems – both state-recognized and non-state systems – can be difficult to reform for three linked reasons. First, where these systems are recognized, it can place the state seal of approval on them, making them harder to reform. Second, plural legal systems are intertwined with the politics of identity, which can make reform efforts highly contentious. And third, because they are complex, in practical terms they are harder to reform.

When States recognize non-state, customary or religious laws, which may be discriminatory but are also evolving, they can effectively 'freeze' what were fluid systems that could have been amenable to progressive reform on gender equality. Governments and courts usually consult experts to ascertain the 'correct' interpretation of certain customary or religious codes. The most visible experts, such as religious scholars, community leaders, elders or academics, usually belong to dominant social groups who may not reflect the views of the silent majority and rarely reflect women's interests.

In Canada, the Indian Act had reduced a complex process of determining kinship, which was potentially more inclusive for Aboriginal women, to one of patriarchal descent, which excluded the children of Aboriginal women who married out of the community. State recognition had inadvertently limited women's rights. This was reversed after a landmark case was taken to the United Nations Human Rights Committee, which established that Sandra Lovelace, a Canadian Aboriginal woman, had the right to return to her reservation and access property, even though she had married a non-Aboriginal man (see Balancing the Scales).

The exemption of customary or religious law from constitutional equality provisions is another example of where plural legal systems can be harder to reform. A growing number of countries recognize women's right to own land and inherit on equal terms to men in their constitutions and laws (see Figure 1.9 and Figure 3.3). However, in a number of countries there are 'claw-back clauses' that stipulate that customary or religious law has precedence over family and property laws and equality provisions do not apply.[26] Amendments are made to constitutions rarely, which means that such discriminatory provisions are very difficult to change.

In 2010, Kenya adopted a new Constitution, which declares that customary laws that are inconsistent with its equality provisions are void. The Constitution specifies that land shall be held, used and managed in accordance with the principle of the elimination of gender discrimination in law, customs and practices. Nevertheless, these provisions explicitly exclude Muslim family laws, indicating that there is further to go to ensure equality for all.[27]

Attempts to reform religion-based family laws in India show how contentious and complex these efforts can be. Article 44 of the Indian Constitution (1950) specifies: 'The State shall endeavour to secure for the citizens a uniform civil code'. But, the political sensitivity of the issue has made it particularly challenging for gender equality advocates to identify and agree upon the most effective strategy for advancing the rights of all Indian women, including minorities. Some local women's rights activists are working to reform identity-based family laws to remove elements of discrimination, while others are promoting a civil code based on egalitarian principles rather than uniformity as such.

The challenges to women's rights and access to justice posed by plural legal systems, as they currently stand, are considerable and should not be ignored. However, there are many examples of governments and women's organizations engaging with plural legal systems to bring about positive change. The most successful efforts are guided by in-depth understanding of the particular context and have challenged some common misconceptions and assumptions (see Box 3.1).

Questioning assumptions about plural legal systems

Over the past decade, there has been growing interest in non-state legal orders by governments and donors on the basis that these offer cheaper, faster, more representative and legitimate justice. However, some of the approaches have been based on general assumptions rather than empirical evidence. Challenging these assumptions is an important starting point for effective policy and programming on women's access to justice in legally plural contexts.

Surveys suggest that in many cases women prefer local justice to the formal system (see Figure 3.1). However, given the weakness of the formal system in many places and the social pressure put on women to keep disputes within the family or community, this may reflect necessity rather than genuine preference. Indeed, at times the disadvantaged want more, not less, state intervention to guarantee their rights (see Box 3.2).[28] In reality, those on the margins of society are also on the margins of legal orders, state or non-state.

The notion that customary or identity-based systems are more legitimate and representative of a community's values may be equally flawed. It is based on the supposition that communities speak with one voice, without examining who has power to define those values, and whose voices remain unheard. Women are often explicitly excluded from shaping non-state justice systems and most religion-based parallel systems are less directly accountable to women because interpretive authority is often presumed to rest with men. In relation to the claim that non-state justice systems are faster, lack of infrastructure and resources in fact often makes them slow and expensive. They may also entail high, non-monetary social costs for women.[29]

Presumptions that non-state legal orders are 'traditional' and are therefore more authentic or legitimate have also been widely challenged. In many parts of the world, colonial powers, post-independence or post-conflict governments have significantly reshaped practices, transplanted them into areas where they did not previously exist, or created new 'traditional authorities', which reflect contemporary political aims rather than age-old customary practices.[30]

By partnering with NGOs and activists to produce locally grounded research, international organizations and donors can counter some of these unhelpful assumptions and ensure that their programming in plural legal environments is based on sound empirical evidence.

Strategies for change

Through guaranteeing equality in constitutions and ratifying CEDAW, governments all over the world have signaled their commitment to ensuring that women can access justice no matter what kind of legal systems are in place.

Women's organizations, which have been on the front line of legal pluralism for decades, have used these guarantees to successfully campaign both to prevent the introduction of a plural system and to have pluralities removed where they feel these reduce women's access to justice. They have also campaigned to retain aspects of pluralism that enhance women's rights and to reform those that do not.

Local women's organizations and human rights NGOs that work on the ground are aware of the benefits and drawbacks of the various legal systems, and their successful interventions are based on the lived realities of the people with whom they work. These organizations have found ways of appropriating international human rights standards into local practices or discovering rights-based aspects of their cultures. They have challenged the presumption that women must choose between rights and culture, and that respect for diversity necessarily entails the sacrificing of women's rights.

Legal empowerment programmes involving both local justice providers and women in the community can be effective in helping to improve accountability.

This section first highlights examples of legal empowerment approaches, which enable women to both navigate plural legal systems and be part of campaigns for change. It then shows how women have worked to catalyse reform within state-recognized plural legal systems and how progressive change can be fostered within non-state justice systems.

Legal empowerment to help women navigate and shape plural legal systems

Legal empowerment initiatives enable people to be active participants not only in using the law, but also in shaping it to their needs. These interventions include the provision of legal services, such as legal aid and paralegals, capacity building and human rights awareness training for both justice system users and providers.[31]

The use of paralegals trained in women's rights is a particularly powerful strategy for ensuring women can access justice where there are multiple formal and non-state systems. Community paralegals play an essential role in ensuring that excluded women know their rights and can negotiate plural legal orders to their advantage, in providing access to the formal system and in helping to enhance the accountability of non-state systems.[32]

When paralegals are located within the community, their knowledge of multiple legal orders and understanding of local social and political structures enables them to bridge the different systems and offer advice with a full understanding of the social and legal context. Paralegals must be fully trained to understand the formal law, and programmes should include capacity for litigation, so that they can refer cases to the formal system where appropriate.

Paralegals have also helped women to shape formal state law and articulate demands for unbiased laws in identity-based or religious justice systems. This can be particularly vital in the case of customary and identity-based legal systems, which may otherwise exclude women's voices. In Pakistan, Shirkat Gah Women's Resource Centre in Lahore has focused on building

women's 'legal consciousness', to enable them to make informed choices about which legal forums to approach, but also to be part of shaping laws and campaigning for change.

Having conducted research on communities' understandings of culture, religion, law and customary practices in relation to women's rights, Shirkat Gah organized paralegal training for members of community-based organizations. When the Government of Pakistan announced a Commission of Inquiry into women's legal status in the 1990s, the paralegals were able to influence its deliberations through a questionnaire that was developed to solicit inputs from the grassroots. The newly trained paralegals were able to give real-life examples of the impact of the law from their experiences in local communities.

They highlighted in particular the fact that customary systems forced women to forgo their inheritance rights in favour of male family members. They also focused attention on the practice of symbolic 'marriage' of women to the Qur'an, which means women cannot marry, ensuring that their share of family property will not leave the family. The Commission's final report included extensive recommendations on women's property rights and, although change has been slow, a bill is being considered by the National Assembly in Pakistan to outlaw the practice of symbolic 'marriage'.[33]

Legal empowerment programmes that involve the training of both local justice providers and women in the community can be effective in helping to improve accountability. Since 2007, UNICEF has been working with village courts in Papua New Guinea. These hybrid courts are created and given jurisdictional powers by the State, but are presided over by village leaders who resolve disputes according to local custom. The programme provides human rights training to village leaders, as well as to youth and women's groups, to enable them to understand and claim their rights. As a result of this work, women are now accepted as village court officials and play an active role in monitoring court decisions.[34]

Box 3.2 Women's access to religious courts in Indonesia

In Indonesia, the religious courts are an important avenue for women seeking justice. Recognizing this, the Supreme Court is working in partnership with civil society to enhance access and monitor their performance.

Legal registration of marriage and divorce is not only important for women's rights within the family, it is also essential for accessing public services. Marriage certificates are often needed to obtain birth certificates for children, which are required to register for school and to claim inheritance rights. For women to access government benefits targeted at poor households, legal divorce documents are needed to prove eligibility.

However, a survey of their members by the women's NGO Pemberdayaan Perempuan Kepala Keluarga (PEKKA), found that the marriages of fewer than 50 percent of respondents were legally recognized, 86 percent had not legally registered their divorce and 56 percent of the women's children did not have birth certificates. One third of PEKKA members living below the poverty line reported difficulties accessing benefits and services such as free health care and cash transfer programmes. Religious courts handle 98 percent of all legal divorces in Indonesia, but the costs can be prohibitive for women. The average total cost of obtaining a divorce through the religious courts is $90, almost four times the monthly income of a person living on the poverty line. Nearly 90 percent of women surveyed said they would be more likely to approach the courts for a divorce if the court fees were waived or if circuit courts were held in nearby towns.

Lack of awareness of rights is also a problem. Working with the World Bank's Justice for the Poor Programme, PEKKA coordinates a network of trained paralegals, who promote legal literacy and provide practical support to enable women to access the religious courts to formalize their marriages and divorces. Multi-stakeholder forums also bring together judges, police, local government and NGOs to improve coordination and increase the responsiveness of justice service providers.

PEKKA has used its experience at community level to lobby local and national governments for change. The Supreme Court has increased the number of circuit courts in rural and remote areas and has introduced a policy of waiving court fees for the poor. Over the last two years, the budget for religious courts has been increased by $3.5 million, an 18-fold annual increase. A web-based data system and monthly SMS communication between the Directorate-General for Religious Courts and the 372 courts across the country is being used to monitor progress, with initial data showing that between 2007 and 2010, the number of poor people accessing religious courts has increased 14 fold.[35]

Catalysing reform in plural legal systems

A number of approaches have been used to challenge discriminatory elements of plural legal systems and bring about progressive change. Women's rights advocates have used the State's obligation to assure the implementation of human rights to demand accountability and change where non-state legal orders or identity-based state laws are discriminatory. This obligation may stem from constitutional guarantees, or international or regional human rights standards.

In an ever-growing body of jurisprudence, customary and religious laws are coming under increased scrutiny, particularly in countries where the legal order is formally plural. Appealing to the formal system, women living under plural legal systems have challenged the aspects that limit their human rights as the landmark Bhe and Lovelace cases show (see Balancing the Scales).

In South Africa, in an important and hard fought victory, women's rights advocates played an instrumental role in ensuring that the equality provisions of the post-Apartheid Constitution applied to customary law. The Centre for Applied Legal Studies (CALS) was closely involved. Subsequently, working with the Rural Women's Movement (RWM), CALS turned its attention to influencing the new law on customary marriage.

At the outset, CALS and RWM took the position that the law must prohibit polygamy. However, a research project to assess the practices, needs and interests of women in relation to customary marriage, raised questions about the protection of women and children in existing polygamous marriages. If polygamy was outlawed outright, their livelihoods would be directly threatened and a significant number of women would be left without legal protection. CALS and RWM therefore shifted their approach to advocate for a framing of the law that would make polygamy expensive, eventually leading to the decline of the practice, while safeguarding women's rights to marital property.[36]

They proposed that each time a man married, existing marital property had to be shared equally with all the wives, old and new. CALS helped draft the regulations for the Customary Marriages Act of 2000 and monitored its implementation. The law ultimately included a provision for equality within customary marriage, giving millions of women legal security and recognizing the equality of husband and wife in terms of status, decision-making, property and children.[37]

In contexts of legal pluralism, women's rights campaigners have found that they gain greater mass support and broaden the scope for reform by using and addressing multiple norms and legal systems at the same time. For instance, Egyptian activists are working towards a rights-based single family code for all religions (replacing the plural state laws) but one that retains *certain* distinct provisions for the various communities.[38] In Nigeria, women's rights advocates have used a combination of arguments from religious, customary, secular and constitutional laws to protect women from extreme punishments under Muslim penal provisions (see Box 3.3).

Progressive change from within

All justice systems and cultures evolve. They can therefore be reformed and shaped according to the needs of the people that they affect. One promising approach aims to support reformers to influence change within their own ethnic or religious community. In many legally plural contexts, rights activists can find themselves battling on several fronts, struggling to promote the right to cultural diversity but also fighting to ensure that any recognition of cultural rights does not exacerbate discrimination against excluded groups within the community.

Box 3.3 Progressive reinterpretation of religious laws in Nigeria

Since 2000, 13 states in northern Nigeria have formally adopted Sharia laws and penal codes in addition to secular laws. Under these laws, a number of women have been convicted of zina (extramarital sex), which carries the death penalty. In one high-profile case, a pregnant rape victim, was sentenced to stoning to death while the perpetrators were set free as no evidence against them was presented or sought.[39]

A Nigerian women's organization, BAOBAB for Women's Human Rights, which has been running programmes focused on women's rights in secular, customary and Muslim laws for a decade, took on the legal defence of these women, collaborating with other organizations and building alliances for broad support.

BAOBAB argues that the current Muslim laws are a product of a particular interpretation of religious laws and that women have been excluded from participating in the process of defining them. Progressive reinterpretation of the laws is therefore key. BAOBAB has critiqued, popularized and integrated women's rights principles from Muslim, secular, customary and international human rights law into local practices and institutions.[40]

BAOBAB briefed lawyers for women in zina cases, enabling them to use arguments from religious frameworks. They also drew on Nigerian secular and constitutional law, as well as international human rights law. As a result of BAOBAB's work, in all cases so far, the Sharia courts of appeal have quashed the convictions.

In Latin America, women have been an important part of indigenous movements demanding the formal acknowledgement of their justice systems as an essential element of their identity and inclusion in the State. The fact that indigenous women experience racist treatment by formal justice institutions does not mean that they are free of discriminatory treatment by indigenous justice systems. However, while women have been part of the struggle to formalize indigenous systems, they have simultaneously contested bias from the inside, as the examples of Ecuador and Mexico show (see Case study: Ecuador and Box 3.4).

The shalish in Bangladesh is a community-based justice system in which small panels of influential local figures help resolve community members' disputes and prescribe penalties if necessary. In the traditional shalish system, arbitrators are exclusively men who tend to maintain conservative cultural norms and practices, which has often resulted in highly discriminatory rulings against women, particularly in matters of sexual conduct.[41] In recent years, Bangladeshi NGOs have engaged with shalish processes to ensure better outcomes for women. The local NGOs, the Maduripur Legal Aid Association and Nagorik Uddyog have trained shalish panels on gender equality, encouraged the participation of women in the process and introduced basic record-keeping so that agreements and other key proceedings are documented.[42]

In Burundi, a country slowly emerging from decades of conflict, UN Women has supported an initiative to incorporate women into the circle of bashingantahe, traditional elders responsible for conflict resolution at the community level, which had previously been a strictly male domain. The bashingantahe are instrumental in the maintenance of community cohesion and the restoration of peace in their collines, the smallest administrative units in the country. Through sensitization of leaders on women's rights and the amendment of the bashingantahe charter, women became accepted as part of the institution, taking part in decision-making. They now make up 40 percent of the committee members of the bashingantahe. As a result, awareness of sexual and gender-based violence and other violations of women's rights has increased. Burundian women's organizations have been campaigning for a new law to guarantee

women's inheritance rights. Although resistant at first, bashingantahe leaders have been speaking out in public in support of the proposed law, including on local radio, and have become important allies in the campaign.[43]

Dialogues to advance women's rights

Dialogues with adjudicators can provide women with a safe place for them to voice concerns over unfairness in the justice system, to take part in determining their own cultural values, and to bring about reform in procedures. Such dialogues are most effective when facilitated by local rights-based organizations with long-standing legal empowerment programmes.

In Pakistan, for example, Shirkat Gah Women's Resource Centre conducted training for marriage registrars, which was run in the form of an interactive discussion rather than top-down teaching. The registrars particularly welcomed the opportunity to share their concerns and seek advice about how to address the fact that, in some cases, customary leaders helped to subvert the law on the minimum age of marriage.[44] The Muslim Women's Research and Action Forum (MWRAF) in Sri Lanka initiated a dialogue with Quazi courts, which hear marriage and divorce cases for the minority Muslim population. This helped women to understand the practical problems and social realities of implementing the law, but also enhanced the Quazi court judges' awareness of how the law can be interpreted and applied in a progressive and gender-sensitive way.[45]

The Kenyan National Commission of Human Rights undertook a project to improve land rights for women. In Luo society in western Kenya, land is always inherited through the male line, meaning that women often lose their livelihood after the death of their husbands. However, the protection of women is perceived to be an important part of Luo culture. In community dialogues, women described their struggle for survival in front of the elders. Confronted with the women's plight and in recognition of social changes and growing awareness of human rights, the elders revitalized their commitment to protective aspects of Luo culture and helped women to gain access to land from their husbands' families.[46]

All justice systems evolve. They can therefore be reformed and shaped according to the needs of the people they affect.

The Federation of Women Lawyers (FIDA-Uganda) has initiated dialogue with local community elders in the Acholi districts of northern Uganda to address the problem of sexual and gender-based violence in their communities. The Ker Kwaro-Acholi (KKA) is a legal-cultural institution comprising 54 traditional leaders who head various clans and are considered cultural custodians of the Acholi people. Starting from the common goal of promoting women's rights in society, FIDA and the paramount chief of the KKA appointed a task force, which worked with FIDA to document local cultural practices. They undertook extensive legal education sessions to raise community awareness of women's rights and mechanisms for redress.

As a result of this work, a set of gender principles was drafted, using language from the Ugandan Constitution, the Domestic Relations Bill and international human rights instruments, to guide the KKA in its future judgments. Varying levels of agreement were reached between local practices and human rights norms on the definition of marriage, the regulation of polygamy, sexual rights, violence against women, and inheritance and property rights. The ongoing process has been important in opening up dialogue between activists and customary leaders, fostering the shared goal of enhancing women's rights.[47]

Box 3.4   Women shaping indigenous courts in Mexico

The pioneering work of Nahua women in Cuetzalan to organize and demand justice represents one of the most significant movements for change among indigenous women in Mexico.

The population of Cuetzalan is 60 percent Nahua and they have been very active in implementing indigenist policies in the fields of health, education and justice. Links between Nahua groups and regional human rights organizations have inspired indigenous women to develop their own understanding of women's rights, with support from Mestizo women, so-called 'rural feminists'. In so doing, they have appropriated and redefined the language of human rights, indigenous rights and women's rights in line with their own cultural contexts.

In 2001, the Mexican Constitution recognized indigenous peoples' rights and forms of social organization, and subsequently an indigenous court was established by the judicial authorities of Puebla in Cuetzalan. At the same time, the House of the Indigenous Woman (Casa de la Mujer Indígena – CAMI) was created to address indigenous women's health issues. However, CAMI soon took on the agenda of access to justice for women survivors of domestic abuse.

CAMI became a place where Nahua women could find practical and psychological support to seek justice and an end to violence.

A methodology known as 'intercultural conciliation with a gender perspective' has been developed, involving health, emotional support and protection, which are addressed in an integrated manner in order to support the survivor and her family. Depending on what the woman wants, cases can be addressed via a legal process or through conciliation. Women are trained as community representatives and promoters of CAMI, providing outreach to women in surrounding communities. CAMI has also developed work on masculinities, to encourage behaviour change among men.

CAMI has started working with the indigenous court, to raise awareness of women's rights with the court's authorities. Women from CAMI form part of the court's governing council and their ongoing dialogue with the indigenous judges aims to ensure that they take women's rights into account in their deliberations, even if this sometimes contravenes patriarchal aspects of local custom. By 2006, women made up more than half of plaintiffs in cases, indicating that the indigenous court plays an important role in adjudicating issues of concern to them.[48]

Conclusion

To make justice systems work for women, governments, policymakers and international organizations need a broader perspective that recognizes the interplay of multiple legal systems, their relation to power and the way that people navigate them.

An effective approach towards justice sector reform in the context of legal pluralism requires rethinking some of the basic assumptions international policymakers have perpetuated. It is important, for example, to avoid discussing legal pluralism in terms of binary oppositions, such as formal and informal justice. The lines are blurred in reality and some of the most successful initiatives illustrate a fine-tuned ability to negotiate the spaces between state and non-state orders to the advantage of the excluded.

As with all laws and justice systems, those based on religious or ethnic identity include elements that discriminate against women. Where there are many different systems in place, the complexity, overlaps and gaps created can exacerbate the challenges that women face in accessing justice and their rights.

Despite the challenges, civil society organizations and governments worldwide are demonstrating how women's rights can be protected, while also fulfilling diverse communities' rights to culture. These approaches are based on an understanding that while cultural practices can be discriminatory, there are many interpretations and practices that fully comply with international human rights standards or national equality guarantees.

Constitutional equality guarantees should apply to all laws and justice systems, in line with international law.

In South Africa, customary law is subject to constitutional equality guarantees, which has enabled women to challenge discriminatory elements of these laws. In Ecuador, indigenous women have secured the right to participate in shaping indigenous justice systems. CEDAW requires governments to take responsibility for gender equality in relation to all legal matters, including family law, and all legal systems, whether they are recognized by the State or not. Furthermore, States have obligations under international law to ensure access to justice, which extends to addressing elements of discrimination within plural legal orders. It is critical that governments ensure that all the legal systems, and their interplay, function at the highest common denominator for women's rights.

Invest in legal empowerment programmes to help women to access justice in plural legal contexts.

Working in partnership with local women's organizations and other NGOs, successful approaches include training community paralegals, supporting dialogue with justice providers and helping women to contest discriminatory elements of laws and practices. In Pakistan, paralegals have supported women to access justice in a plural legal context, but have also enabled them to campaign for reform of family laws.

Ensuring that women can participate in defining and delivering justice is critical to countering discrimination and increasing accountability.

All over the world, women have been demanding a seat at the table when it comes to defining and delivering justice in plural legal contexts. In Burundi, women are now part of the bashingantahe customary justice institution, gaining the respect of male leaders, as well as their support for the campaign for equal inheritance rights. Governments can play a key role in supporting women to participate on an equal basis with men in shaping legal systems, empowering them to bring their interpretations of culture to the forefront.

Chapter 4:
Justice for Women During and After Conflict

CASE STUDY: Liberia

For 14 years, women in Liberia bore the brunt of two brutal wars characterized by the use of child soldiers, mass displacement and widespread sexual and gender-based violence. Women were also instrumental in ending the fighting in the country and bringing peace to its people.

One such woman, Leymah Gbowee, a social worker and mother of six, brought together several dozen women in 2002 to pray for peace after watching her country descend into a war that made violence, rape and murder a part of daily existence. In doing so, she launched a movement of ordinary women who campaigned to help put an end to Liberia's civil war and pave the way for the election of Africa's first female Head of State, Ellen Johnson Sirleaf.

The women came together in their thousands, with the support of the Women in Peacekeeping Network (WIPNET), to push for a meeting with then President Charles Taylor to extract a promise from him to attend peace talks in Ghana. Leymah Gbowee subsequently led a delegation of Liberian women to Ghana to continue to apply pressure on the warring factions during the peace process. They monitored the talks and staged a silent protest outside the presidential palace in Accra. When the talks stalled, the women barricaded the room, refusing to let the men out until a peace agreement was signed. Eventually, an agreement was reached but the real work of engendering justice and reconciliation had only just begun.

In West African culture, a palava hut is a round structure with a thatched roof usually located in the middle of the compound of a community elder. In palava huts, chiefs and elders would traditionally resolve disputes and settle conflicts. In the context of post-conflict Liberia, palava huts became a forum where individuals could admit their 'wrongful acts' and seek a pardon from the community.

WIPNET has co-opted and reinvented the concept of the palava hut to support the process of disarmament, demobilization and reintegration of combatants. Liberian women decided to build palava huts and call them peace huts instead, a place for women to meet, to discuss problems, to provide support to one another and to build peace in their communities.

The women act as mediators, meeting regularly to share information about problems in the community and to make plans to resolve them. The number of participants varies, from a few dozen to two hundred women. Community members come to the peace huts with grievances, including cases of rape, as well as those related to land and religious or ethnic disputes.

The peace huts are a place of sanctuary and safety for women escaping domestic violence. Members of the peace huts work with the local police to identify those suspected of crimes against women, ensuring that they are arrested and interrogated. The women address child support issues, monitor early warning signs of conflict, expose corrupt politicians, lead peaceful demonstrations, engage in adult literacy and income-generating programmes, and pray and sing together.

The peace hut movement is growing, with at least nine in existence in five counties of Liberia. The movement has shown the power of women working together to build and maintain peace in their communities.[1]

'Conflict can provide women with opportunities to break out of stereotypes and stifling societal patterns... If women seize these opportunities, transformation is possible. The challenge is to protect the seeds of transformation sown during the upheaval and to use them to grow the transformation in the transitional period of reconstruction.'

Anu Pillay

Liberian women gather inside a peace hut.

Introduction

In the space of a few decades, international justice has progressed from failing to recognize, prosecute and redress women's experiences in conflict, to the gains made in the Rome Statute of the International Criminal Court.

Prioritizing justice for women is an essential part of rebuilding trust in state institutions and establishing sustainable peace.

Building on the pioneering work of the international tribunals for the former Yugoslavia and Rwanda, the Rome Statute codifies as international crimes a broad range of sexual and gender-based violations including rape, sexual slavery, enforced prostitution, forced pregnancy, enforced sterilization, gender persecution and trafficking in women and children. The inclusion of these atrocities as crimes to be prosecuted by the international community is a very significant gain.

The major challenge of translating these gains into justice for women on the ground, a challenge for all law reform, is exacerbated where the justice infrastructure is shattered and mass atrocities have taken place. The building blocks for the rule of law – a strong legal framework and a functioning justice system – are weak or absent in conflict and post-conflict settings.

Prioritizing justice for women, to deal with the crimes of war and to build a justice system that can meet women's needs in post-conflict contexts, is an essential part of rebuilding trust in state institutions, establishing inclusive citizenship and ultimately sustainable peace.

The first part of this chapter explores the gendered impact of conflict. The second part focuses on the gains that have been made in international law and analyses what needs to happen to increase the number of successful prosecutions, both at international and domestic levels.

As well as retributive justice through prosecutions, women demand other forms of accountability and reparative justice, to recognize what they have suffered and give them the means to rebuild their lives. The final part of the chapter highlights how truth commissions and comprehensive reparations can play an important part in meeting these demands.

There is a growing recognition that rather than reinforcing the pre-conflict status quo, post-conflict remedies and reparations should address the underlying inequalities that women faced before the conflict, aiming for transformative change for women and girls. As well as ensuring that reparations are broad in scope and accessible, enabling women to participate in the reshaping of the post-conflict State is a key element of transformative justice.

Post conflict is not just when transformative justice is most needed, it is also the moment when there is the most potential to deliver. During conflict, traditional gender roles are unseated, women take on new roles and the foundations for a new society are established through new constitutions, institutions and legal frameworks. There are enormous opportunities during these periods to promote women's leadership, enhance access to justice and build more just and stable societies for all.

The impact of conflict on women

Everyone suffers during conflict. Severe violations and human rights abuses, including killings, abductions and forced displacement wreak havoc and destruction in everyone's lives. However, the impact is different for women and men.

The blurring of the lines between the battlefield and the 'home front' in many contemporary conflicts means that civilians are increasingly targeted. While men are more likely to be killed, women are always disproportionately singled out for sexual violence and abuse. In Sierra Leone, some men reported sexual abuse to the Truth and Reconciliation Commission, but all cases of rape and sexual slavery were reported by women (see Figure 4.1).[2] Furthermore, it is widely recognized that these crimes against women are always substantially under-reported.

Sexual violence as a tactic of warfare has been used systematically and deliberately for centuries. It creates shame and stigma and has in the past been perpetrated with almost complete impunity. Sexual violence is used against civilian populations to destroy the social fabric of communities, as a deliberate vector of HIV, for the purpose of forced impregnation, to drive the forcible displacement of populations and to terrorize whole communities.[3]

The true extent of these atrocities is generally not known because they are not fully documented, investigated or prosecuted (see Box 4.1). But the best estimates suggest their scale is vast. In Rwanda, it is estimated that between 250,000 and 500,000 women were raped in less than 100 days, as part of the 1994 genocide, in which 800,000 people were killed.[4] In Bosnia and Herzegovina, between 20,000 and 60,000 mostly Muslim women were subjected to sexual violence in 'rape camps'.[5]

FIGURE 4.1: Violations reported to the Sierra Leone Truth and Reconciliation Commission, by sex

Women were more likely than men to report forced displacement and abduction. All reports of rape and sexual slavery were made by women.

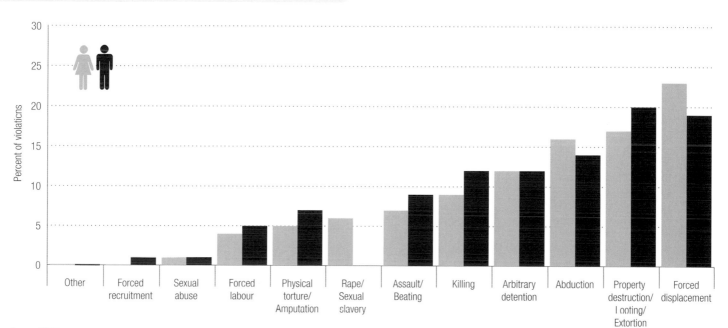

Source: UN Women calculations using data from Benetech 2010.

Note: The Sierra Leone Truth and Reconciliation Commission received statements detailing 40,242 violations. Men reported 67.3 percent (27,065) of these violations, women reported 32.4 percent (13,038). The victim's sex was not recorded for the remaining 0.3 percent (139 violations). Values represent the ratio of each category of violation to the total number of violations suffered by that group.

While peace agreements may stop the killing, failure to address sexual violence in ceasefires or peace accords mean that crimes against women often do not stop when the guns fall silent.

In eastern Democratic Republic of the Congo, at least 200,000 cases of sexual violence, mostly involving women and girls, have been documented since 1996.[6]

While peace agreements may stop the killing, failure to address sexual violence in ceasefires or peace accords means that crimes against women often do not stop when the guns fall silent. Violence is 'normalized' during conflict and as demobilized combatants return home, post-conflict contexts are often characterized by ongoing and sometimes increased levels of violence and insecurity for women. A study in Liberia in 2007, four years after the end of the conflict, found that in Nimba County, 26 percent of single women and 74 percent of married or separated women had been raped in the previous 18 months.[7] A study in the Democratic Republic of the Congo found that while the number of rapes by combatants declined between 2004 and 2008, the number of reported civilian rapes increased 17-fold.[8]

The massive upheavals and social dislocation caused by conflict also have particular impacts on women, who bear the disproportionate burden of social and economic rights violations. When men go off to fight, in many cases, women are left behind to secure the basic requirements for survival, for themselves and their families. The destruction of social infrastructure and reduction of government spending on social services places additional burdens on women as caregivers and exacerbates existing poverty.

Mass displacement is a consequence of violent conflict and women represent the majority of internally displaced people (IDPs) and refugees globally.[9] By 2009, there were more than 3 million displaced people in Colombia, the majority of them women and girls.[10] Of the violations reported by women to the Sierra Leone Truth and Reconciliation Commission, nearly a quarter were related to forced displacement (see Figure 4.1).

Sexual violence is both a cause and consequence of displacement. Around the world, women fleeing from conflict are at risk of abuse during transit, in camps and during return and reintegration. In a 2008 survey in Colombia, nearly 18 percent of the women questioned said that physical aggression and sexual violence were the drivers for their displacement.[11] In camps for displaced people in Darfur (the Sudan), inappropriate design of facilities and the need to travel long distances outside the camp for firewood or other necessities have increased the risks of violence for women.[12]

In research on women's justice priorities in post-conflict contexts, where the struggle for everyday survival is paramount, their demands are often for basic services and the means to rebuild shattered lives. In Cambodia, for example, 83 percent of women and men prioritized jobs, while 37 percent said that the delivery of services, including health care and food was most important.[13] In Timor-Leste, half of the women surveyed identified education for their children as their top priority.[14] In the Central African Republic, women said they needed money, access to services and housing. But they also demanded punishment for perpetrators of human rights abuses, as well as recognition of suffering and apologies. They identified the need for psychological counselling as part of the justice process (see Figures 4.4 and 4.5).

Accountability for crimes is a critical part of building a peaceful, stable and democratic society. In eastern Democratic Republic of the Congo, a survey found that while only 1 to 2 percent of respondents said that providing justice, arresting and punishing those responsible for violence or encouraging reconciliation are among their immediate priorities, 82 percent of respondents believed that accountability is necessary to achieve peace in the longer term.[15]

Ensuring that accountability is sought for gender-based crimes must be a central part of this quest for justice. The next section summarizes the advances in international law that have finally made this possible and then examines what can be done at the international and national levels to increase prosecutions and close the impunity gap.

Documentation of violations during and in the immediate aftermath of conflict can play a vital part in making prosecutions more likely, by collecting evidence for future investigation, by mapping crimes and identifying and maintaining links with potential witnesses.

Security Council resolutions 1820 and 1888 call for the gathering of information on trends, patterns and perpetrators of sexual violence in conflict to inform future Security Council responses. In the wake of the violence that engulfed Kenya after the 2007 presidential election, former United Nations Secretary-General Kofi Annan brokered a power-sharing agreement, which included the appointment of the Commission of Inquiry on Post Election Violence, known as the Waki Commission, named after its chair, Justice Philip Waki, an appeal court judge. The Commission was specifically mandated to investigate and document widespread incidents of sexual violence. The investigation was supported by an inter-agency gender-based violence group, consisting of United Nations agencies including the United Nations Population Fund (UNFPA) and UN Women, and civil society partners such as the Federation of Women Lawyers (FIDA-Kenya). Working with two women investigators with extensive expertise in dealing with cases of sexual violence, this group formulated gender-sensitive investigation methods, helped to locate victims and provided counselling services.[16]

The Commission received testimony from victims of sexual violence in public, in private and through statements collected by investigators, including from those who did not wish to appear before the Commission but nevertheless wanted their experiences taken into account.

In October 2008, the Waki Commission published its report, finding that sexual violence was perpetrated by all sides including by members of the security forces. It recommended that a special tribunal be created to 'seek accountability against persons bearing the greatest responsibility for crimes, particularly crimes against humanity'.[17] The names of perpetrators of violence were passed to the Prosecutor at the International Criminal Court, who received the Court's permission in 2010 to launch an investigation into the events.[18]

There have been many challenges for survivors of sexual violence seeking justice in Kenya, with problems reported in relation to witness protection, allegations of judicial corruption and lack of support for internally displaced women. But, it is nevertheless hoped that the documentation gathered by the Waki Commission will help to ensure that sexual violence crimes are prosecuted in any cases taken forward by the International Criminal Court as well as in any domestic investigation and prosecution of post-election violence.

Advances in international law

In the past, the impact of conflict on women has barely been acknowledged in international law and as a result, women's experiences have been largely denied, kept private and written out of history. However, in the past two decades, significant advances have been made in the recognition and prosecution of gender-based crimes committed during conflicts (see Display: Women, conflict and international law).

As far back as the 18th century, military codes have prohibited sexual violence, although in practice, rape of women has been tacitly accepted as 'conquerors' rights'.[19] Following the First World War, the 1929 Geneva Convention stated that 'prisoners of war are entitled to respect for their persons and honour. Women shall be treated with all consideration due to their sex'. Sexual violence was treated as a matter of moral defamation, rather than a violent crime.[20]

The London and Tokyo Charters, which established the Nuremburg and Tokyo Tribunals in the aftermath of the

There has been an extraordinary shift from a time when rape was rendered invisible...to the recognition that it is a threat to international peace and security.

Second World War, claimed jurisdiction over war crimes, crimes against humanity and crimes against the peace, without specifically mentioning rape.[21] No indictments or evidence were presented on the systematic military sexual slavery of tens of thousands of Asian women, the so-called 'comfort women', by the Japanese army (see Box 4.4).[22] An estimated 2 million women were raped in Europe, but rape was never charged in the Nuremburg trials.[23] When asked about sexual violence, the prosecutor said: 'The tribunal will forgive me if I avoid citing the atrocious details'.[24]

In 1949, the revised Geneva Conventions were adopted and, for the first time, one Convention was devoted to protecting civilians, stipulating that women should be 'protected... in particular against rape, forced prostitution and any other form of indecent assault'. However, it perpetuated the relative invisibility of crimes against women, categorizing rape as an attack on a woman's honour, not explicitly listing it as a 'grave breach' of the Conventions. In 1977, the first and second Additional Protocols to the Geneva Conventions of 1949 were signed, which further expanded the scope of the Conventions, to include legal protection of women civilians and combatants against sexual violence, including in civil conflicts.[25]

The atrocities committed in the former Yugoslavia and Rwanda prompted the establishment of two International Criminal Tribunals in the 1990s, which saw great leaps forward in international law on women and conflict. The governing statutes of these courts included the first explicit formulation of rape as a crime against humanity to be prosecuted, and the jurisprudence in these tribunals has recognized sexual violence as a serious war crime.[26] The Akayesu case at the International Criminal Tribunal for Rwanda was the first time in history that a defendant was convicted of rape as an instrument of genocide and as a crime against humanity (see Balancing the Scales).[27]

A number of groundbreaking cases at the International Criminal Tribunal for the former Yugoslavia have expanded the scope of international law on sexual violence, including the Furundžija case in which it was established that a single act of rape in the context of a widespread attack can constitute a crime against

humanity, as well as the Delalic case, which recognized sexual violence as torture.[28] The Krstic decision stated that sexual violence could be a foreseeable consequence of other wartime violations, reversing the assumption that sexual abuse in conflict is inevitable, the result of spontaneous acts of individuals and therefore not the responsibility of military superiors.[29] In 2008, a further landmark development was the Brima, Kamara and Kanu case at the Special Court for Sierra Leone, which found that forced marriage was an inhumane act constituting a crime against humanity.[30]

The International Criminal Tribunal for the former Yugoslavia and the International Criminal Tribunal for Rwanda also established important changes in the rules of evidence, limiting the use of the defence of consent in sexual assault cases and prohibiting evidence of the survivor's past sexual history being used. In the Gacumbitsi case at the International Criminal Tribunal for Rwanda, the prosecutor stated that proving non-consent did not require evidence on the words or conduct of the victim, the victim's past relationship with the perpetrator, or evidence of force. Instead, the trial chamber was asked to infer non-consent from the circumstances surrounding the case, such as the context of an ongoing campaign of genocide or the detention of the victim.[31]

Gender justice advocates have noted that sexual assault against men is usually charged as torture, persecution or inhumane acts, crimes for which the need to establish coercive circumstances or the lack of consent is not considered necessary.[32] This highlights the need for continued scrutiny of laws and rules of evidence that discriminate against women or are based on a male standard of justice.

The sex crimes cases ongoing at the International Criminal Tribunal for the former Yugoslavia and the International Criminal Tribunal for Rwanda influenced the Rome Statute, ratified by 114 States, which established the International Criminal Court in 2002. The Statute defines crimes against humanity and war crimes broadly to include rape, sexual slavery, enforced prostitution, forced pregnancy, enforced sterilization and any other form of sexual violence of comparable gravity. All constitute serious violations of the laws or customs of war.[33] As of

April 2011, the International Criminal Court is engaged or conducting investigations in six countries. No cases have yet been completed, but of the 23 indictments issued by the Court, 12 contain sexual violence crimes.[34]

These advances have been accompanied by five United Nations Security Council resolutions over the past decade that have, for the first time, recognized rape as a tactic of warfare and called for an end to impunity for these crimes (see Box 4.2).

There has been an extraordinary shift from a time when rape was rendered invisible, a mere 'by-product' of war, or conceived as a crime against family honour, to the recognition from the courts and the international community that sexual violence cannot be consented to, is a war crime, a crime against humanity, may be a constituent part of genocide and is a threat to international peace and security. It is also testament to the advocacy and leadership of a handful of judges and the many women who have survived brutal sexual attacks and refused to keep quiet. Increasing the number of successful prosecutions for sexual and gender-based crimes at international and national levels remains both a challenge and an urgent priority.

Box 4.2 United Nations Security Council resolutions on women, peace and security

Five United Nations Security Council resolutions have together recognized the impact of conflict on women, established that sexual violence in conflict is a matter of international peace and security and have put in place concrete measures to ensure accountability.

When the United Nations Security Council passed the groundbreaking resolution 1325 in 2000, it was the first time that the importance of women's role in peacebuilding was recognized. The resolution emphasized the need for women's equal and full participation in all efforts to maintain and promote peace and security. It also called for attention to the special needs of women and girls during repatriation and resettlement, rehabilitation, reintegration and post-conflict reconstruction.[35]

This resolution was followed in 2008 by Security Council resolution 1820, which recognized that sexual violence has been used 'as a tactic of war, to humiliate, dominate, instil fear in, disperse and/or forcibly relocate civilian members of a community or ethnic group'.[36] It called for effective steps to prevent and respond to acts of sexual violence as a central part of maintaining international peace and security. It urged Member States to comply with their obligations to prosecute the perpetrators of sexual violence, ensuring that all victims, particularly women and girls, have equal protection under the law and equal access to justice. It called for an end to impunity for sexual violence as part of a comprehensive approach to seeking sustainable peace, justice, truth and national reconciliation.

Three further resolutions provided building blocks for the implementation of these commitments. In 2009, resolution 1888 laid the ground for the appointment of the Special Representative of the Secretary-General on Sexual Violence in Conflict. It called upon the Secretary-General to ensure the rapid deployment of teams of experts and advisers to situations of concern and to ensure that peace talks address sexual violence.[37] In the same year, resolution 1889 called for a strategy to increase women's representation in conflict resolution decision-making, including indicators and proposals for a monitoring mechanism. Among other things, States must track money spent on women in post-conflict and recovery planning.[38]

Resolution 1960, agreed in December 2010, called for a monitoring and reporting framework to track sexual violence in conflict. It mandated that the names of those 'credibly suspected of committing or being responsible for patterns of rape and other forms of sexual violence in situations of armed conflict on the Security Council agenda' be included in annual reports on the implementation of resolutions 1820 and 1888.[39]

Women, conflict and international law

The past century has been characterized by very high levels of armed conflict. Since time immemorial, sexual violence has been used as a tactic of war.

This display gives just five examples of conflicts since 1960 in which the 'widespread' or 'systematic' use of sexual violence against women and girls has been reported by the United Nations. It also tracks the developments in international law over the past century that have finally made it possible to prosecute these crimes.

Colombia
1964 onwards

According to the UN Human Rights Council: 'Colombia has endured decades of armed conflict and gross human rights violations that have caused a protracted humanitarian crisis'. The Special Rapporteur on violence against women noted: 'Sexual violence by armed groups has become a common practice'. A 2010 survey of 407 municipalities, in which there is an active presence of armed actors, found that between 2001 and 2009, 95,000 women had been raped.

Timor-Leste
1975–1999

The UN Secretary-General noted: 'It is clear that the highest level of the military command in East Timor knew… that there was widespread violence against women in East Timor. There were cases of sexual slavery, sexual violence as a means of intimidation and sexual violence as a result of the climate of impunity created by the security forces operating in the island.'

1939–1945
Second World War: Two million women were raped in Germany. Tens of thousands of Asian women were sexually enslaved as 'comfort women' by the Japanese army.

1900 · 1910 · 1920 · 1930 · 1940 · 1950 · 1960 · 1970 · 1980

1899 and 1907
The Hague Conventions: Stipulate that during periods of military occupation 'family honour…must be respected.'

1929
The Geneva Convention: States that 'Women [prisoners of war] shall be treated with all consideration due to their sex'.

1945–1946
Nuremberg and Tokyo Tribunals: The Charters included war crimes, crimes against humanity and crimes against the peace, without mentioning rape. No indictments or evidence was presented on the 'comfort women'. Rape was never charged at the Nuremburg trials.

1949
The Geneva Conventions: Extended protection to women civilians, stating that they must be 'especially protected against any attack on their honour in particular against rape, enforced prostitution, or any form of indecent assault'. But rape was not listed as a 'grave breach'.

1977
Protocol I and II Additional to the Geneva Conventions: Further extended legal protection against sexual violence to apply to women civilians and combatants, including in civil conflicts.

'Women and girls are particularly targeted by the use of sexual violence, including as a tactic of war to humiliate, dominate, instil fear in, disperse and/or forcibly relocate civilian members of a community or ethnic group.'

— Security Council resolution 1820

Source: See endnotes.

Countries that have been primary parties to one or more conflicts, 1960–2008 (112 countries in total).

Bosnia and Herzegovina 1992–1995

The UN Security Council noted: 'Grave breaches… of international humanitarian law have been committed, including…"ethnic cleansing" and mass killings' and was 'appalled by reports of the massive, organized and systemic detention and rape of women, in particular Muslim women, in Bosnia and Herzegovina'. It is estimated that 20,000 to 60,000 women and girls were subjected to sexual violence in 'rape camps'.

Rwanda 1994

The UN Commission on Human Rights estimated that between 250,000 and 500,000 women were raped during the Rwandan genocide. 'Rape was systematic and was used as a "weapon" by the perpetrators of the massacres... rape was the rule and its absence the exception.' In 2000, a survey of 1,125 women who survived rape during the genocide found that 67 percent were HIV positive.

Darfur, Sudan 2003 onwards

The UN International Commission of Inquiry on Darfur found that 'rape and sexual violence have been used by the Janjaweed and Government soldiers… as a deliberate strategy with a view to… terrorizing the population, ensuring control over the movement of the IDP population and perpetuating its displacement'. In July 2008, the UN reported that there were 2.5 million internally displaced people in Darfur.

1960   2000   2010

1993
Establishment of the International Criminal Tribunal for the former Yugoslavia (ICTY): The ICTY Statute explicitly includes rape within its definition of crimes against humanity. The convictions secured at the ICTY entrenched sexual violence, rape and sexual enslavement as international crimes and confirmed that they could amount to torture and genocide. There have been 29 convictions for sexual violence (see Table 4.1).

1994
Establishment of the International Criminal Tribunal for Rwanda (ICTR): Followed the ICTY in including sexual violence within its Statute. *Prosecutor v Akayesu* in 1998 saw the first ever conviction for rape as an instrument of genocide and a crime against humanity. There have been 11 convictions for sexual violence (see Table 4.1).

1998
The General Assembly meets in Rome to develop the Statute of the International Criminal Court (ICC): Ratified by 114 States, the Statute broadly defines sexual violence as crimes against humanity and war crimes. It provides for reparations and protection for victims.

2000
Security Council resolution 1325: Groundbreaking resolution on women and conflict (see Box 4.2).

2002
Establishment of the ICC: As of April 2011, the Court is engaged or conducting investigations in the Central African Republic, the Democratic Republic of the Congo, Kenya, Libya, the Sudan and Uganda. Of 23 indictments issued, 12 contain sexual violence charges.

2002
Establishment of the Special Court for Sierra Leone: In *Prosecutor v Brima et al.*, it was found that forced marriage is a crime against humanity. There have been six convictions for sexual violence (see Table 4.1).

2010
Jean-Pierre Bemba case opens at the ICC: The trial of the former Vice-President of the Democratic Republic of the Congo, for his alleged role in the conflict in the Central African Republic, is the first ICC case being tried primarily on sexual violence charges, and is the first time that all three judges, the senior trial lawyer prosecuting and almost half of the victims making representations in the case are women.

2008
Security Council resolution 1820: Recognized sexual violence in conflict as a matter of international peace and security (see Box 4.2).

2009–2010
Security Council resolutions 1888, 1889 and 1960: Provide concrete building blocks for the implementation of resolutions 1325 and 1820 (see Box 4.2).

Increasing prosecutions and closing the impunity gap

Despite impressive advances in international law, overall the number of prosecutions remains low. At the International Criminal Tribunal for the former Yugoslavia, the International Criminal Tribunal for Rwanda and the Special Court for Sierra Leone, in those cases that have been completed, as of April 2011, a total of 155 individuals had been indicted, of which 71 have been indicted for sexual violence crimes. There have been 46 convictions in which the judgments contained findings of sexual violence, including as war crimes or crimes against humanity (see Table 4.1).

It is widely acknowledged that winning convictions for sexual violence is difficult. In the Court of Bosnia and Herzegovina and the International Criminal Tribunal for the former Yugoslavia, where sexual violence was included in charges, conviction rates were lower than for cases that did not include this kind of crime (see Figure 4.2). However, women's rights advocates report that some international investigators avoid pursuing these charges, citing reasons such as lack of evidence and women's reluctance to testify about rape.[40] Successful prosecutions of sexual and gender-based violence cases require a comprehensive strategy and commitment at the highest levels from the outset.

At the Special Court for Sierra Leone, for example, the Chief Prosecutor ensured that sexual violence was incorporated into all aspects of the Court's prosecution strategy from the beginning and devoted 2 out of 10 investigators to deal with sexual violence crimes. At the International Criminal Tribunal for Rwanda, only 1 to 2 percent of investigators were dedicated to this area.[41]

Given the social stigma that they face, persuading women to come forward to testify is a significant challenge. Of the more than 3,700 witnesses who testified at the International Criminal Tribunal for the former Yugoslavia between 1996 and 2006, only 18 percent were women.[42] The experience of testifying can be deeply traumatic for women. In one case at the International Criminal Tribunal for Rwanda involving six defendants, a prosecution lawyer noted that a rape survivor was asked 1,194 questions by the defence counsel.[43]

Addressing the procedural and institutional barriers that women face in testifying is not only essential for upholding the rights and dignity of those who come before the courts, but is also necessary for the effective functioning of the courts themselves.[44] Ensuring that women are represented among court staff, in legal teams and as judges can play a part in making courts more accessible to women. A study on the International Criminal Tribunal for the former Yugoslavia found that defence lawyers

TABLE 4.1: Prosecutions for sexual violence in international courts

Given the widespread use of sexual violence in these conflicts, the number of prosecutions and convictions is very low.

Court	Number of accused indicted in completed cases*	Number indicted for crimes involving sexual violence in completed cases	Number of judgments in which conviction involved evidence or findings of sexual violence**
International Criminal Tribunal for the former Yugoslavia (ICTY)	93	44	29
International Criminal Tribunal for Rwanda (ICTR)	54	21	11
Special Court for Sierra Leone (SCSL)	8	6	6

Source: ICTY data are UN Women analysis using data from Mischkowski and Mlinarevic 2009 and information collected from court documents. Data for the ICTR and the SCSL are based on UN Women analysis of court documents. Data as of April 2011.

Note: *This column does not include cases that have been dropped, the indictment was withdrawn, or the accused died before or during trial, or cases transferred to the national courts. The indictment count for the SCSL does not include the five indicted for contempt of court or the two for professional misconduct. Open cases where the trial is ongoing or the accused remains a fugitive are also not included in the table, of which there are 19 in the ICTY, 32 in the ICTR and two in the SCSL. **For the ICTY, the figure includes 19 judgments currently on appeal, similarly for the ICTR, 10 judgments are currently on appeal.

FIGURE 4.2: Convictions at the Court of Bosnia and Herzegovina and the International Criminal Tribunal for the former Yugoslavia

Conviction rates are lower where the charges include sexual violence.

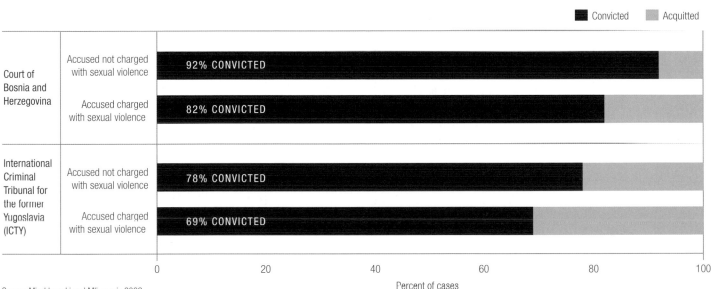

■ Convicted ■ Acquitted

Court of Bosnia and Herzegovina
- Accused not charged with sexual violence: **92% CONVICTED**
- Accused charged with sexual violence: **82% CONVICTED**

International Criminal Tribunal for the former Yugoslavia (ICTY)
- Accused not charged with sexual violence: **78% CONVICTED**
- Accused charged with sexual violence: **69% CONVICTED**

Percent of cases
0   20   40   60   80   100

Source: Mischkowski and Mlinarevic 2009.

Note: ICTY data are based on a total of 71 accused in concluded cases. Of the 11 acquitted of charges of sexual violence, only three were acquitted of all charges. The remaining nine accused were found guilty of other non-sexual charges. Court of Bosnia and Herzegovina data are based on a total of 35 accused in concluded cases.

were more respectful when questioning a female witness in front of a female judge and women spoke more freely.[45]

Financial assistance, childcare and transport are basic requirements to help women to overcome the practical obstacles to their participation in the justice process.[46] Long-term support is also essential, including psychosocial counselling and appropriate health care such as antiretroviral treatment for those living with HIV. The Victims and Witnesses Unit of the Special Court for Sierra Leone developed a comprehensive package of protection and support.[47] Follow-up research with male and female witnesses found that those who had been briefed and supported had a largely positive experience of the Court.[48]

Learning from these experiences, the International Criminal Court has placed a strong emphasis on the procedures needed to ensure gender-based crimes are dealt with appropriately. The Court established the Victims and Witnesses Unit — whose remit it is to ensure the personal safety, physical and psychological well-being, dignity and privacy of those testifying — and the

Trust Fund for Victims, which has a dual mandate to assist victims and administer court-ordered reparations.[49] In the past two years, a number of women have been appointed at a senior level, including to the post of Special Gender Advisor to the Prosecutor, helping to achieve gender parity among professional staff and judges (see Figure 4.3).[50]

The much anticipated trial of Jean-Pierre Bemba, former Vice-President of the Democratic Republic of the Congo, which started in November 2010, holds the potential to be a watershed case for women's access to justice at the Court. Jean-Pierre Bemba, who is being tried for his alleged part in crimes in the Central African Republic is the most senior official to be brought before the Court so far. It is the first case before the International Criminal Court to be tried primarily on sexual violence charges, including rape as a war crime and as a crime against humanity. The case will also be the first time in the history of international war tribunals where all three judges, the senior trial lawyer prosecuting and almost half of the victims making representations in the case are women.[51]

Strengthening national justice systems

While international courts have played an important role in furthering justice for gender-based crimes in conflict, most are only mandated to deal with those most responsible for atrocities. Strengthening justice systems and building national capacity is therefore critical for closing the impunity gap and to fostering long-term peace and stability. All of the institutional challenges of the justice chain described in Chapter 2 are exacerbated during and after conflict, which is why Security Council resolution 1820 urges United Nations entities to 'support the development and strengthening of the capacities of national institutions' (see Box 4.2).[52]

In a survey in eastern Democratic Republic of the Congo, half of the respondents said they wanted justice delivered through the national court system, double the proportion that endorsed the International Criminal Court. However, 82 percent of respondents also wanted the international community to assist in national prosecutions.[53] The use of mobile courts is a promising example of this approach (see Box 4.3).

In post-conflict Rwanda, UN Women and UNDP have supported the gender desk at the Rwanda National Police headquarters. The desk handles cases of gender-based violence, including receiving and interviewing survivors, investigating cases, servicing a complaints hotline, arranging for the collection of medical evidence and preparing case files to be submitted for prosecution. It is assisted by specially trained police officers located in every one of the 69 police stations throughout the country. Since the gender desk was established, the number of cases adjudicated has increased and research has found that the stigma associated with sexual violence has been reduced.[54]

In the Sudan, UNDP has worked with partners to provide 12 legal aid centres across Darfur, Kassala and the Three Areas (Abyei, Blue Nile and South Kordofan). Raising awareness of gender-based violence has been prioritized and each centre runs women-only legal advice sessions. Displaced women have been trained as paralegals, empowering them with new skills and providing legal advice to many others. A legal aid network, made up of 61 Darfurian lawyers, was established to take on cases referred by the legal aid centres. In 2007, they took on 550 new cases, achieving convictions for rape and murder, acquittals of women charged with zina (extramarital sex) and the release of people arbitrarily detained. A third of the cases were related to gender-based violence.[55]

In many conflict and post-conflict countries, domestic legislation is silent on the broad range of crimes of sexual and gender-based violence covered in the Rome Statute, sometimes leaving victims with no legal recourse. It is vital to ensure that national laws reflect these provisions and that measures on witness and victim protection,

FIGURE 4.3: Women judges in international courts

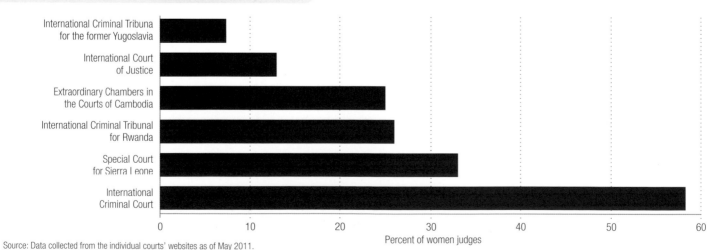

Only in the International Criminal Court have women judges achieved parity.

Source: Data collected from the individual courts' websites as of May 2011.

Note: Ad litem judges are not included.

Eastern Democratic Republic of the Congo continues to suffer from insecurity and conflict, characterized by the use of brutal sexual violence. Partnering with the Government and working with local police, lawyers, judges and psychologists, the American Bar Association and the Open Society Justice Initiative have provided mobile courts to bring justice to remote areas.

In 2010, nine mobile courts adjudicated 186 cases. Of these, 115 were rape cases that resulted in 95 convictions, with prison sentences ranging from 3 to 20 years. More than 260 judicial officers have been trained, including 150 police officers, 80 lawyers and 30 magistrates.

In February 2011, the Fizi rape case was heard, at the official request of the President of the Military Court. Eleven Congolese soldiers, including Lieutenant Colonel Kibibi Mutware, were indicted for crimes against humanity for their part in the mass rape of more than 40 women and girls in Fizi on New Year's Day. The court staff responded very quickly, travelling to the remote area and working with United Nations agencies and NGOs to collect evidence and testimony.

Forty-nine women testified during the trial, which was the first time that a crimes against humanity case has been heard in a mobile court. Closed session hearings were held to enable women to testify in private and a counsellor was provided to give them psychosocial support. Hundreds of people from the surrounding areas observed the trial proceedings.

Kibibi and three fellow officers were found guilty and sentenced to 20 years imprisonment and five other soldiers received sentences of between 10 and 15 years. The soldiers were also ordered to pay the women reparations. Although enforcing these orders will be very challenging, new legal clinics are being set up to provide greater support for women before, during and after the trials, including helping them to claim their reparation payments.

While rapes are still being committed on a major scale, some women have been able to seek justice, a small but nevertheless significant strike against impunity.[56]

reparations, and rules of procedure and evidence are adopted to enable women to have their claims heard by domestic courts. In Uganda, following the long-running civil war, legislation has been adopted to implement the provisions of the Rome Statute, including the establishment of a war crimes chamber and training in international law for judges, prosecutors and bar association members.[57]

As domestic judicial reform takes time, hybrid (mixed international and national) courts can help fill the gap and support reform, providing on-the-job training opportunities for lawyers, investigators and judges. Hybrid courts can leave in their wake a revitalized justice structure and a legacy of jurisprudence upon which to build.[58] Examples of hybrid mechanisms include the Court of Bosnia and Herzegovina, a war crimes chamber staffed with international and national judges, and the Special Court for Sierra Leone, a stand-alone tribunal with jurisdiction over international and certain national crimes. Hybrid courts have also been set up in Cambodia, Timor-Leste and Kosovo (under UNSCR 1244).[59] In October 2010, the Government of the Democratic Republic of the Congo announced its intention to create 'specialized chambers' integrated into the national judicial system, but with participation from international magistrates, with jurisdiction over grave violations of human rights.[60]

Community justice mechanisms

Non-state or community-based justice mechanisms are often the only form of justice available to women in post-conflict settings. As the Liberian peace huts show, these mechanisms can be instrumental in achieving conflict resolution, reconciliation and a degree of accountability, particularly where state institutions are very weak. As discussed in Chapter 3, these justice systems can however also be problematic for women.

In Rwanda, gacaca, a local dispute resolution process was partially reformed and used by the Government to hear cases of lesser crimes related to the genocide as well as to gather evidence to categorize crimes. Since 2001, gacaca courts have dealt with over 1.5 million cases.[61]

*The period
following conflict is
characterized not
just by enormous
challenges, but
also by significant
opportunities.*

Advocacy by local and international civil society ensured that gacaca courts were explicitly excluded from dealing with sexual violence cases, except during the evidence-gathering stage. However, as the backlog in the formal courts has persisted, the law was reformed in 2009 to allow sexual violence cases to be heard before gacaca courts. The reform was meant to be accompanied by measures to enable women to give evidence in closed session hearings. But, concerns have been raised that women's privacy has not been adequately protected and that sentences for those convicted have not been enforced.[62]

Despite the challenges to securing justice for women through these mechanisms, the majority of cases will continue to be dealt with in these forums. Therefore, it is important to support women to shape and define them, including through engagement with customary and religious leaders.

After years of conflict in Timor-Leste, elements of customary justice were incorporated into transitional justice processes, in order to localize justice and accountability at the community level. In addition to the Serious Crimes Process, the Commission for Reception, Truth and Reconciliation (Comissão de Acolhimento, Verdade e Reconciliação – CAVR) was created to hear

testimonies and document a range of conflict-related crimes. Serious crimes were referred to the courts for prosecution while offences considered less serious, such as looting and burning of property were dealt with through community-level reintegration and reconciliation processes implemented by the Commission. Among the CAVR's activities was a community reconciliation programme based on the customary practice of nahe biti boot (spread out the big mat). It involved the public confession and apology of perpetrators who came forward. A local panel moderated the process and facilitated the negotiation of an act of reconciliation acceptable to the victim, such as community service, reparation, or other forms of compensation. After the session was concluded, a community reconciliation agreement was registered with the appropriate district court and once it had been fulfilled, the accused were granted immunity from criminal and civil liability.

Women's representation was mandatory on the arbitration panels to ensure that they had a role in shaping them. The women who participated stated that it took time to build trust among the male elders and to convince them that women could be involved in conflict resolution. Gradually however, acceptance of their participation grew and the women became respected in these new roles.[63]

Beyond prosecutions: Transformative justice

Increasing the numbers of prosecutions for sexual violence is a priority for ending impunity and ensuring accountability to women in post-conflict contexts. However, the sheer scale of the crimes committed during conflict and the fragility of post-conflict institutions means that prosecutions alone are not enough to ensure justice for women.

Moreover, women themselves do not necessarily equate justice with prosecutions: recognition of what they have endured and the means to rebuild their lives often takes precedence over going to court. It is increasingly acknowledged that post-conflict justice mechanisms have the potential not only to redress the specific crimes that women have suffered, but can also bring about

transformative change in their lives. This section analyses two elements of transitional justice – truth commissions and reparations – to show how they can be part of achieving these broader justice outcomes for women.

The period following conflict is characterized not just by enormous challenges, but also by significant opportunities.

It is a time of profound political transformation in which important groundwork for achieving women's rights can be laid. The final part of the chapter shows how women's participation in post-conflict contexts, including in peace talks and legal and constitutional reform, places women in a position to influence the shaping of the new State.

Truth commissions

Truth commissions are officially sanctioned, temporary, non-judicial bodies established to investigate a history of past violations in countries emerging from conflict or moving from authoritarian rule to democracy. There have been approximately 40 truth commissions to date with varying mandates to foster accountability; officially acknowledge crimes and victims' experiences; to establish an inclusive history; to identify recipients for reparations; and to make recommendations for institutional change.

The recommendations of truth commission reports have the potential for longer-term, transformative impacts on societies. The final report of the Sierra Leone Truth and Reconciliation Commission identified a continuum of violence against women before, during and after the conflict. The subordinate status of women before the conflict, who under customary law were viewed as property to be inherited, was one of the factors that drove the targeting of women for sexual slavery and forced marriage during the war, as well as their stigmatization afterwards. The Commission issued strong recommendations for legal, political, educational and economic reforms to strengthen the status of women and address ongoing sexual violence. It called on the Government to address structural gender inequalities through law reform, access to justice and quotas for women's representation.[64]

Despite the potential for transformative impact, truth commission mandates have historically been gender blind. They commonly focus on violations of political and civil rights such as death, torture and disappearances, which can exclude the experience of secondary victims including female relatives. In addition, broader socio-economic violations, such as displacement and loss of livelihoods, which affect women disproportionately,

are often excluded from commission mandates. Where there has been no official truth-telling process or women have felt excluded from truth commissions, they have organized their own tribunals to ensure that their voices are heard (see Box 4.4).

The same factors that prevent women from testifying before courts present obstacles to their participation in truth-seeking initiatives. No commission to date has put in place the range of measures necessary to ensure the safety, physical and psychological well-being, dignity and privacy of victims and witnesses. As a result, many women who testify tell the stories of their male relatives, not their own experiences. In South Africa, for example, women gave 55 percent of all testimonies at the Truth and Reconciliation Commission, but the majority of these concerned what had happened to their husbands or sons, downplaying the violence they had personally suffered.[65]

In recent years, there have been significant advances in relation to gender sensitivity. The truth commissions in Peru, Timor-Leste and Sierra Leone have drawn special attention to gender issues, employed more women staff members and involved local women's organizations to a much greater extent than before. The 2001 Peruvian Truth Commission (Comisión de la Verdad y Reconciliación — CVR) was the first in which sexual violence was fully acknowledged, with a commitment made to mainstream gender into the proceedings, overseen by a special unit.[66]

In Sierra Leone, UN Women supported the work of the Truth and Reconciliation Commission to ensure that there was a comprehensive gender strategy. Women's organizations were funded to facilitate outreach to local communities and provide transport, medical assistance and childcare for women witnesses. A data system was set up to collect sex disaggregated statistics.[67]

The Timor-Leste CAVR had a dedicated gender unit, which worked closely with women's organizations. Community-based hearings allowed women to talk about their experiences in the conflict, including in their roles supporting the resistance movement. At the national hearings for women, for the first time in the history of Timor-Leste, women spoke out publicly, with people across the country following the hearings on television and radio.[68] Similarly, in Sierra Leone, some women

Recommendations of truth commission reports have the potential for longer-term, transformative impacts on society.

wanted to narrate their experiences in public, rejecting the notion that they should bear the stigma alone or keep their experiences private.[69] However, for many others, particularly survivors of sexual violence, closed session hearings are vital to guarantee the confidentiality and safety necessary to enable women to come forward.

Despite progress, substantial challenges remain. Truth seeking bodies may not be effective in all cultural or political contexts and the positive benefits that are assumed to derive from publicly revealing pain and suffering are questioned by some gender justice advocates. The Trauma Centre for Survivors of Violence and Torture in Cape Town found that 50 to 60 percent of victims who testified before the South African Truth and Reconciliation Commission had been re-traumatized, with the experience re-opening wounds and leaving them more embittered.[70]

Box 4.4 Demanding accountability: Women's tribunals

In contexts where official processes have not addressed women's justice demands, civil society organizations have held their own tribunals to highlight women's experiences. Although the judgments of these tribunals are not binding, they help to end the silence that surrounds sexual violence crimes and can create moral pressure for formal recognition of women's rights violations.

In Tokyo, in December 2000, the Women's International War Crimes Tribunal on Japan's Military Sexual Slavery was held. The Tribunal aimed to highlight the systematic sexual enslavement of tens of thousands of Asian women, the so-called 'comfort women' during the Second World War. More than a thousand people took part in the Tribunal, which heard testimony from 64 survivors from nine countries, as well as from two Japanese veterans, who were themselves perpetrators of sexual violence.

The judges, who included the former President of the International Criminal Tribunal for the former Yugoslavia, found both the Japanese State and the Emperor Hirohito guilty of war crimes and crimes against humanity. The Tribunal recommended that the Government of Japan make a full apology and provide compensation to the survivors. While the Government has taken some steps to apologize, the measures taken to date have been deemed insufficient by the survivors.[71] In 2009, the CEDAW committee recommended that the Government should 'urgently endeavour to find a lasting solution for the situation of "comfort women" which would include the compensation of victims, the prosecution of perpetrators and the education of the public about these crimes'.[72]

In March 2010, two women's tribunals took place. In New York, the Nobel Women's Initiative and the Women's League of Burma organized the International Tribunal on Crimes against Women of Burma. As far back as 2006, the United Nations General Assembly urged the Government of Myanmar to 'take urgent measures to put an end to the military operations targeting civilians…including widespread rape and other forms of sexual violence persistently carried out by members of the armed forces'.[73] At the Tribunal, 12 women testified about rape, torture and murder in front of 200 people, with a further 2,000 people watching by live webcast. The four judges, who included human rights experts and Nobel Laureates, found both the Government and the military responsible for the crimes.[74]

In Guatemala, indigenous women recounted their experiences in the Tribunal of Conscience against Sexual Violence during Internal Armed Conflict. It was organized by Equipo de Estudios Comunitarios y Acción Psicosocial (ECAP), La Unión Mujeres Transformando el Mundo (MTM), Union Nacional de Mujeres Guatemaltecas (UNAMG), Coordinadora Nacional de Viudas de Guatemala (CONAVIGUA) and La Cuerda, with support from United Nations partners, including UN Women.[75] The Commission for Historical Clarification (Comisión para el Esclarecimiento Histórico – CEH), which was set up in the aftermath of the civil war found that sexual violence was widespread during more than three decades of conflict in the country, estimating that around 90 percent of these crimes were committed by military personnel. However, to date there have been no prosecutions.[76] Some women had waited almost 30 years to talk about their experiences, including of rape, forced pregnancy and sterilization, forced marriage and sexual and domestic slavery. The magistrates of the Tribunal held the State accountable for the ongoing affects of these crimes on the lives of women, their families and communities.[77]

As it becomes more widely accepted that women should be part of truth commissions, it is essential to ensure that women are involved from the outset in framing and shaping them. Measures are required to ensure that testifying is a positive experience and is linked to long-term support and reparations. Follow up research is needed to discover the impact of truth telling and other informal accountability processes, to ensure that they meet women's needs.[78]

Reparations

Reparations are measures adopted by States that are intended to 'repair' past harms, in particular the systematic violation of human rights associated with periods of conflict or repression. The right to redress is enshrined in numerous human right treaties.[79]

Administrative reparations programmes, which are put in place by governments for a large group of victims, can include individual compensation, pensions, opportunities for education and training, access to health and psychological rehabilitation, measures of collective reparation, as well as memorials, official apologies or other symbolic measures. They provide acknowledgement of violations, a reassertion of the rights of survivors and practical means to redress the impact of crimes.

While reparations are first and foremost an obligation to the individual by the State, lack of political will and capacity at the national level cannot be an excuse for the non-fulfilment of this right. The international community has strived to provide accountability and retributive justice through the courts: there is growing recognition that it also has a role in supporting reparative justice for crimes under international law (see Box 4.5).

As the most victim-centred of justice measures, reparations are especially important for women, who are typically least able to mitigate the impacts of conflict. In the Central African Republic, in common with many post-conflict contexts, women say that reparations are needed to help them recover losses and alleviate poverty, but they are also important for recognizing their suffering (see Figure 4.5). To date, however, few reparations programmes have adequately met women's needs.

Ensuring women benefit means paying close attention to how programmes are designed and delivered, as well as ensuring that resources are made available for reparations.

It is important to look at what kinds of violations are included. Sexual violence has been inadequately covered and to date, no reparations programme has explicitly included forms of reproductive violence, such as forced impregnation, abortion or sterilization.[80] Recipients of reparations should include family members, as well as the direct victim, and take into account ongoing issues that women face, for example in dealing with the material consequences of stigma. Where payments are awarded, it is important to ensure that women can actually access the money, in contexts where they may not have bank accounts, the necessary forms of identification, or exercise little control over their own income.

Payments can also create tensions if they are not administered sensitively. In Timor-Leste, victims of sexual violence were awarded the same amount as those who suffered other violations, to minimize the risk of women being identified based on what they received. Recognizing that women were more likely to claim benefits for their children than themselves and prioritized their children's schooling, women claiming education grants were also given literacy training, livelihoods skills and reproductive health care.[81]

Given the challenges of the burden of proof in cases of sexual violence, consideration could be given to designing reparations programmes that do not require evidence, which may be difficult to provide or place women at further risk. In Chile, for example, the payment of reparations for torture did not require victims to disclose or prove their experiences. The fact that they had been detained in a location known for its extensive use of torture meant that compensation was paid automatically.[82] Such innovative thinking could be applied in cases where mapping or documentation have found the incidence of sexual violence to be exceptionally high, without demanding proof from individual victims.

In the 2010 thematic report on reparations, the United Nations Special Rapporteur on violence against women identified the growing demand for 'transformative justice'

There is a growing recognition that the international community has a role in supporting reparative justice for crimes under international law.

in response to gender-based violations. In particular, she noted that measures for redress need to 'subvert instead of reinforce pre-existing patterns of cross-cutting structural subordination, gender hierarchies, systemic marginalization and structural inequalities that may be the root causes of the violence that women experience before, during and after the conflict'.[83] The recent Cotton Field case, heard at the Inter-American Court of Human Rights, has helped to establish a framework for such transformative measures (see Balancing the Scales).

Reparations that support women's economic empowerment can contribute to transformative justice by placing them in a better position to break with historic patterns of subordination and social exclusion.[84] Enabling women to access land is one example of this. In recognition of the barriers that Mayan women have historically faced in accessing land, Guatemala's National Reparations Programme (Programa Nacional de Resarcimiento – PNR) included land awards and regularization of land titles as a measure of reparation.[85] In Colombia, rural women who have been displaced or had their land seized have had problems reclaiming it without written proof of tenancy or a formal marriage certificate. Measures to simplify procedures and lower thresholds of evidence, such as recognizing labour and productive histories as evidence of ownership, are needed in these cases to enable women to reclaim their land.[86]

In Sierra Leone, the Government's National Commission for Social Action, supported by the United Nations Trust Fund to End Violence against Women and the United Nations Peacebuilding Fund, is implementing a reparations programme targeting 650 women survivors of sexual violence. Women's organizations conducted surveys with the women to assess their marketable skills and on the basis of their findings, skills training,

Box 4.5 Reparative justice for the women of Songo Mboyo

In 2003, dozens of women were raped by soldiers in Songo Mboyo in the Democratic Republic of the Congo. Their case highlights both the severe challenges for women seeking justice and the urgent need for comprehensive reparations.

On the night of 21 December 2003, troops attacked the villages of Songo Mboyo and Bongandanga. In all, 119 reports of rape and 86 of looting were recorded and sent to the military prosecution department, but no action was taken for nearly two years, during which time the women were repeatedly threatened by soldiers. In 2005, 12 men were indicted and a year later, seven were convicted and sentenced to life imprisonment. The case set an important legal precedent as the first time in the country's history that rape was tried as a crime against humanity as defined in the Rome Statute. The women were awarded a total of $165,317 in reparations. However, within two months, the convicted men had escaped from prison and the women have never received any of the damages awarded.[87]

In an effort to address the rights of sexual violence survivors, a high-level panel was convened in 2010 by the United Nations Office of the High Commissioner for Human Rights to investigate the remedies and reparations available to victims of sexual violence. In September and October 2010, panel members held dialogues with survivors, NGOs and local officials, meeting a total of 61 victims, ranging in age from 3 to 61 years old in six towns, including Songo Mboyo.[88]

The women from Songo Mboyo have formed an association of survivors and asked the high-level panel to provide a boat for them to transport their goods down river to the market, to secure their livelihoods and contribute to their recovery. UN Women has responded to this request for collective redress and the boat was delivered to the women in February 2011. Working with local and national Government and civil society partners, this measure is just the first step in implementing the recommendations of the high-level panel to deliver reparative justice for survivors of sexual violence in the Democratic Republic of the Congo.

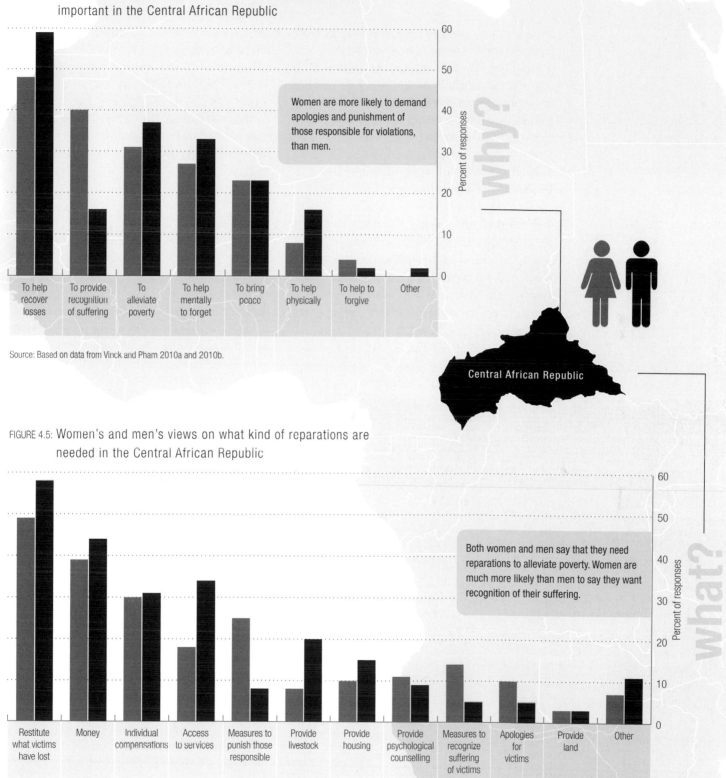

FIGURE 4.4: Women's and men's perceptions of why reparations are important in the Central African Republic

Women are more likely to demand apologies and punishment of those responsible for violations, than men.

Percent of responses

60
50
40
30
20
10
0

To help recover losses | To provide recognition of suffering | To alleviate poverty | To help mentally to forget | To bring peace | To help physically | To help to forgive | Other

Source: Based on data from Vinck and Pham 2010a and 2010b.

why?

Central African Republic

FIGURE 4.5: Women's and men's views on what kind of reparations are needed in the Central African Republic

Both women and men say that they need reparations to alleviate poverty. Women are much more likely than men to say they want recognition of their suffering.

Percent of responses

60
50
40
30
20
10
0

Restitute what victims have lost | Money | Individual compensations | Access to services | Measures to punish those responsible | Provide livestock | Provide housing | Provide psychological counselling | Measures to recognize suffering of victims | Apologies for victims | Provide land | Other

what?

Source: Based on data from Vinck and Pham 2010a and 2010b.

micro-grants and support to set up small businesses are being provided. To date, 300 women are participating in programmes in 14 districts of the country. In March 2011, at a ceremony in Freetown, the first 90 women graduated from training courses including literacy, driving, computer skills, soap-making and hairdressing.[89]

Women's participation in rebuilding the post-conflict State

One important way to ensure that truth commissions and reparations programmes meet women's needs is to ensure that they participate in the shaping of transitional justice measures. Inclusive national consultations are a key precondition of the success of these mechanisms.

Women's involvement is vital for building their autonomy and political power in post-conflict societies. In the context of ingrained gender inequality such participation can be a form of reparation in itself.[90]

Women's participation, starting with peace negotiations, is also critical for bringing about lasting and fundamental change in post-conflict societies. Peace agreements establish the overarching framework for the transition and democratization process, often defining who has power and how it will be exercised. They can address the establishment of accountability mechanisms, access to land rights, return of internally displaced people and refugees, and constitutional guarantees for women's rights and political participation.[91]

However, the number of women participating in peace processes remains small and provisions within peace agreements often fail to address women's rights adequately. A study of 585 peace agreements since 1990 found that only 16 percent contain any references to women and only 7 percent include mention of gender equality or women's human rights. Although much more progress is needed, since the passing of Security Council resolution 1325 in 2000, the percentage of agreements that contain references to women has risen significantly, from 11 to 27 percent.[92]

Despite these challenges, women have seized the post-conflict moment to reshape societies and advance women's rights. In sub-Saharan Africa, for example, some of the most significant changes with respect to women's rights have occurred when there were opportunities to 'rewrite the rules' of the political order, often after major civil conflicts. Of the countries that have passed legislation on women's land rights in recent years, five out of seven did so as part of post-conflict reform: Mozambique, Namibia, Rwanda, South Africa and Uganda. Similarly, many of the countries with more than 30 percent women's representation in parliament in sub-Saharan Africa have come out of conflicts, including Angola, Burundi, Mozambique, Rwanda, South Africa and Uganda.[93] In all cases, as mandated by CEDAW, temporary special measures including quotas, have been used to boost women's representation (see Figure 4.6).

FIGURE 4.6: Laws and policies on gender equality and women's representation in parliaments in sub-Saharan Africa

Post-conflict countries have higher levels of women's political representation and are more likely to have gender equality laws and policies.

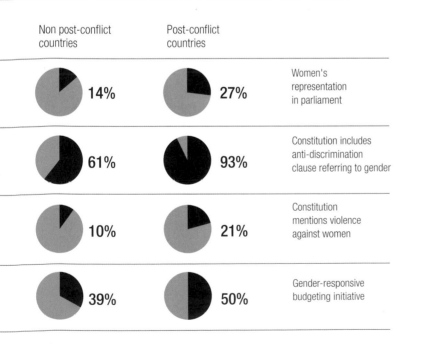

Non post-conflict countries	Post-conflict countries	
14%	27%	Women's representation in parliament
61%	93%	Constitution includes anti-discrimination clause referring to gender
10%	21%	Constitution mentions violence against women
39%	50%	Gender-responsive budgeting initiative

Source: Tripp et al. 2009; UN Women calculations using data from IPU 2011a.

Note: N= 46 countries in sub-Saharan Africa.

Conclusion

Women have the least access to justice precisely when they need it most – in periods of conflict and post-conflict. All the problems associated with weak infrastructure, social barriers and stigma described elsewhere in this report are severely exacerbated, at a time when crimes on a massive scale have taken place and in many cases are ongoing.

There have been great leaps forward in the recognition of gender-based crimes in the past two decades. From a time when rape was accepted as an inevitable part of conflict, to the codification of gender-based crimes in the Rome Statute of the International Criminal Court and the recognition by the United Nations Security Council that sexual violence is a threat to international peace and security, the shift has been seismic and the message clear: impunity for crimes against women must stop.

Increasing prosecutions is a priority.

Vast challenges remain in bringing justice to the millions of women who have suffered severe violations of their rights. International prosecutions can be agonizingly slow and gender-based crimes still do not receive the priority and investment needed. To ensure that women can come forward to testify, a range of actions is needed, from providing money for transport and accommodation, long-term psychosocial support and HIV treatment, to witness protection and closed hearings in courts. Efforts to strengthen domestic justice systems through police reform, legal aid and mobile courts are showing results in challenging conflict and post-conflict settings.

Gender-sensitive truth commissions.

Prosecutions will never be enough on their own. Even with all these measures in place, many women will not seek justice in this way. Women want recognition of what they have endured and the means to pick up their lives and move on. When truth commissions are well designed and gender-sensitive, they can provide this recognition and ensure that women's stories are written into history. The recommendations of truth commissions can also catalyse reform of laws and institutions to promote women's rights. There has been a rapid evolution in these mechanisms, but to ensure they meet women's needs, it is essential that women are part of the process of designing them from the outset.

Transformative reparations programmes.

Comprehensive reparations programmes have perhaps the most potential to make a difference in women's lives in post-conflict contexts. If appropriately designed and delivered, with the aim of addressing underlying gender inequalities, they can play a significant role in bringing about transformative change in the lives of women and girls. Programmes must be broad in scope, to encompass all the violations that women face and be available for female relatives as well as victims. The practical barriers that women face in accessing reparations should be a priority for policymakers. As yet, the transformative potential of reparations is largely unrealized.

The post-conflict moment opens up the possibility of reframing political and civic leadership, with women at the centre. Women's participation in the design of all post-conflict justice mechanisms, in peace processes and in political decision-making is essential for ensuring the post-conflict State advances women's rights and justice for all.

Part II:
Gender Justice and the Millennium Development Goals

The Millennium Declaration and the eight Millennium Development Goals (MDGs) collectively herald a vision for a more just and equal world: a promise by Governments in 189 countries to achieve social justice for all. While advances have been made, data show that overall progress masks inequalities based on gender, income and location. Women and girls, especially those living in rural areas, have been the least likely to share in this progress, with millions continuing to live in poverty and exclusion.

Ending gender-based injustices that create barriers to women's and girls' opportunities must be the centrepiece of further action to achieve the MDGs.

The MDGs are interdependent and each one depends on making progress on gender equality and advancing women's rights. Reducing poverty and hunger (MDG 1) depends on improving access to decent work, particularly for women and young people, and on securing access to assets, including land. The MDG targets on health and education (MDGs 2, 3, 4, 5 and 6) cannot be met unless all girls have the chance to go to school and women's sexual and reproductive health and rights are addressed.

Reducing child mortality (MDG 4) depends on improving the status and well-being of women. Progress on combatting HIV and AIDS (MDG 6) requires recognition of how gender inequality and violence against women fuel the pandemic. Since millions of women, particularly in rural areas depend on natural resources for their livelihoods, they must be a central part of efforts to achieve environmental sustainability (MDG 7). Progress on all of these Goals underpins women's social and economic empowerment and access to decision-making at all levels (MDG 3). There has been a growing consensus since 2000 that gender equality must be at the heart of all global development partnerships (MDG 8).[1]

Part I of this report has shown how law and justice systems can play a central role in achieving women's rights. Over recent decades, legal reform, including on protection from violence, equality within the family and access to economic resources, has transformed the landscape for women's rights. However, institutional obstacles and services that fail to respond to women's needs have hampered implementation and have created barriers to women's access to justice. Women's lack of autonomy, lower levels of education and limited opportunities outside the home also make it harder for them to navigate complex and under-resourced justice systems. The MDGs provide the development framework to achieve gender equality, empowering women to claim their rights and access justice.

To build on the progress already made towards meeting the targets of the MDGs, it is increasingly important to focus on those left behind, especially the most excluded women and girls. Part II of this report evaluates each of the Goals from a gender perspective, focusing on where country averages conceal marked disparities in outcomes between women and men, and between different groups of women. It highlights the successful approaches that governments and civil society are taking to tackle these inequalities.

Scaling up investment and action on the gender equality dimensions of all the Goals has the dual advantage of addressing widespread inequality and accelerating progress overall. With only four years left until the target date of 2015, ending gender-based injustices that create barriers to women's and girls' opportunities must be the centrepiece of further action.

The MDGs provide the development framework to achieve gender equality, empowering women to claim their rights and access justice.

Students at an adult literacy class in Morocco. The lessons are part of an income generating programme for women.

Efforts to achieve MDG 1 must target women and girls, who continue to bear the disproportionate burden of extreme poverty and hunger.

According to the most recent data, global poverty rates have declined significantly, due largely to progress in China and India. The number of people in developing countries living on less than $1.25 a day fell from 1.8 billion in 1990 to 1.4 billion in 2005.[2]

The full impact of the global economic crisis on poverty is not yet known. However, unemployment has increased in all regions. The ILO estimates that in 2010, there were 87 million unemployed women globally, up from 76 million in 2007.[3]

In addition, major spikes in the prices of rice, wheat and maize since 2008 have led to large increases in the number of people going hungry.[4] The Food and Agriculture Organization (FAO) estimates that 906 million people were under-nourished in 2010, compared to 827 million in 1990 to 1992.[5] Control over land and other productive resources are the foundation for the food security, income and social status of millions of women and their families, especially in rural areas.

The FAO estimates that the productivity gains from ensuring equal access to fertilizers, seeds and tools for women could reduce the number of hungry people by between 100 and 150 million.[6]

The Economic Commission for Latin America and the Caribbean analysed household surveys to show that, compared to men, women are more likely to live in a poor household. The difference is especially marked for those of working age living in rural areas. For example, it estimates that there are 110 women aged 20 to 59 living in poor rural households for every 100 men in Colombia and 114 women for every 100 men in Chile.[7]

UN Women's analysis for sub-Saharan Africa found a similar pattern. For example, in Cameroon, Malawi, Namibia, Rwanda and Zimbabwe there are more than 120 women aged 20 to 59 living in poor households for every 100 men (see Figure 5.1).

These calculations do not take into account the fact that the distribution of income *within* households is typically unequal between women and men. In Malawi, for example, according to household surveys, only 18

FIGURE 5.1: Ratio of women to men of working age in the poorest households in sub-Saharan Africa

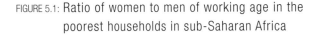

Women are more likely than men to live in poverty in 22 out of the 25 countries for which data are available.

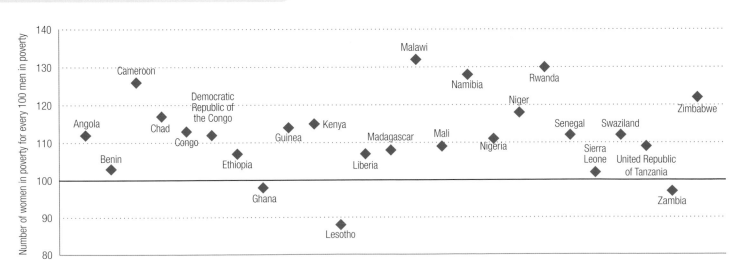

Source: UN Women calculations using MEASURE DHS latest available (2004–2009), based on methodology presented in ECLAC 2004.

Note: Sample includes working age population aged 20 to 59 years.

1A: Halve, between 1990 and 2015, the proportion of people whose income is less than one dollar a day.	1B: Achieve full and productive employment and decent work for all, including women and young people.	1C: Halve, between 1990 and 2015, the proportion of people who suffer from hunger.

FIGURE 5.2: Proportion of the workforce in agriculture and unpaid family work, by sex

In South Asia and sub-Saharan Africa, the majority of women are farm workers. Women do more unpaid work than men in all regions.

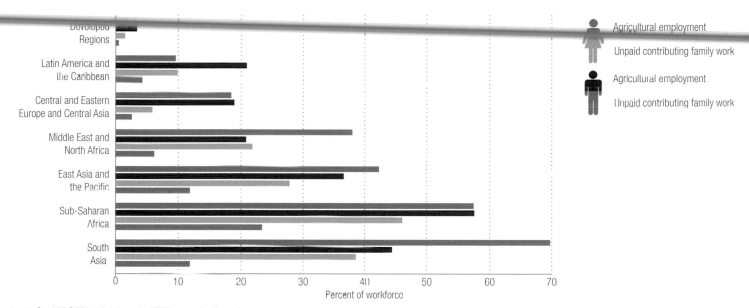

Source: Special ILO 2011 tabulation using UN Women regional groupings

Note: Based on ILO estimates for 2009, see ILO 2011. Unpaid contributing family work is defined as work performed in a market-oriented establishment operated by a related person living in the same household.

percent of married women aged 15 to 49 earned cash income, compared to 57 percent of men. Of the women who earned their own income, 34 percent said they have no say in how it is spent.[8] Therefore, there are likely to be a large number of women living in poverty in households that are not categorized as poor.

Much more research and analysis is needed, including collecting sex disaggregated household data to discover an accurate picture of women's poverty.

Poverty is not just about income. Millions of women face 'time poverty' due to the double work burden of providing for families in addition to shouldering a large share of unpaid and time-intensive domestic labour (see Figure 5.2). This limits women's time for leisure activities and impacts on their well-being, as well as curtailing their opportunities for education and paid employment.

Investments in labour-saving technologies and infrastructure, such as fuel-efficient stoves and water pumps, can reduce workloads, particularly of rural women.[9] Provision of affordable childcare and policies to encourage a more equitable division of caring responsibilities, such as paid paternity leave, are also important (see Chapter 1 and Annex 2).

The Beijing Platform for Action called for governments to ensure that the contribution of women's unpaid work to the economy is recognized.[10] More recently, the Commission on the Measurement of Economic Performance and Social Progress, established by the Government of France in 2008, recommended that governments prioritize the comprehensive and periodic accounting of household activity, including measuring the differences in the quantity and quality of unpaid work between women and men, as part of efforts to move beyond narrow GDP measures to capture broader well-being and quality of life indicators.[11]

Education is a critical foundation for gender equality and women's empowerment. Despite progress, many socially excluded girls continue to miss out on primary education.

Girls' education prevents the intergenerational transmission of poverty and spurs progress on other MDGs, including reducing maternal and infant mortality. Educated women have fewer children and later, and are more likely to send their children to school.[12]

Significant advances have been made towards achieving universal primary education, with the number of out-of-school children falling from 106 million in 1999 to 67 million in 2009. In developing regions, there were 96 girls for every 100 boys enrolled in primary school, up from 91 in 1999. In 2009, girls accounted for 53 percent of all out-of-school children.[13]

Progress is uneven across regions and within countries. Enrolment rates are lowest in sub-Saharan Africa, although this region has made the most progress since 2000, making the leap from 62 percent to 78 percent enrolment for girls and 67 percent to 80 percent for boys (see Figure 5.3).

While enrolment is rising, many girls will not complete their primary education. In almost every region, young women are significantly more likely to be 'education poor' (to have four years or less of primary education) than young men. In the Middle East and North Africa, a quarter of women aged 17 to 22 have less than four years of schooling compared to one in eight men (see Figure 5.4).

FIGURE 5.3: Primary school adjusted net enrolment rates, by region and sex

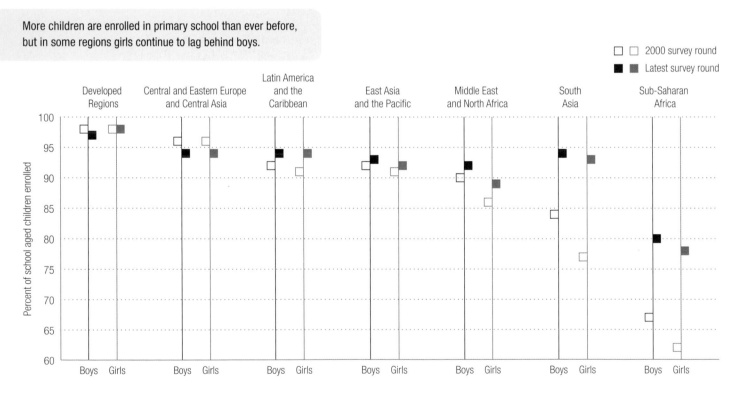

More children are enrolled in primary school than ever before, but in some regions girls continue to lag behind boys.

Source: UNESCO Institute of Statistics 2011.

Note: Unweighted averages, based on a sample of 111 countries, using UN Women regional groupings. The primary school adjusted net enrolment rate measures the number of primary school-age children enrolled in either primary or secondary education. 'Latest survey round' includes survey data from 2008–2009.

2A: Ensure that, by 2015, children everywhere, boys and girls alike, will be able to complete a full course of primary schooling.

To achieve universal primary education, greater attention should be paid to excluded children who have been left behind. Data show that poor girls from rural areas and from ethnic minority or indigenous groups often have the lowest education and literacy levels.[14]

In the Plurinational State of Bolivia, multilingual satellite schools are helping to ensure that indigenous girls in remote jungle and highland areas have access to education. Supported by a central school, the satellite schools send teachers out to isolated communities to provide classes that promote multiculturalism and provide indigenous children with language skills. Between 1992 and 2001, the proportion of rural girls completing six years of schooling increased from 11 percent to 74 percent.[15]

FIGURE 5.4: Share of the population aged 17 to 22 with fewer than 4 years of schooling

Women are more likely than men to be 'education poor' in most regions.

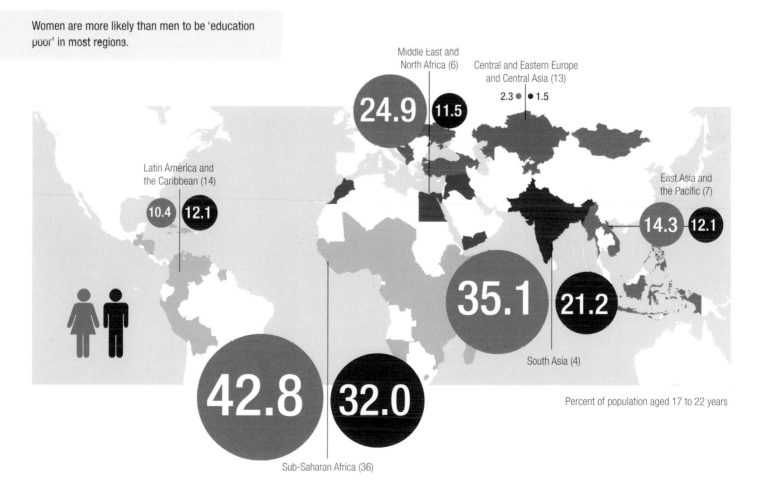

Middle East and North Africa (6)
24.9   11.5

Central and Eastern Europe and Central Asia (13)
2.3 ● ● 1.5

Latin America and the Caribbean (14)
10.4   12.1

East Asia and the Pacific (7)
14.3   12.1

South Asia (4)
35.1   21.2

Sub-Saharan Africa (36)
42.8   32.0

Percent of population aged 17 to 22 years

Source: UNESCO 2010a.

Note: Based on most recent available data (1999–2007) for a sample of 80 countries. Numbers in parentheses represent the number of countries included in the regional (unweighted) average. The threshold of four years or less is used to define absolute deprivation in education. The benchmark for 'education poverty' was first established in UNESCO 2010b.

MDG 3: Promote gender equality and empower women

Secondary education, decent work and ensuring women's voices are heard in decision-making are essential for tackling gender discrimination and accelerating progress on all the MDGs.

To achieve gender equality and women's empowerment, MDG 3 focuses on gender parity in education at all levels, women's employment outside the agricultural sector and women's representation in national parliaments. While there has been good overall progress on girls' education, progress on women's employment and representation has been much slower.

Men's labour force participation is higher than that of women in all regions of the world.[16] The global share of women in wage employment in the non-agricultural sector was 40 percent in 2009, an increase of just 5 percentage points since 1990.[17] When women access the labour market they are often unable to secure decent jobs. Globally, more than half of women (53 percent) work in vulnerable employment, rising to more than 80 percent of women in South Asia and sub-Saharan Africa.[18]

Achieving gender equality requires women's active participation and involvement in decision-making at all levels, starting in the home and extending to the highest levels of government. But in many countries, women have no say over basic household decisions, including on purchases and their own health care (see Figure 2.3). At the national level, women's representation in parliaments has increased in the last decade, but globally less than one in five members of parliament is a woman (see Figure 5.5).

Secondary education is critical for women to be able to claim rights and participate in decision-making, as well as being a route to decent work. Progress has been made on the goal of gender parity in secondary schooling, with 96 girls for every 100 boys enrolled in secondary school in 2009, up from 88 girls for every 100 boys in 1999.[19] However, overall secondary school attendance rates are very low in many countries, with significant levels of inequality between urban rich and rural poor girls (see Figure 5.6).

FIGURE 5.5: Women's representation in political decision-making

Developed regions have reached 30 percent critical mass for share of women in ministerial positions, but no region has achieved the mark for the proportion of women in parliament.

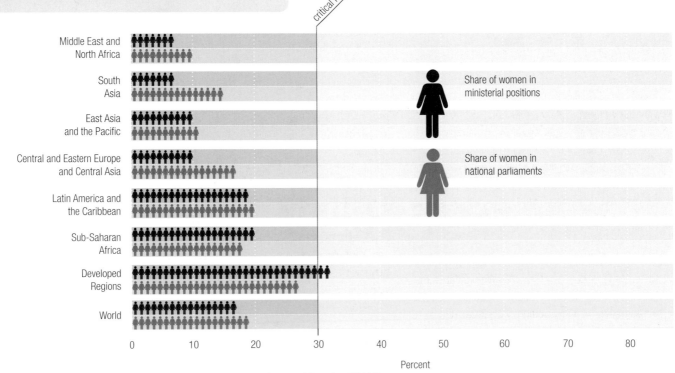

Source: UN Women calculations based on women in parliament data from IPU 2011a and women ministers from IPU 2010c.

Note: Data for the share of women in ministerial positions are as of January 2010; data for the share of women in parliament are as of 31 January 2011. See Annex 1 for detailed country information.

TARGET

3A: Eliminate gender disparity in primary and secondary education, preferably by 2005, and in all levels of education no later than 2015.

FIGURE 5.6: Secondary school attendance rates for girls in urban rich and rural poor households

Gender parity has been achieved in secondary attendance in 17 out of 40 countries. However, for some this has been achieved at very low overall rates and poor girls from rural areas are missing out.

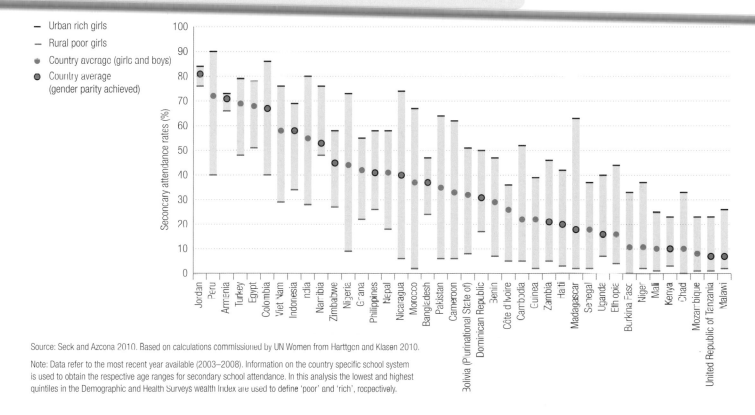

— Urban rich girls
— Rural poor girls
● Country average (girls and boys)
○ Country average (gender parity achieved)

Source: Seck and Azcona 2010. Based on calculations commissioned by UN Women from Harttgen and Klasen 2010.

Note: Data refer to the most recent year available (2003–2008). Information on the country specific school system is used to obtain the respective age ranges for secondary school attendance. In this analysis the lowest and highest quintiles in the Demographic and Health Surveys wealth Index are used to define 'poor' and 'rich', respectively.

Poverty, early marriage and discriminatory attitudes that place a lower value on their education keep girls out of school. Laws prohibiting early marriage, coupled with financial incentives, can make a difference (see Figure 1.2). Countries such as Bangladesh and Ethiopia have had success in providing stipends to girls who stay in school and delay marriage until after they have completed their education.[20]

The Beijing Platform for Action called for gender balance in governmental bodies, while CEDAW mandates the use of temporary special measures, including quotas, to increase the voice of women in political decision-making.[21]

The 30 percent critical mass mark for women's representation has been reached or exceeded in 28 countries, of which at least 23 have used quotas.[22] The impressive strides of some of the world's poorest countries – including those emerging from conflict – show that progress depends on political will more than level of development. In a number of countries, including Costa Rica, the former Yugoslav Republic of Macedonia and Rwanda, increases in women's representation in parliament have coincided with significant legal reform on women's rights (see Display: Women in parliaments and legal reform).

MDG 4: Reduce child mortality

There have been some impressive gains in child survival, but children from poor households, and in some countries girls, remain disproportionately likely to die before their fifth birthday.

The mortality rate for children under the age of five has dropped by more than a third from 89 deaths per 1,000 live births in 1990 to 60 per 1,000 in 2009.[23] But the poorest children are not always benefitting from this progress and are significantly less likely to survive than their richer counterparts in all regions of the developing world (see Figure 5.7).

Reducing child mortality is contingent on improving the rights and status of women. Early marriage puts mothers and children at risk. Pregnancy and childbirth are the leading causes of death for girls aged 15 to 19 in developing countries.[24] Child mortality increases by 60 percent if the mother is under the age of 18, attributed to health complications in pregnancy and labour, and a lack of knowledge of and access to reproductive health care services.[25]

Entrenched gender discrimination continues to underpin the 'missing women' phenomenon. The economist Amartya Sen estimated that 100 million women were 'missing' in Asia in 1990 as a result of prenatal sex selection, infanticide and neglect. New estimates put the figure at 134 million.[26] Under-five mortality rates for girls are significantly higher in several countries in Asia, even though girls are physiologically predisposed to have higher survival rates than boys.[27] For example, the under-five mortality rate for girls in India in 2008 was 73 per 1,000 live births, compared to 65 for boys. In China, the rate for girls was 24, compared to 18 for boys.[28]

FIGURE 5.7: Under-five mortality rate, by region (deaths per 1,000 live births)

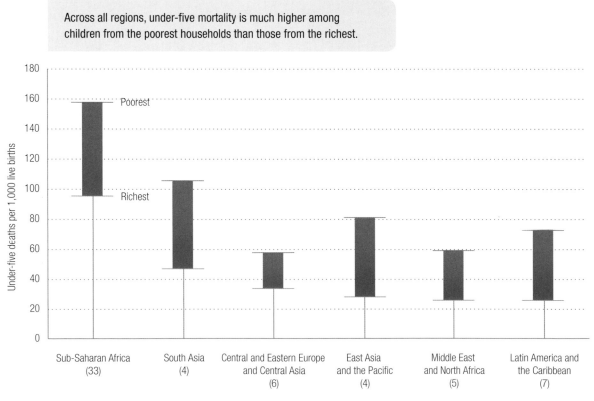

Across all regions, under-five mortality is much higher among children from the poorest households than those from the richest.

Source: WHO 2010.

Note: Based on the most recent available data (2000–2008) for a sample of 59 countries. Numbers in parentheses represent the number of countries included in the regional (unweighted) average. In this analysis the lowest and highest quintile in the Demographic and Health Surveys wealth index are used to define 'poorest' and 'richest', respectively.

TARGET

4A: Reduce by two thirds, between 1990 and 2015, the under-five mortality rate.

FIGURE 5.8: Sex ratios at birth, for countries with large female deficits (1980–2010)

Sex ratios remain high in countries where sons are traditionally preferred over daughters.

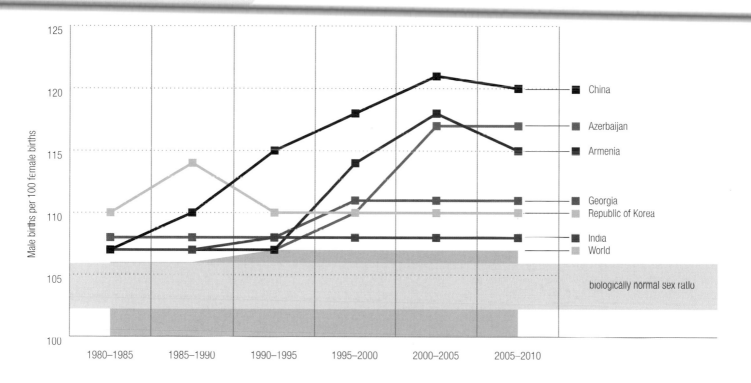

Source: UN DESA 2011b.

Note: The biologically normal sex ratio at birth is approximately 102–106 boys for every 100 girls.

Furthermore, according to United Nations estimates, the sex ratio at birth has increased globally from a stable 105 in the early 1970s to a recent peak of 107 (see Figure 5.8). This is partly attributed to a rise in prenatal sex selection in some countries.[29]

Women often resort to sex selection under immense social and family pressure to produce sons. Discriminatory social norms, patrilineal inheritance and the reliance on sons for economic support in old age lead families to place higher value on having boys. Governments have an obligation to address this systemic discrimination, without exposing women to the risk of serious injury or death by denying them access to safe abortion.[30]

The Republic of Korea has had some success in addressing high sex ratios, which peaked at 114 in the 1980s. Through investing in girls' education and promoting women's employment, the discriminatory perception that daughters are a financial burden has been challenged. Popular campaigns, including one with the slogan 'One daughter raised well is worth 10 sons', have been mounted to change attitudes. A survey found that, while in 1985, 48 percent of women reported they 'must have a son', this had dropped to less than 20 percent by 2003.[31]

Of all the Goals, MDG 5 depends the most on improving women's status. But progress has been very slow, with poor women and those in rural areas much less likely to receive the services they need.

After years of neglect, maternal mortality is finally becoming a development priority, spurred on by the launch of the United Nations Secretary-General's Global Strategy for Women's and Children's Health in September 2010.

The scale of the challenge is significant. In 2008, it is estimated that 358,000 women died in pregnancy or childbirth. The number of maternal deaths has decreased by 2.3 percent per year since 1990, far below the 5.5 percent needed to reduce maternal deaths by three quarters by 2015. On current trends only 14 countries will meet the target.[32] In addition to deaths, over 300 million women worldwide suffer long-term health problems and disability arising from complications in pregnancy or delivery.[33]

It is estimated that up to 70 percent of maternal deaths could be prevented through the availability of maternal and reproductive health care services and adequate family planning.[34] Unmet need for family planning, however, remains high in most regions, particularly in sub-Saharan Africa, where one in four women aged 15 to 49, who are married or in a union and have expressed

FIGURE 5.9: Skilled attendance at delivery, urban rich and rural poor women

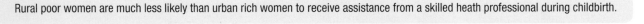

Rural poor women are much less likely than urban rich women to receive assistance from a skilled heath professional during childbirth.

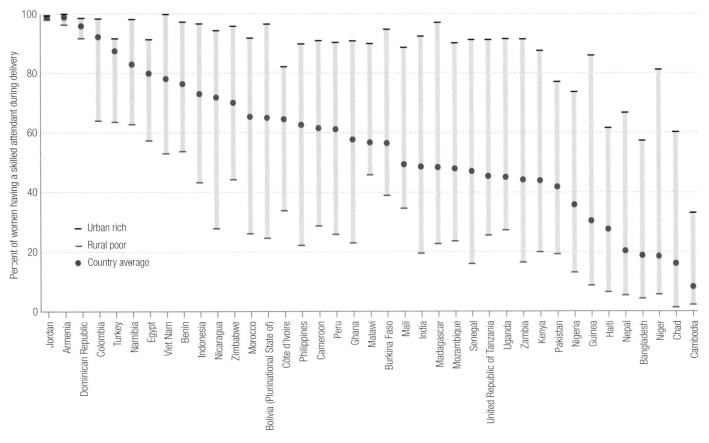

Source: Seck and Azcona 2010. Based on calculations commissioned by UN Women from Harttgen and Klasen 2010.

Note: Data refer to the most recent year available (2001–2008). Skilled assistance at delivery refers to live births attended by trained health personnel such as a doctor or nurse. In this analysis the lowest and highest quintiles in the Demographic and Health Surveys wealth index are used to define 'poor' and 'rich', respectively.

5A:	Reduce by three quarters, between 1990 and 2015, the maternal mortality ratio.	5B:	Achieve, by 2015, universal access to reproductive health.

FIGURE 5.10: Barriers to women accessing health care, in selected countries with high rates of maternal mortality

Women cite not having a female health provider, along with the cost of treatment as among the top reasons for not seeking health care.

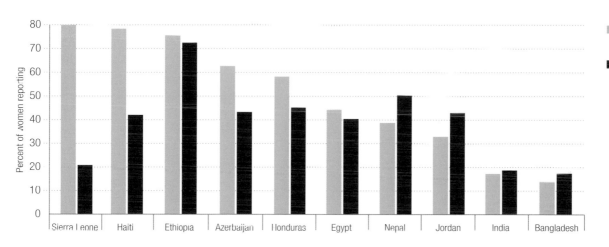

Source: UN Women elaboration using MEASURE DHS 2010.

Note: Data refer to the most recent year available (2004–2008). Values calculated for women aged 15 to 49 years.

the desire to use contraceptives, do not have access to them. Despite this demand, aid for family planning as a proportion of total aid to health declined from 8.2 percent to 3.2 percent between 2000 and 2008.[35]

Rural location and poverty combine to make childbirth a serious risk for many women. In Bangladesh and Nepal, only around 5 percent of poor rural women have access to skilled birth attendance, essential for reducing maternal mortality. In both countries, wealthy urban women are over 10 times more likely to receive this service than poor rural women (see Figure 5.9).

User fees and a lack of female staff are major barriers to women accessing health care services. Household survey data show that in Sierra Leone, 80 percent of women report concern about cost as a reason for not seeking health care (see Figure 5.10). Eliminating these cost barriers can greatly boost skilled attendance for poor women: in Burundi, the removal of fees resulted in a 61 percent increase in births in hospitals.[36]

Since 1994, the proportion of births attended by skilled personnel in Indonesia has doubled to 73 percent.[37] The maternal mortality rate has also been cut in half since 1989, the result of the Government's 'midwife in every village' programme, through which 54,000 midwives have been trained, certified and deployed in just seven years.[38]

MDG 6: Combat HIV/AIDS, malaria and other diseases

While there have been significant advances towards the targets on HIV and AIDS, further progress is contingent on addressing poverty, gender inequality and violence against women, which continue to fuel the pandemic.

Globally, there were 33.3 million people living with HIV in 2009 and women were 53 percent of those in developing countries and 21 percent in developed regions. Almost 80 percent of all women living with HIV are in sub-Saharan Africa. More than 5 million people received antiretroviral treatment in 2009. Although this represents a 30 percent increase since 2008, it is only 35 percent of those who needed it.[39]

Poverty increases vulnerability to HIV infection, in rich and poor countries alike. In the United States, over a quarter of African-American women live on or below the poverty line and they are 15 times more likely to be infected with HIV than are white women.[40]

Most women contract HIV from their husbands or intimate partners. In India, for example, around 90 percent of women living with HIV acquired the virus while in a long-term relationship.[41] Women's risk of infection is increased by their lack of decision-making power. Household survey data show that women in a number of countries report not being able to ask their partner to use a condom (see Figure 5.11).

Violence against women is both a cause and consequence of HIV. A study in South Africa found that women who had been physically and sexually abused were 66 percent more likely to be living with HIV, compared to women who had not been abused.[42] A survey in China found that twice as many women as men reported being physically harassed or threatened because of their HIV status and they are more likely to be verbally abused, excluded from the house and socially outcast (see Figure 5.12).

FIGURE 5.11: Women who reported not being able to ask their husband or partner to use a condom

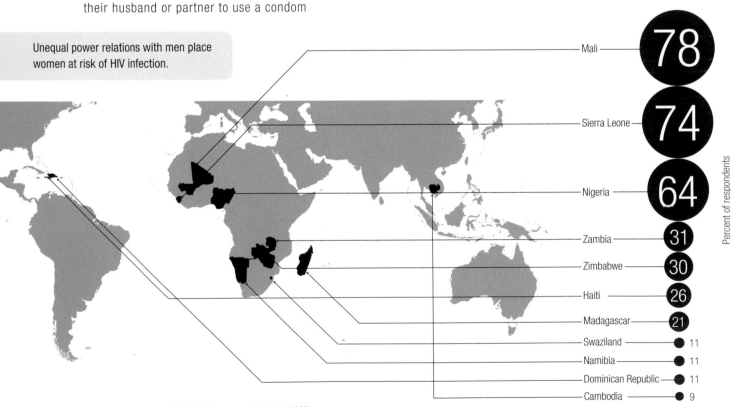

Unequal power relations with men place women at risk of HIV infection.

Country	Percent of respondents
Mali	78
Sierra Leone	74
Nigeria	64
Zambia	31
Zimbabwe	30
Haiti	26
Madagascar	21
Swaziland	11
Namibia	11
Dominican Republic	11
Cambodia	9

Source: UN Women calculations using MEASURE DHS latest available (2004–2009).

6A: Have halted by 2015 and begun to reverse the spread of HIV/AIDS.	6B: Achieve, by 2010, universal access to treatment for HIV/AIDS for all those who need it.	6C: Have halted by 2015 and begun to reverse the incidence of malaria and other major diseases.

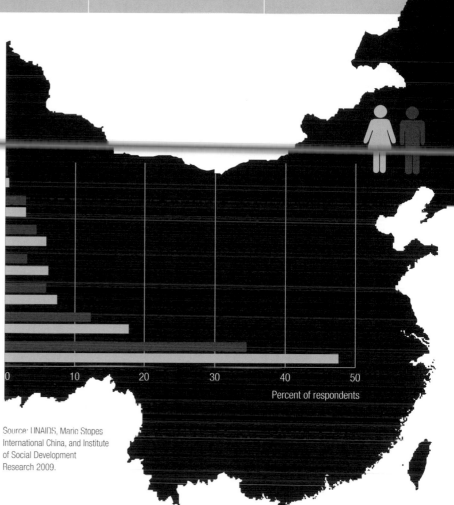

FIGURE 5.12: Discrimination reported by people living with HIV in China

Women are more likely than men to experience stigma and discrimination because of their HIV status.

Excluded from religious activities
Physically attacked
Excluded from day-to-day family life
Physically harassed or threatened
Excluded from social events
Verbally insulted or threatened
Clearly noticed being gossiped about

0   10   20   30   40   50
Percent of respondents

Source: UNAIDS, Marie Stopes International China, and Institute of Social Development Research 2009.

The Government of China has taken a number of important steps to raise awareness of HIV and AIDS. In 2008, the Ministry of Labour and Social Security and the China Enterprises Confederation (CEC) launched the HIV Workplace Education Programme in three pilot provinces to reduce stigma and discrimination. Meanwhile, the All China Women's Federation (ACWF) is spearheading a national programme on 'HIV Prevention for a Healthy Family', involving 120,000 volunteers who, by 2008, had trained nearly 10 million participants on HIV prevention and care.[43]

In South Africa, Intervention with Microfinance for AIDS and Gender Equity (IMAGE) is a programme that provides small loans for women to set up businesses. This is combined with gender and HIV education to help them better negotiate sexual relationships and challenge negative attitudes within communities.

A study found that the programme had contributed to a 55 percent reduction in the incidence of intimate partner violence among the women who participated in the programme.[44]

Guaranteeing women's inheritance and property rights is another important element of the fight against HIV and AIDS. Studies have shown that women who own property are less likely to report domestic violence, which in turn may make them less vulnerable to infection. Furthermore, ensuring women can inherit property in the event of widowhood is essential for safeguarding their livelihoods and mitigating the impacts of HIV and AIDS.[45]

Environmental degradation has negative repercussions for millions of women, especially those in rural areas who rely on natural resources to survive. Yet, women are often denied the right to participate in the conservation and management of these resources.

MDG 7 aims to ensure that the principles of sustainable development are integrated into countries' policies and programmes. This Goal also includes targets on improving access to drinking water and basic sanitation, and on conditions of slum dwellers.

The MDGs were agreed before the impacts of climate change were widely recognized, but there is growing evidence that rising temperatures and changing weather patterns are posing major threats to social justice and development. Poor women are likely to bear the impacts of climate change as they perform the majority of the world's agricultural work and are most affected by weather-related disasters.[46]

However, policies and programmes often fail to target rural women. On climate adaptation, few country-level plans include women as key stakeholders or primary participants in adaptation activities (see Figure 5.13).

The challenges posed by climate change make it especially important that agricultural extension services reach women, to help them adapt to climate change, and that new technologies such as solar-powered drip irrigation and drought-resistant crops are made available.[47]

In Pintadas, in Bahia, one of the poorest states of Brazil, the SouthSouthNorth network and the Association of Women of Pintadas have developed an irrigation project designed to harness solar power and improve water management. Women have been trained in the technical skills to manage and adapt new agricultural systems to deal with the consequences of climate change and drought.[48]

FIGURE 5.13: **Proportion of National Adaptation Programmes of Action (NAPAs) that mention women, by sector**

Despite the disproportionate impact of climate change on women, they are mentioned as key stakeholders or primary participants in adaptation activities in few NAPAs.

Percent of NAPAs

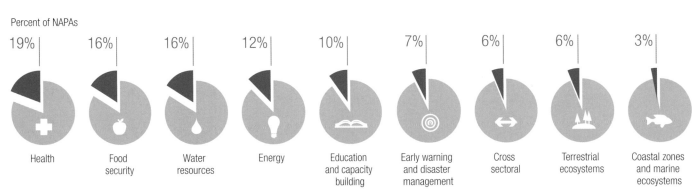

| 19% | 16% | 16% | 12% | 10% | 7% | 6% | 6% | 3% |
| Health | Food security | Water resources | Energy | Education and capacity building | Early warning and disaster management | Cross sectoral | Terrestrial ecosystems | Coastal zones and marine ecosystems |

Source: UNFCCC 2008.

Note: Based on UN Women analysis of 423 NAPA reports by least developed countries (as of October 2010). There are 36 NAPAs on infrastructure, insurance and tourism none of which include women as key stakeholders or primary participants in adaptation activities.

TARGETS

| 7A: Integrate the principles of sustainable development into country policies and programmes and reverse the loss of environmental resources. | 7B: Reduce biodiversity loss, achieving, by 2010, a significant reduction in the rate of loss. | 7C: Halve, by 2015, the proportion of people without sustainable access to safe drinking water and basic sanitation. | 7D: By 2020, to have achieved a significant improvement in the lives of at least 100 million slum dwellers. |

Scaling up investment in gender equality and women's empowerment is essential for making progress on all the Goals and for donors to meet their own policy commitments.

MDG 8 calls for a global partnership for development, which addresses the needs of the least developed countries, improves trading and financial systems, tackles global debt and spreads the use of new technology.

Overseas aid is an important part of this global partnership. Over the past ten years, progress has been made on increasing levels of bilateral official development assistance (ODA). Despite the recent economic crisis, ODA flows have continued to rise and are expected to reach $126 billion per year in 2010.[49]

But to date, only five countries – Denmark, Luxembourg, the Netherlands, Norway and Sweden – have reached the United Nations target of 0.7 percent of gross national income (GNI) to be spent on aid.[50]

Moreover, funding for gender equality is consistently low. The proportion of aid allocated by OECD-DAC donors to programmes in which gender equality was a primary aim rose to 4 percent in the years 2007 to 2009. Programmes in which gender equality was a significant but secondary aim accounted for 28 percent of funding.[51] Financial commitments to organizations working on gender equality have increased by a third, from 0.4 percent in 2002 to 0.6 percent in 2008 (see Figure 5.14).

In November and December 2011, the fourth High Level Forum on Aid Effectiveness will be held in Busan, in the Republic of Korea. The Forum will be an important opportunity to recognize efforts to integrate gender into public finance management systems and adopt concrete actions to build on the commitments on gender equality made at the last High Level Forum in Ghana in 2008.[52] It will be important to ensure that any monitoring framework for aid effectiveness agreed at the Busan meeting includes performance indicators in relation to gender equality.

FIGURE 5.14: Official Development Assistance (ODA) for women's equality organizations and institutions

Donor support for women's organizations has risen, but still makes up a very small proportion of ODA.

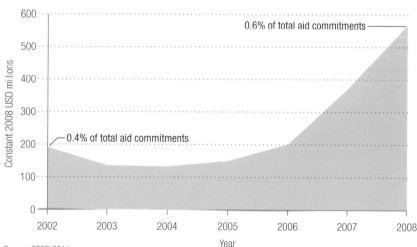

Source: OECD 2011.

Note: ODA for women's equality organizations is defined as support for institutions and organizations (governmental and non-governmental) working for gender equality and women's empowerment. The analysis is based on a review of sector-allocable aid for 24 OECD-DAC members who reported on their commitment levels.

TARGETS

8A: Develop further an open, rule-based, predictable, non-discriminatory trading and financial system.

8B: Address the special needs of the least developed countries.

8C: Address the special needs of landlocked developing countries and small island developing States.

8D: Deal comprehensively with the debt problems of developing countries.

8E: Provide access to affordable essential drugs in developing countries.

8F: Make available the benefits of new technologies.

Ten Recommendations to Make Justice Systems Work for Women

The past century has seen a transformation in women's legal rights, with countries the world over expanding the scope of women's legal entitlements. However, for millions of women worldwide, the laws that exist on paper do not translate into equality and justice.

Despite progress, discriminatory laws and critical gaps in legal frameworks remain a problem in every region. Moreover, governments are responsible for providing a functioning and accessible justice system, but too often they fall short, with major institutional barriers denying women's access to justice.

Progress of the World's Women shows that where laws and justice systems work well, they can provide an essential mechanism for women to realize their human rights. Laws and justice systems shape society, by providing accountability, by stopping the abuse of power and by creating new norms.

This report highlights the ways in which governments and civil society are working together to reform laws and create new models for justice service delivery that meet women's needs. They have risen to the challenge of ensuring that women can access justice in the most challenging of situations, including after conflict and in the context of legal pluralism. Women themselves play a central role as agents for change, as legislators, judges, lawyers, campaigners and community activists.

These ten recommendations to make justice systems work for women are proven, achievable and, if implemented, they hold enormous potential to increase women's access to justice and advance gender equality.

1

Support women's legal organizations

Women's legal organizations are at the forefront of making justice systems work for women. Where government-funded legal aid is limited, women's organizations step in to provide the advice and support that women need to pursue a legal case, to put a stop to violence, to seek a divorce or claim the land that is rightfully theirs.

These organizations have been leaders in successful interventions in plural legal environments, showing that it is possible to engage with plural legal systems while simultaneously supporting local cultures, traditions and practices.

Women's organizations have also spearheaded law reform efforts and strategic litigation cases that have transformed the landscape for women's rights nationally, regionally and internationally. These cases, including those on violence against women, sexual and reproductive health, citizenship and inheritance have enforced or clarified laws already on the books, challenged laws that should be repealed and created new laws to fill legislative gaps.

Supporting these organizations is an urgent priority and a vital investment to increase women's access to justice.

② Support one-stop shops and specialized services to reduce attrition in the justice chain

The justice chain, the series of steps that a woman must take to seek redress, is characterized by high levels of attrition, whereby cases are dropped as they progress through the system. As a result, only a fraction of cases end in a conviction or a just outcome.

One way to reduce attrition, especially in cases of violence against women, is to invest in one-stop shops, which bring together vital services under one roof to collect forensic evidence, and provide legal advice, health care and other support. The Thuthuzela Care Centres (TCCs) in South Africa are one successful example of this approach, now being replicated in other countries, including Chile and Ethiopia. Conviction rates for rape cases dealt with by the TCC in Soweto have reached up to 89 percent, compared to a national average of 7 percent.

A study in the United States found that women supported by specialized advocates for survivors of rape, who helped them navigate the justice system, were more likely to make police reports, more likely to receive health care and less likely to report distress in their dealings with the different service providers.

③ Implement gender-sensitive law reform

Gender-sensitive law reform is the foundation for women's access to justice. CEDAW provides the internationally agreed gold standard for legal reform to achieve gender equality. Action is needed to repeal laws that explicitly discriminate against women; to extend the rule of law to protect women in the private domain, including from domestic violence; and to address the actual impact of laws on women's lives.

While CEDAW is among the most widely ratified of United Nations treaties, it also has one of the largest number of reservations. The most common are on article 16, which guarantees women's rights within marriage and the family. Removing these reservations is a critical step to putting in place a legal framework that supports women's rights.

To have the most impact, laws must be drafted to drive implementation, including clear mandates, procedures, funding and accountability mechanisms. For example, in 45 countries, laws on domestic violence include guarantees of free legal aid for women. In Nepal, financial incentives have ensured implementation of laws on equal inheritance, which has led to a threefold increase in women's property ownership. In Sweden, non-transferable 'daddy months' have increased the uptake of paternity leave, helping to address the gender pay gap.

④ Use quotas to boost the number of women legislators

In countries where women's representation in parliament increases substantially, it is often accompanied by new laws that advance women's rights.

From the United Republic of Tanzania to Costa Rica, Rwanda to Spain, where quotas have been used to boost the number of women legislators, progressive laws on violence against women, land rights, health care and employment have followed. Where women have organized, sometimes across party lines, to ensure women's interests are represented, change has followed.

The Beijing Platform for Action called for gender balance in governmental bodies, while CEDAW mandates the use of temporary special measures, including quotas, to increase the voice of women in decision-making at all levels. Of the 28 countries that have reached or exceeded the 30 percent critical mass mark in national parliaments, at least 23 have used some form of quota.

⑤ Put women on the front line of law enforcement

Employing women on the front line of justice service delivery can help to increase women's access to justice. Data show that there is a correlation between the presence of women police officers and reporting of sexual assault.

In post-conflict Liberia, the presence of the all-women Indian police brigade has increased reporting of sexual violence and has also boosted recruitment of women into the force. Despite these benefits, women's average representation in the police does not exceed 13 percent in any region of the world.

The gains from employing women in the police are not automatic: investment is essential. The experience from Latin America and elsewhere is that women's police stations and gender desks must be adequately resourced, and staff expertly trained, properly rewarded and recognized for their work. Furthermore, recruitment of women police officers and resourcing of gender desks must be part of a broader strategy to train and incentivize *all* police to adequately respond to women's needs.

⑥ Train judges and monitor decisions

Balanced, well-informed and unbiased judicial decision-making is an essential part of ensuring that women who go to court get justice. However, even where laws are in place to guarantee women's rights, they are not always properly or fairly applied by judges.

Organizations such as the International Association of Women Judges and the Indian NGO Sakshi provide judges, both women and men, with specialized training and space to discuss the challenges they face, which can help to build understanding of and commitment to gender equality. Judges who have been trained also come up with simple but effective ways to make courts more accessible, such as waiving court fees, providing forms free of charge or prioritizing sensitive cases.

Systematic tracking of judicial decision-making is needed at the national level to provide accountability to women seeking justice and to enable civil society and governments to monitor the performance of the courts on women's rights.

⑦ Increase women's access to courts and truth commissions during and after conflict

Very significant advances in international law in the past two decades have, for the first time, made it possible to redress sexual violence crimes. However, prosecutions are rare. To increase the number of convictions, it is vital that international courts prioritize gender-based crimes in their prosecution strategies.

Courts and other justice forums such as truth commissions must be made more accessible to women. The only way to guarantee this is to ensure that women play a central part in defining the scope, remit and design of all post-conflict justice mechanisms.

Measures that make a difference include financial assistance, childcare and transport to help women overcome the practical obstacles to their participation; psychosocial counselling, health care and other long-term support; and provision of closed session hearings to enable women to testify about sexual violence.

In the Democratic Republic of the Congo, mobile courts are bringing justice to women, responding rapidly to investigate and prosecute cases of sexual violence. Although currently small-scale, these pioneering courts are helping to end impunity for these crimes.

8

Implement gender-responsive reparations programmes

Reparations are the most victim-focused justice mechanism and can be a critical vehicle for women's recovery post-conflict. However, while the international community has dedicated substantial funding to international courts and other transitional justice mechanisms, this has not been matched by an equal commitment to assist States to fulfil their obligations for reparative justice.

To benefit women, reparations programmes must take account of all forms of sexual and gender-based violence, and include individual, community and symbolic measures, as well as access to services and land restitution. Packages of benefits can be designed to promote victim empowerment and self-sustainability to address underlying gender inequality.

In Sierra Leone, women survivors of gender-based violence are benefitting from a Government reparations programme. Supported by United Nations partners, this programme provides skills training and micro-grants to women to set up their own businesses.

9

Invest in women's access to justice

Strengthening the rule of law has been a major priority for governments for several decades, but only a fraction of this funding is being spent on justice for women and girls.

Analysis of the major bilateral donors' funding for justice shows that of the $4.2 billion that was allocated to justice in 2009, $206 million (5 percent) was spent on projects in which gender equality was a primary aim. Over the decade 2000 to 2010, the World Bank has allocated $126 billion to public administration, law and justice, of which only $7.3 million was allocated to the gender equality components of rule of law and access to justice projects.

To ensure governments are meeting their international commitments to put in place a legal framework that guarantees women's rights and a functioning justice system, a significant scaling up of investments is needed.

10

Put gender equality at the heart of the Millennium Development Goals

More than a decade since 189 Governments signed up to the MDGs, there has been impressive progress, especially on poverty and education. However, with four years left to achieve the Goals, it is clear that further advances depend on accelerating progress on gender equality and ensuring that excluded women and girls are not left behind.

Achieving these Goals is also an essential precondition for women to access justice. Without education, awareness of rights and decision-making power, women are often unable to claim their rights, obtain legal aid or go to court.

Some practical approaches to putting women's rights at the heart of the MDGs include: abolishing user fees for health care, which has been shown to increase women's and girls' access to services, including for reproductive health; using stipends and cash transfers to encourage girls to go to school, delay marriage and continue their education for the critical secondary years; putting women on the front line of service delivery to make public services more accessible; and amplifying women's voices in decision-making, from the household up to local and national levels, to ensure that policies reflect the realities of women's lives.

Annexes

ANNEX 1: Women's political rights

	Year women obtained the right[a]		Women's political participation					Quotas for women's political participation[b]		
	To vote	To stand for election	Year first woman elected (E) or appointed (A) to parliament	Year first woman presided over parliament[c]	Share of women in ministerial positions[d] (%) 2010	Share of women in parliament[e] (%) 1997	(%) 2011	Constitutional quota for national parliaments	Election law quota for national parliaments	Constitutional or legislative quota at sub-national level[f]
Central and Eastern Europe and Central Asia					10 t	9 t	17 t			
Albania	1920	1920	1945 E	2005 g	7	12	16	No	Yes h	..
Armenia	1921	1921	1990 E i	–	11	6	9	No	Yes	..
Azerbaijan	1921	1921	1990 E i	–	3	12	16	No	No	..
Belarus	1919	1919	1990 E i	–	3	..	32	No	No	..
Bosnia and Herzegovina	1949	1949	1990 E i	2009 g	0	..	16	No	Yes	Yes
Bulgaria	1944	1944	1945 E	2009 g	18	11	21	No	No	..
Croatia	1945	1945	1992 E i	1993	16	7	24	No	No	..
Cyprus	1960	1960	1963 E	–	9	5	13	No	No	..
Czech Republic	1920	1920	1992 E i	1998 g	18	14	21	No	No	..
Estonia	1918	1918	1919 E	2003 g	8	11	23	No	No	..
Georgia	1918, 1921	1918, 1921	1992 E i	2001	6	7	7	No	No	..
Hungary	1918	1918	1920 E	1963	0	11	9	No	No	..
Kazakhstan	1924, 1993	1924	1990 E i	–	5	11	14	No	No	..
Kyrgyzstan	1918	1918	1990 E i	–	10	5	23	No	Yes h	..
Latvia	1918	1918	..	1995 g	21	9	20	No	No	..
Lithuania	1919	1919	1920 A	2009 g	14	18	19	No	No	..
Montenegro	..	..	..	..	5	..	11	No	No	..
Poland	1918	1918	1919 E	1997	28	13	18	No	No	..
Republic of Moldova	1978, 1993	1978	1990 E	2001	5	5	19	No	No	..
Romania	1929, 1946	1929, 1946	1946 E	2008 g	6	6	10	No	No	..
Russian Federation	1918	1918	1993 E i	–	17	7	11	No	No	..
Serbia	..	..	..	2008 g	19	..	22	Yes	Yes h	Yes
Slovakia	1920	1920	1992 E i	–	13	15	15	No	No	..
Slovenia	1945	1945	1992 E i	–	22	8	11	No	Yes h	Yes
Tajikistan	1924	1924	1990 E i	–	6	3	18	No	No	..
The former Yugoslav Republic of Macedonia	1946	1946	1990 E i	–	10	3	33	No	Yes h	Yes
Turkey	1930	1934	1935 A	–	8	2	9	No	No	..
Turkmenistan	1927	1927	1990 E i	2006 g	6	18	17	No	No	..
Ukraine	1919	1919	1990 E i	–	4	4	8	No	No	..
Uzbekistan	1938	1938	1990 E	2008 g	3	6	19	No	Yes	Yes
Developed Regions					31 t	17 t	27 t			
Andorra	1970	1973	..	–	33	7	36	No	No	..
Australia	1902, 1962	1902, 1962	1943 E	1987	23	21	28	No	No	..
Austria	1918	1918	1919 E	1927 g	39	25	28	No	No	..
Belgium	1919, 1948	1921, 1948	1921 A	2004	33	16	38	No	Yes h	Yes
Canada	1917, 1951 k	1920, 1960	1921 E	1972	30	21	25	No	No	..
Denmark	1915	1915	1918 E	1950	42	33	38	No	No	..
Finland	1906	1906	1907 E	1991	63	34	40	No	No	..
France	1944	1944	1945 E	–	26	9	20	Yes	Yes h	Yes
Germany	1918	1918	1919 E	1972 g	33	26	32	No	No	..
Greece	1949, 1952	1949, 1952	1952 E	2004	31	6	17	No	No	Yes
Iceland	1915, 1920	1915, 1920	1922 E	1974 g	46	25	43	No	No	..
Ireland	1918, 1928	1918, 1928	1918 E	1982	21	14	16	No	No	..
Israel	1948	1948	1949 E	2006	7	8	19	No	No	..
Italy	1945	1945	1946 E	1979	22	10	20	No	No	..
Japan	1945, 1947	1945, 1947	1946 E	1993	12	8	14	No	No	..
Liechtenstein	1984	1984	..	–	40	4	24	No	No	..
Luxembourg	1919	1919	1919 E	1989	27	20	20	No	No	..
Malta	1947	1947	1966 E	1996	25	6	9	No	No	..
Monaco	1962	1962	..	–	20	6	26	No	No	..
Netherlands	1919	1917	1918 E	1998 g	24	28	39	No	No	..
New Zealand	1893	1919	1933 E	2005	29	29	34	No	No	..
Norway	1913	1907, 1913	1911 A	1993	53	36	40	No	No	..
Portugal	1931, 1934, 1976	1931, 1934, 1976	1934 E	–	31	13	27	No	Yes h	Yes

	Year women obtained the right[a]		Women's political participation					Quotas for women's political participation[b]		
	To vote	To stand for election	Year first woman elected (E) or appointed (A) to parliament	Year first woman presided over parliament[c]	Share of women in ministerial positions[d] (%) 2010	Share of women in parliament[e] (%) 1997	(%) 2011	Constitutional quota for national parliaments	Election law quota for national parliaments	Constitutional or legislative quota at sub-national level[f]
San Marino	1959	1973	..	1981	20	12	17	No	No	..
Spain	1931	1931	1931 E	1999	53	20	34	No	Yes h	Yes
Sweden	1919, 1921	1919, 1921	1921 E	1991	45	40	45	No	No	..
Switzerland	1971	1971	1971 E	1977	43	20	28	No	No	..
United Kingdom	1918, 1928	1918, 1928	1918 E	1992 g	23	12	21	No	No	..
United States of America	1920 l	1788 l	1917 E	2007	33	11 m	17 m	No	No	..
East Asia and the Pacific					**9 t**	**8 t**	**11 t**			
Brunei Darussalam	–	..	..	..	0	..	..	No	No	..
Cambodia	1955	1955	1958 E	–	10	6	19	No	No	..
China	1949	1949	1954 E	–	12	21	21	No	No	..
Democratic People's Republic of Korea	1946	1946	..	–	6	20	16	No	No	..
Fiji	1963	1963	1970A	..	9	6	..	No	No	..
Hong Kong, China (SAR)	..	..	..	..	..	..	..	No	No	..
Indonesia	1945	1945	1950 A	–	14	11	18	No	Yes	..
Kiribati	1967	1967	..	–	8	0	4	No	No	..
Lao People's Democratic Republic	1958	1958	1958 E	–	10	9	25	No	No	..
Malaysia	1957	1957	1959 E	–	7	10	14	No	No	..
Marshall Islands	1979	1979	..	..	10	..	3	No	No	..
Micronesia (Federated States of)	1979	1979	..	–	17	0	0	No	No	..
Mongolia	1924	1924	1951 E	–	7	8	4	No	No	..
Myanmar	1935	1946	1947 E	..	..	..	4	No	No	..
Nauru	1968	1968	..	–	0	6	0	No	No	..
Palau	1979	1979	..	–	25	3	7	No	No	..
Papua New Guinea	1964	1963	1977 E	–	4	2	1	No	No	..
Philippines	1937	1937	1941 E	–	14	12	21	No	No	Yes
Republic of Korea	1948	1948	1948 E	–	13	3	15	No	Yes	Yes
Samoa	1948, 1990	1948, 1990	1976 A	–	23	4	8	No	No	..
Singapore	1947	1947	1963 F	–	5	5	23	No	No	..
Solomon Islands	1974	1974	1993 E	..	0	2	0	No	No	..
Thailand	1932	1932	1948 A	–	13	7	14	No	No	..
Timor-Leste	..	..	..	..	21	..	29	No	Yes h	..
Tonga	1960	1960	..	–	8	0	4 n	No	No	..
Tuvalu	1967	1967	..	–	0	8	0	No	No	..
Vanuatu	1975, 1980	1975, 1980	1987 E	–	0	..	4	No	No	..
Viet Nam	1946	1946	1976 E	–	4	26	26	No	No	..
Latin America and the Caribbean					**19 t**	**12 t**	**20 t**			
Antigua and Barbuda	1951	1951	1984 A	1994 g	11	11	19	No	No	..
Argentina	1947	1947	1951 E	1973	20	23	38	Yes	Yes h	Yes
Bahamas	1961, 1964	1961, 1964	1977 A	1997 g	0	20	18	No	No	..
Barbados	1950	1950	1966 A	–	6	18	20	No	No	..
Belize	1954	1954	1984 E+A	1984 g	0	11	11	No	No	..
Bolivia (Plurinational State of)	1938, 1952	1938, 1952	1966 E	1979 g	20	4	30	No	Yes h	Yes
Brazil	1932	1932	1933 F	–	7	7	10	No	Yes h	..
Chile	1931, 1949	1931, 1949	1951 E	2002 g	46	7	14	No	No	..
Colombia	1954	1954	1954 A	..	21	10	14	No	No	..
Costa Rica	1949	1949	1953 E	1986	35	16	39	No	Yes h	Yes
Cuba	1934	1934	1940 E	–	25	23	43	No	No	..
Dominica	1951	1951	1980 E	1980 g	20	9	13	No	No	..
Dominican Republic	1942	1942	1942 E	1999	9	10	19	No	Yes	Yes
Ecuador	1929, 1967	1929, 1967	1956 E	–	33	4	32	No	Yes h	Yes
El Salvador	1939	1961	1961 E	1994	15	15	19	No	No	..
Grenada	1951	1951	1976 E+A	1990 g	19	11 j	21	No	No	..
Guatemala	1946	1946, 1965	1956 E	1991	0	13	12	No	No	..
Guyana	1953	1945	1968 E	–	31	20	30	No	No	..
Haiti	1950	1950	1961 E	–	22	3 j	11 j	No	No	..
Honduras	1955	1955	1957 F	–	36	8	18	No	Yes	Yes
Jamaica	1944	1944	1944 E	1984	13	12	16	No	No	..
Mexico	1947	1953	1952 A	1994	11	14	25	No	Yes h	Yes

Women's political rights

	Year women obtained the right[a]		Women's political participation					Quotas for women's political participation[b]		
	To vote	To stand for election	Year first woman elected (E) or appointed (A) to parliament	Year first woman presided over parliament[c]	Share of women in ministerial positions[d] (%) 2010	Share of women in parliament[e] (%) 1997	(%) 2011	Constitutional quota for national parliaments	Election law quota for national parliaments	Constitutional or legislative quota at sub-national level[f]
Nicaragua	1955	1955	1972 E	1990	39	11	21	No	No	..
Panama	1941, 1946	1941, 1946	1946 E	1994	27	10	8	No	Yes	..
Paraguay	1961	1961	1963 E	–	22	6	14	No	Yes h	Yes
Peru	1955	1955	1956 E	1995	22	11	28	No	Yes h	Yes
Saint Kitts and Nevis	1951	1951	1984 E	2004	0	13	7	No	No	..
Saint Lucia	1951	1951	1979 A	2007 g	8	14	21	No	No	..
Saint Vincent and the Grenadines	1951	1951	1979 E	–	21	10	14	No	No	..
Suriname	1948	1948	1975 E	1997 g	..	16	10	No	No	..
Trinidad and Tobago	1946	1946	1962 E+A	1991	35	19	27	No	No	..
Uruguay	1932	1932	1942 E	1963 g	21	7	15	No	Yes h	Yes
Venezuela (Bolivarian Republic of)	1946	1946	1948 E	1998 g	26	6	17	No	No	..
Middle East and North Africa					7 t	..	10 t			
Algeria	1962	1962	1962 A	–	4	3	7	No	No	..
Bahrain	1973 p	1973 p	2002 A	–	11	..	15	No	No	..
Egypt	1956	1956	1957 E	–	9	2	13 j	No	Yes	..
Iraq	1980	1980	..	–	10	6	25	Yes	Yes	..
Jordan	1974	1974	1989 A	–	7	2	12	No	Yes	..
Kuwait	2005	2005	..	–	7	0	8	No	No	..
Lebanon	1952	1952	1991 A	–	7	2	3	No	No	..
Libyan Arab Jamahiriya	1964	1964	..	–	0	..	8	No	No	..
Morocco	1963	1963	1993 E	–	11	1	7	No	No	..
Occupied Palestinian Territory	..	..	..	..	..	..	..	No	No	..
Oman	1994, 2003	1994, 2003	..	–	9	..	9	No	No	..
Qatar	..	..	..	–	0	..	0	No	No	..
Saudi Arabia	–	–	..	–	0	..	0	No	No	..
Syrian Arab Republic	1949, 1953	1953	1973 E	–	6	10	12	No	No	..
Tunisia	1959	1959	1959 E	–	4	7	23	No	No	..
United Arab Emirates	–	..	..	–	17	0	23	No	No	..
Yemen	1967, 1970	1967, 1970	1990 E i	–	6	1	1	No	No	..
South Asia					7 t	5 t	16 t			
Afghanistan	1963	1963	..	..	7	..	28	Yes	Yes h	Yes
Bangladesh	1972	1972	1973 E	–	16	9	19	Yes	No	Yes
Bhutan	1953	1953	1975 E	–	0	2	14	No	No	..
India	1950	1950	1952 E	2009 g	10	7	11	No	No	Yes
Iran (Islamic Republic of)	1963	1963	1963 E+A	–	3	5	3	No	No	..
Maldives	1932	1932	1979 E	–	7	6	6	No	No	..
Nepal	1951	1951	1952 A	–	8	5	33	Yes	Yes h	Yes
Pakistan	1947	1947	1973 E i	2008 g	8	3	21	Yes	Yes	Yes
Sri Lanka	1931	1931	1947 E	–	6	5	5	No	No	..
Sub-Saharan Africa					20 t	9 t	18 t			
Angola	1975	1975	1980 E	–	28	10	39	No	Yes	..
Benin	1956	1956	1979 E	–	13	7	11	No	No	..
Botswana	1965	1965	1979 E	2009 g	12	9	8	No	No	..
Burkina Faso	1958	1958	1978 E	–	18	11	15	No	Yes h	Yes
Burundi	1961	1961	1982 E	2005	29	..	36	Yes	Yes h	..
Cameroon	1946	1946	1960 E	–	12	6	14	No	No	..
Cape Verde	1975	1975	1975 E	–	53	11	18	No	No	..
Central African Republic	1986	1986	1987 E	–	12	4	..	No	No	..
Chad	1958	1958	1962 E	–	7	2	5	No	No	..
Comoros	1956	1956	1993 E	–	0	0	3	No	No	..
Congo	1963	1963	1963 E	–	14	..	9	No	No	..
Côte d'Ivoire	1952	1952	1965 E	–	13	8	9	No	No	..
Democratic Republic of the Congo	1967	1970	1970 E	–	13	..	8	No	No	..
Djibouti	1946	1986	2003 E	–	11	0	14	No	Yes h	..
Equatorial Guinea	1963	1963	1968 E	–	4	9	10	No	No	..

	Year women obtained the right[a]		Women's political participation					Quotas for women's political participation[b]		
	To vote	To stand for election	Year first woman elected (E) or appointed (A) to parliament	Year first woman presided over parliament[c]	Share of women in ministerial positions[d] (%) 2010	Share of women in parliament[e] (%) 1997	(%) 2011	Constitutional quota for national parliaments	Election law quota for national parliaments	Constitutional or legislative quota at sub-national level[f]
Eritrea	1955　q	1955	1994 E	–	25	21	22	No	Yes	Yes
Ethiopia	1955	1955	1957 E	1995	7	2　j	26	No	No	..
Gabon	1956	1956	1961 E	2009　g	21	10	16	No	No	..
Gambia	1960	1960	1982 E	2006	31	2	8	No	No	..
Ghana	1954	1954	1960	2009　g	22	9	8	No	No	..
Guinea	1958	1958	1963 E	..	16	7	..　r	No	No	..
Guinea-Bissau	1977	1977	1972 A	–	24	10	10	No	No	..
Kenya	1919, 1963	1919, 1963	1969 E+A	–	15	3	10	Yes	No	..
Lesotho	1965	1965	1965 A	2000　g	32	11	23	No	No	Yes
Liberia	1946	1946	..	2003	30	6　j	14	No	No	..
Madagascar	1959	1959	1965 E	..	17	4	12	No	No	..
Malawi	1961	1961	1964 E	–	27	8	21	No	No	..
Mali	1956	1956	1959E	–	21	12	10	No	No	..
Mauritania	1961	1961	1975 E	–	23	1	19	No	Yes　h	Yes
Mauritius	1956	1956	1976 E	–	..	8	19	No	No	..
Mozambique	1975	1975	1977 F	2010　g	26	25	39	No	No	..
Namibia	1989	1989	1989 E	–	24	17	25	No	No	Yes
Niger	1948	1948	1989 E	..	23	1	..	No	Yes	..
Nigeria	1958, 1978	1958, 1978	..	2007	10	..	7	No	No	..
Rwanda	1961	1961	1981	2008　g	33	17	51	Yes	No	Yes
São Tomé and Príncipe	1975	1975	1975 E	1980	39	7	18	No	No	..
Senegal	1945	1945	1963 E	–	13	12	30	Yes	No	..
Seychelles	1948	1948	1976 E+A	–	20	27	24	No	No	..
Sierra Leone	1961	1961	..	–	8	..	13	No	No	Yes
Somalia	1956	1956	..	–	..	..	7	Yes	No	..
South Africa	1930, 1984, 1994	1930, 1984, 1994	1933 E	1994	34	24	43　s	No	No	Yes
Sudan	1964	1964	1964 E	–	6	5	24	No	Yes	..
Swaziland	1968	1968	1972 F+A	2006　g	26	9	22	No	No	..
Togo	1945	1945	1961 E	–	14	1	11	No	No	..
Uganda	1962	1962	1962 A	–	32	18	31	Yes	Yes	Yes
United Republic of Tanzania	1959	1959	..	2010　g	27	17	36	Yes	Yes	Yes
Zambia	1962	1962	1964 E+A	–	17	10	14	No	No	..
Zimbabwe	1919, 1957	1919, 1978	1980 E+A	2005　g	19	15	18	No	No	..
World					17　t	11　u	19　u			

SOURCES:

Columns 1-2: IPU 2010d; Column 3: IPU 2011b, UNDP 2009; Column 4: IPU 2011b; Column 5: IPU 2010c; Column 6: IPU 2010a; Column 7: IPU 2011a; Columns 8-10: International IDEA, Stockholm University and IPU 2010.

NOTES

".." indicates that data are not available.

a. Data refer to the year in which the right to vote or stand for national election on a universal and equal basis was recognized. Reference to several dates reflects the stages in the granting of rights. In some countries, women were granted the right to vote or stand in local elections before obtaining these rights for national elections. Data on local election rights are not included in this annex. "–" indicates where women are not allowed to vote and/or stand for election. In the case of the United Arab Emirates, the right to vote is limited for both women and men, and in Brunei Darussalam neither women nor men are allowed to vote.

b. Quota systems are defined as mandatory or targeted measures put in place to promote gender balance in political positions. Quotas typically take the form of a target percentage which varies across countries from 20 to 40 percent. Sometimes a gender neutral 50:50 quota is used, which sets a maximum for women's representation as well as for men's. Quota types include: legislated candidate quota, where a number of places for women are reserved on electoral lists; reserved seats, where a share of seats in the legislative assembly are reserved for women; and political quotas, where a target for a certain percentage of women as election candidates is set by individual parties. The annex does not include quotas used by political parties on a voluntary basis, which have been used in a number of countries that have reached or exceeded the 30 percent critical mass mark. For more information on quotas, including definitions, see International IDEA, Stockholm University and IPU 2010.

c. Date at which, for the first time in the country's parliamentary history, a woman became speaker/presiding officer of parliament or of one of its houses. As of 31 December 2010, there were 270 posts, of which women occupied 14.1 percent. "–" indicates where no women has presided over parliament.

d. Data are as of 1 January 2010. The total includes deputy prime ministers and ministers. Prime ministers who hold ministerial portfolios and heads of government who exercise a ministerial function are also included. Vice presidents and heads of governmental or public agencies have not been included.

e. 1997 data are as of 25 December 1997. 2011 data are as of January 2011. The calculation is based on the total number of seats filled in parliament at that time.

f. Information about sub-national level quotas is not exhaustive.

g. At time of writing, a woman presided over parliament or a house of parliament. In two countries (Antigua and Barbuda and Saint Lucia) a woman is at the head of both chambers of parliament.

h. Legal sanctions for non-compliance with election law quotas are applicable.

i. Refers to the year women were elected to the current parliamentary system.

j. Based on available information for lower/single house only.

k. Data are from Parliament of Canada 2010. In 1917, women with relatives in the armed forces were allowed to vote on behalf of their male relatives. In 1951, the Northwest Territories passed an elections ordinance granting women the right to vote.

l. The Constitution of the United States establishes the right of all persons to stand for election. However, it was only in 1920 that women were explicitly granted the right to vote and stand for election.

m. The total refers to all voting members of the House.

n. No women were elected in 2010, however one woman was appointed to the cabinet. As cabinet ministers also sit in parliament, there is one woman out of a total of 28 members.

p. According to the Constitution in force (1973), all citizens are equal before the law. However, women were not able to exercise electoral rights in the first legislative elections held in 1973. The first legislature was dissolved by decree of the Emir on 26 August 1975. Women were allowed to vote in the referendum of 14–15 February 2001 which approved the National Action Charter. Subsequently, women exercised their full political rights as both voters and candidates in the 2002 national elections.

q. In November 1955, Eritrea was part of Ethiopia. The Constitution of Sovereign Eritrea adopted on 23 May 1997 stipulates that: 'All Eritrean citizens, of eighteen years of age or more, shall have the right to vote'.

r. The parliament was dissolved following the December 2008 coup.

s. The figures on the distribution of seats do not include the 36 special rotating delegates appointed on an ad hoc basis.

t. Data are UN Women calculated unweighted averages.

u. World average is from IPU 2011a.

ANNEX 2: Women's economic opportunities

	Employment laws					Employment					Wage disparities
	Women can work in all industries	Women can work the same night hours as men	Paid or unpaid maternity leave	Length of paid maternity leave[a]	Mandatory paid or unpaid paternity leave	Labour force participation[b]		Unemployment[c]		Female unemployment as a share of total[c]	Wages in manufacturing[d]
				(calendar days)		Female (%) 2009	Male (%) 2009	Female (%) 2000-2008	Male (%) 2000-2008	(% of total) 2000-2008	(women's as a % of men's wages)
Central and Eastern Europe and Central Asia				**174 h**		**50 h**	**68 h**	**8 h**	**8 h**	**47 h**	
Albania	Yes	Yes	Yes	365	No	49	70	28	19	51	..
Armenia	Yes	Yes	Yes	140	No	60	75	40	32	53	62
Azerbaijan	Yes	Yes	Yes	126	Yes	60	67	5	8	40	56
Belarus	Yes	Yes	Yes	126	No	55	67	..	..	..	67
Bosnia and Herzegovina	No	Yes	Yes	365	Yes	55	68	33	27	41	..
Bulgaria	Yes	Yes	Yes	135	Yes	48	61	6	6	48	70
Croatia	Yes	Yes	Yes	365	Yes	46	60	11	8	52	76
Cyprus	..	..	Yes	126	..	54	71	4	3	52	65
Czech Republic	Yes	Yes	Yes	196	Yes	49	68	6	3	55	65
Estonia	Yes	Yes	Yes	140	Yes	55	69	5	6	47	..
Georgia	Yes	Yes	Yes e	126 e	Yes	55	74	13	14	45	51
Hungary	Yes	Yes	Yes	168	Yes	43	59	8	8	47	73
Kazakhstan	Yes	Yes	Yes	126	No	66	76	10	7	57	68
Kyrgyzstan	Yes	Yes	Yes	126	Yes	55	79	9	8	46	..
Latvia	Yes	Yes	Yes	112	Yes	54	70	7	8	45	81
Lithuania	Yes	Yes	Yes	126	Yes	50	62	6	6	48	70
Montenegro	No	No	Yes e	365 e	Yes	..	..	36	26	52	..
Poland	Yes	Yes	Yes	112	Yes	46	62	8	6	51	..
Republic of Moldova	Yes	Yes	Yes	126	Yes	46	53	3	5	42	..
Romania	Yes	Yes	Yes	126	Yes	45	60	5	7	36	75
Russian Federation	No	Yes	Yes	140	Yes	57	69	6	6	44	..
Serbia	No	Yes	Yes	365	Yes	..	..	21	16	50	..
Slovakia	Yes	Yes	Yes	196	Yes	51	69	11	8	51	..
Slovenia	No	No	Yes	365	No	53	65	5	4	50	..
Tajikistan	..	..	..	..	..	57	78	..	..	..	..
The former Yugoslav Republic of Macedonia	..	..	..	..	..	43	65	34	34	39	..
Turkey	No	No	Yes	112	No	24	70	9	9	27	..
Turkmenistan	..	..	..	..	..	62	74	..	..	..	..
Ukraine	No	No	Yes	126	Yes	52	65	6	7	45	71
Uzbekistan	No	Yes	Yes	126	Yes	58	71	..	..	..	..
Developed Regions				**150 h**		**54 h**	**70 h**	**6 h**	**6 h**	**49 h**	
Andorra	..	..	..	..	..	..	..	..	..	..	71
Australia	Yes	Yes	Yes	126	Yes	58	72	5	4	49	90
Austria	Yes	Yes	Yes	112	Yes	53	68	4	4	50	62
Belgium	Yes g	Yes	Yes	105	Yes	47	61	8	6	49	79
Canada	Yes	Yes	Yes	119	Yes	63	73	6	7	43	..
Denmark	Yes	Yes	Yes	365	Yes	60	71	4	3	52	87
Finland	Yes	Yes	Yes	147	Yes	57	65	7	6	51	84
France	Yes	Yes	Yes	112	Yes	51	62	8	7	51	83
Germany	Yes	Yes	Yes	98	Yes	53	67	8	7	46	76
Greece	Yes	Yes	Yes	119	Yes	43	65	11	5	61	..
Iceland	Yes	Yes	Yes	90	Yes	72	83	3	3	39	72
Ireland	Yes	Yes	Yes	182	Yes	54	73	5	7	33	72
Israel	Yes	Yes	Yes	98	Yes	52	62	7	6	50	..
Italy	Yes	Yes	Yes	150	Yes	38	61	9	6	52	..
Japan	Yes	Yes	Yes	98	Yes	48	72	4	4	40	61
Liechtenstein	..	..	Yes	140	..	..	..	..	..	..	..
Luxembourg	..	..	Yes	112	..	48	63	6	4	52	73
Malta	..	..	Yes	98	..	32	68	7	6	38	89
Monaco	..	..	Yes	112	..	..	..	5	3	58	..
Netherlands	Yes	Yes	Yes	112	Yes	59	73	3	3	50	83
New Zealand	Yes	Yes	Yes	98	Yes	62	76	4	4	47	81
Norway	Yes	Yes	Yes	322	Yes	63	71	2	3	44	90
Portugal	Yes	Yes	Yes	120	Yes	56	69	9	6	54	68

	Employment laws					Employment					Wage disparities
	Women can work in all industries	Women can work the same night hours as men	Paid or unpaid maternity leave	Length of paid maternity leave[a]	Mandatory paid or unpaid paternity leave	Labour force participation[b]		Unemployment[c]		Female unemployment as a share of total[c]	Wages in manufacturing[d]
				(calendar days)		Female (%) 2009	Male (%) 2009	Female (%) 2000-2008	Male (%) 2000-2008	(% of total) 2000-2008	(women's as a % of men's wages)
San Marino	..	..	Yes	150	..	..	..	5	1	73	..
Spain	Yes	Yes	Yes	112	Yes	49	68	13	10	49	..
Sweden	Yes	Yes	Yes	480	Yes	61	69	7	6	50	91
Switzerland	Yes	Yes	Yes	98	No	61	74	5	3	56	77
United Kingdom	Yes	Yes	Yes	273	Yes	55	70	5	6	41	82
United States of America	Yes	Yes	Yes	84 f	No	58	72	5	6	43	..
East Asia and the Pacific				85 h		65 h	80 h	6 h	6 h	43 h	
Brunei Darussalam	..	..	..	..	..	60	75				
Cambodia	Yes	Yes	Yes	90	Yes	74	86	7	8	61	
China	No	Yes	Yes	90	No	67	80				
Democratic People's Republic of Korea	..	..	..	..	..	55	77	..	..	..	
Fiji	..	..	Yes	84	..	39	78	6	4	39	
Hong Kong, China (SAR)	Yes	Yes	Yes	70	No	52	69	3	5	39	60
Indonesia	Yes	Yes	Yes	90	Yes	52	86	11	8	47	68
Kiribati	..	..	Yes	84	..						
Lao People's Democratic Republic	Yes	Yes	Yes	90	No	78	79	1	1	50	
Malaysia	No	Yes	Yes	60	No	44	79	3	3	38	..
Marshall Islands	..	..	..	..	..						
Micronesia (Federated States of)	..	..	..	..	..	..	..	..	..		
Mongolia	No	Yes	Yes	120	No	68	78	4	3	56	71
Myanmar	..	..	Yes	84	..	63	85				88
Nauru	..	..	..	..	..						
Palau	..	..	..	..	..	..	..	..	..		
Papua New Guinea	No	No	Yes	42 f	No	72	74	1	4	22	..
Philippines	Yes	No	Yes	60	Yes	49	78	7	8	37	92
Republic of Korea	Yes	Yes	Yes	90	Yes	50	72	3	4	34	57
Samoa	..	..	..	..	..	38	75	6	4	38	..
Singapore	Yes	Yes	Yes	84	No	54	76	4	3	47	65
Solomon Islands	..	..	Yes	84	..	24	50	..	..	..	
Thailand	No	Yes	Yes	90	No	66	81	1	1	42	75
Timor-Leste	..	..	..	..	..	59	83				
Tonga	..	..	..	..	..	55	75	7	4	60	
Tuvalu	..	..	..	..	..	..	..	9	5	18	
Vanuatu	..	..	Yes	90	..	79	88	..	..	..	
Viet Nam	No	Yes	Yes	120	No	68	76	2	2	56	
Latin America and the Caribbean				93 h		53 h	80 h	9 h	6 h	50 h	
Antigua and Barbuda	..	..	Yes	91	..	..	..	9	8	52	
Argentina	Yes	Yes	Yes	90	Yes	52	78	12	8	53	
Bahamas	..	..	Yes	91	..	68	79	9	7	56	
Barbados	..	..	Yes	84	..	66	78	11	9	52	
Belize	..	..	Yes	98	..	47	81	17	7	57	
Bolivia (Plurinational State of)	No	Yes	Yes	60	No	62	82	7	4	56	..
Brazil	Yes	Yes	Yes	120	Yes	60	82	10	6	58	61
Chile	Yes	Yes	Yes	126	Yes	42	73	10	7	45	..
Colombia	No	Yes	Yes	84	Yes	41	78	15	9	53	60
Costa Rica	Yes	No	Yes	120	No	45	80	7	3	55	95
Cuba	..	..	Yes	126	..	41	67	2	2	40	
Dominica	..	..	Yes	84	..	..	..	10	12	34	
Dominican Republic	Yes	Yes	Yes	84	Yes	51	80	25	9	63	
Ecuador	No	Yes	Yes	84	Yes	47	78	11	6	58	
El Salvador	Yes	Yes	Yes	84	No	46	77	4	8	25	64
Grenada	..	..	Yes	90	..						
Guatemala	No	Yes	Yes	84	Yes	48	88	2	1	49	
Guyana	..	..	Yes	91	..	45	81	15	10	40	
Haiti	..	..	Yes	84	..	58	83	..	..	..	

Women's economic opportunities

	Employment laws					Employment					Wage disparities
	Women can work in all industries	Women can work the same night hours as men	Paid or unpaid maternity leave	Length of paid maternity leave[a]	Mandatory paid or unpaid paternity leave	Labour force participation[b]		Unemployment[c]		Female unemployment as a share of total[c]	Wages in manufacturing[d]
				(calendar days)		Female (%) 2009	Male (%) 2009	Female (%) 2000-2008	Male (%) 2000-2008	(% of total) 2000-2008	(women's as a % of men's wages)
Honduras	Yes	Yes	Yes	84	No	40	80	4	3	47	..
Jamaica	No	No	Yes	84	No	56	74	15	7	62	..
Mexico	Yes	Yes	Yes	84	No	43	81	4	4	39	72
Nicaragua	Yes	Yes	Yes	84	No	47	78	5	5	35	..
Panama	No	Yes	Yes	98	No	48	81	9	5	52	97
Paraguay	Yes	Yes	Yes	84	Yes	57	87	8	4	55	108
Peru	Yes	Yes	Yes	90	No	58	76	8	6	54	..
Saint Kitts and Nevis	..	..	Yes	91	..	..	..	..	..	..	..
Saint Lucia	..	..	Yes	90	..	51	76	25	17	55	71
Saint Vincent and the Grenadines	..	..	Yes	91	..	56	79	..	..	..	..
Suriname	..	..	..	..	..	39	66	0	0	53	..
Trinidad and Tobago	..	..	Yes	91	..	55	78	10	4	60	..
Uruguay	Yes	Yes	Yes	84	Yes	54	75	10	5	60	..
Venezuela (Bolivarian Republic of)	Yes	Yes	Yes	126	No	52	80	8	7	41	..
Middle East and North Africa				**61 h**		**26 h**	**77 h**	**16 h**	**8 h**	**31 h**	
Algeria	Yes	No	Yes	98	Yes	37	80	18	13	22	..
Bahrain	..	..	Yes	45	..	32	85	10	4	41	77
Egypt	No	No	Yes	90	No	22	75	19	6	50	66
Iraq	..	..	Yes	62	..	14	69	13	10	20	..
Jordan	No	No	Yes	70	No	23	74	24	10	18	69
Kuwait	No	No	Yes	70	Yes	45	82	..	..	..	..
Lebanon	No	Yes	Yes	49	No	22	72	..	..	..	..
Libyan Arab Jamahiriya	..	..	Yes	50	..	25	79	..	..	..	..
Morocco	No	Yes	Yes	98	No	26	80	10	10	27	..
Occupied Palestinian Territory	..	..	..	..	..	17	68	24	26	16	50
Oman	No	No	Yes e	42 e	No	25	77	..	..	..	..
Qatar	..	..	Yes	50	..	50	93	13	2	40	142
Saudi Arabia	No	No	Yes	70	Yes	21	80	13	4	36	..
Syrian Arab Republic	No	No	Yes	50	No	21	79	21	8	39	..
Tunisia	..	..	Yes	30	..	26	71	17	13	32	..
United Arab Emirates	No	No	Yes	45	No	42	92	7	3	31	..
Yemen	No	No	Yes	60	No	20	73	..	..	..	..
South Asia				**85 h**		**37 h**	**81 h**	**6 h**	**5 h**	**44 h**	
Afghanistan	..	..	Yes	90	..	33	85	9	8	53	..
Bangladesh	Yes	No	Yes	112	No	59	83	7	3	41	..
Bhutan	..	..	..	..	..	53	71	3	3	38	..
India	No	Yes	Yes	84	No	33	81	5	5	30	..
Iran (Islamic Republic of)	No	Yes	Yes	90	No	32	73	16	9	29	90
Maldives	..	..	..	..	..	57	77	24	8	68	..
Nepal	Yes	No	Yes	52	No	63	80	11	7	51	45
Pakistan	No	No	Yes	84	No	22	85	9	4	34	..
Sri Lanka	Yes	No	Yes	84	No	34	75	8	4	56	77
Sub-Saharan Africa				**88 h**		**66 h**	**83 h**	**10 h**	**8 h**	**51 h**	
Angola	Yes	Yes	Yes	84	No	74	88	..	..	..	..
Benin	No	Yes	Yes	98	No	67	78	(.)	1	31	..
Botswana	Yes	Yes	Yes	84	No	72	81	20	15	56	66
Burkina Faso	Yes	Yes	Yes	98	No	78	91	..	..	..	..
Burundi	..	..	Yes	84	..	91	88	..	..	..	..
Cameroon	No	No	Yes	98	No	53	81	7	8	44	..
Cape Verde	..	..	Yes	60	..	53	81	..	..	..	..
Central African Republic	..	..	Yes	98	..	72	87	..	..	..	..
Chad	No	No	Yes	98	No	63	78	..	..	..	..
Comoros	..	..	Yes	98	..	74	85	..	..	..	..
Congo	..	..	Yes	105	..	63	83	..	..	..	..
Côte d'Ivoire	No	Yes	Yes	98	No	51	82	..	..	..	..

	Employment laws					Employment					Wage disparities
	Women can work in all industries	Women can work the same night hours as men	Paid or unpaid maternity leave	Length of paid maternity leave[a]	Mandatory paid or unpaid paternity leave	Labour force participation[b]		Unemployment[c]		Female unemployment as a share of total[c]	Wages in manufacturing[d]
				(calendar days)		Female (%) 2009	Male (%) 2009	Female (%) 2000-2008	Male (%) 2000-2008	(% of total) 2000-2008	(women's as a % of men's wages)
Democratic Republic of the Congo	No	No	Yes	98	No	57	86	..	..	..	..
Djibouti	..	..	Yes	98	..	62	79	..	..	..	..
Equatorial Guinea	..	..	Yes	84	..	40	92	..	..	..	..
Eritrea	..	..	..	..	..	63	83	..	..	..	..
Ethiopia	No	Yes	Yes	90	No	81	90	23	12	64	..
Gabon	..	..	Yes	98	..	70	81	..	..	..	..
Gambia	..	..	Yes	84	..	71	85	..	..	..	..
Ghana	Yes	Yes	Yes	84	No	74	75	11	10	51	..
Guinea	No	Yes	Yes	98	No	79	89	..	..	..	..
Guinea-Bissau	..	..	Yes	60	..	60	84	..	..	..	..
Kenya	No	Yes	Yes	90	Yes	76	88	..	..	..	..
Lesotho	No	Yes	Yes	84 f	No	71	78	..	..	..	..
Liberia	..	..	..	..	..	67	76	4	7	37	..
Madagascar	Yes	No	Yes	98	No	84	89	3	2	66	85
Malawi	Yes	Yes	Yes	56	No	75	79	10	5	53	..
Mali	No	No	Yes	98	Yes	38	67	11	7	53	..
Mauritania	No	No	Yes	98	No	59	81	41	9	73	..
Mauritius	..	..	Yes	84	..	41	75	13	4	65	..
Mozambique	..	..	Yes	60	..	85	87	..	..	..	..
Namibia	Yes	Yes	Yes	84	No	52	63	25	19	52	..
Niger	No	Yes	Yes	98	No	39	87	1	2	21	..
Nigeria	No	No	Yes	84	No	39	73	..	..	..	..
Rwanda	Yes	Yes	Yes	84	No	87	85	..	..	..	..
São Tomé and Príncipe	..	..	Yes	60	..	44	76	25	11	61	..
Senegal	No	No	Yes	98	No	65	89	14	8	50	..
Seychelles	..	..	Yes	98	..	..	..	5	6	47	..
Sierra Leone	..	..	..	..	..	65	67	2	5	32	..
Somalia	..	..	Yes	98	..	56	85	..	..	..	..
South Africa	Yes	Yes	Yes	120	Yes	47	63	26	20	53	..
Sudan	No	No	Yes	56	No	31	74	..	..	..	..
Swaziland	..	..	Yes	84 f	..	53	75	..	..	..	57
Togo	Yes	Yes	Yes	98	No	64	86	..	..	..	..
Uganda	Yes	Yes	Yes	84	Yes	78	91	4	3	63	..
United Republic of Tanzania	Yes	Yes	Yes	84	Yes	86	91	6	3	68	..
Zambia	Yes	Yes	Yes	84	No	59	79	11	14	36	..
Zimbabwe			Yes	98	..	60	74	4	4	50	..
World				**110 h**		**53 i**	**78 i**	**7 i**	**6 i**	**47 h**	

Columns 1, 2, 5. World Bank 2010f.

Columns 3-4: UN Statistics Division 2010a.

Columns 6-10: ILO 2009b.

Column 11: UN Statistics Division 2010b.

NOTES

".." indicates that data are not available.

(.) indicates a value less than 1 percent.

a. Days may be paid at less than full pay and in some cases a portion of the leave may be unpaid.

b. The labour force participation rate is a measure of the proportion of a country's working-age population that engages actively in the labour market, either by working or looking for work. It is calculated by expressing the number of persons in the labour force as a percentage of the working-age population. The labour force is the sum of the number of persons employed and the number of unemployed.

c. Unemployment is the share of the labour force without work but available for and seeking employment. The data refer to the latest year available during the period specified.

d. This indicator refers to the ratio of women's to men's wages in manufacturing, expressed as a percentage. In general, the wage statistics from which the indicator has been calculated refer to average earnings per month per employee. It is calculated by the UN Statistics Division based on ILO data and covers a wider range of countries than other gender wage gap indicators.

e. Data are from World Bank 2010f.

f. Leave is not paid.

g. Data for Belgium are from ELLN 2010.

h. Data are UN Women calculated averages. Where appropriate, they are weighted using the relevant population.

i. ILO 2011.

ANNEX 3: Women's reproductive health and rights

	Legal abortion[a]							Reproductive health			
	To save the woman's life	To preserve physical health	To preserve mental health	In cases of rape or incest	In cases of foetal impairment	Economic or social reasons	On request	Maternal Mortality Ratio (per 100,000 live births)		Contraceptive use[b,d] (%)	Skilled assistance at delivery[c,d] (%)
								1990	2008	2000-2008	2000-2008
Central and Eastern Europe and Central Asia								63 q	31 q	51 q	97 q
Albania	Yes	Yes	Yes	Yes	Yes	Yes	Yes	48	31	10	99
Armenia	Yes	Yes	Yes	Yes	Yes	Yes	Yes	51	29	19	100
Azerbaijan	Yes	Yes	Yes	Yes	Yes	Yes	Yes	64	38	13	88
Belarus	Yes	Yes	Yes	Yes	Yes	Yes	Yes	37	15	56	100 e
Bosnia and Herzegovina	Yes	Yes	Yes	Yes	Yes	Yes	Yes	18	9	11	100 e
Bulgaria	Yes	Yes	Yes	Yes	Yes	Yes	Yes	24	13	40 f	99
Croatia	Yes	Yes	Yes	Yes	Yes	Yes	Yes	8	14	..	100
Cyprus	Yes	Yes	Yes	Yes	Yes	No	No	17	10	..	100 e
Czech Republic	Yes	Yes	Yes	Yes	Yes	Yes	Yes	15	8	63 f	100
Estonia	Yes	Yes	Yes	Yes	Yes	Yes	Yes	48	12	56 f	100
Georgia	Yes	Yes	Yes	Yes	Yes	Yes	Yes	58	48	27	98
Hungary	Yes	Yes	Yes	Yes	Yes	Yes	Yes	23	13	71 f	100
Kazakhstan	Yes	Yes	Yes	Yes	Yes	Yes	Yes	78	45	49	100 e
Kyrgyzstan	Yes	Yes	Yes	Yes	Yes	Yes	Yes	77	81	46	98 e
Latvia	Yes	Yes	Yes	Yes	Yes	Yes	Yes	57	20	56 f	100
Lithuania	Yes	Yes	Yes	Yes	Yes	Yes	Yes	34	13	33 f	100
Montenegro	Yes	Yes	Yes	Yes	Yes	Yes	Yes	15	15	17	99 e
Poland	Yes	Yes	Yes	Yes	Yes	No	No	17	6	28 f	100
Republic of Moldova	Yes	Yes	Yes	Yes	Yes	Yes	Yes	62	32	43	100 e
Romania	Yes	Yes	Yes	Yes	Yes	Yes	Yes	170	27	38	98
Russian Federation	Yes	Yes	Yes	Yes	Yes	Yes	Yes	74	39	70	100
Serbia	Yes	Yes	Yes	Yes	Yes	Yes	Yes	13	8	19	99 e
Slovakia	Yes	Yes	Yes	Yes	Yes	Yes	Yes	15	6	66 f	100
Slovenia	Yes	Yes	Yes	Yes	Yes	Yes	Yes	11	18	63 f	100
Tajikistan	Yes	Yes	Yes	Yes	Yes	Yes	Yes	120	64	33	88
The former Yugoslav Republic of Macedonia	Yes	Yes	Yes	Yes	Yes	Yes	Yes	16	9	10	99
Turkey	Yes	Yes	Yes	Yes	Yes	Yes	Yes	68	23	43	91
Turkmenistan	Yes	Yes	Yes	Yes	Yes	Yes	Yes	91	77	45	100 e
Ukraine	Yes	Yes	Yes	Yes	Yes	Yes	Yes	49	26	48	99
Uzbekistan	Yes	Yes	Yes	Yes	Yes	Yes	Yes	53	30	59	100 e
Developed Regions								11 q	14 q	66 q	99 q
Andorra	Yes g	No g	No g	No g	No g	No g	No g	..	..	..	..
Australia	Yes	Yes	Yes	Yes	Yes	Yes	Yes	10	8	71	100 e,f
Austria	Yes	Yes	Yes	Yes	Yes	Yes	Yes	10	5	47 f	100 e,f
Belgium	Yes	Yes	Yes	Yes	Yes	Yes	Yes	7	5	73	..
Canada	Yes	Yes	Yes	Yes	Yes	Yes	Yes	6	12	72	98 e
Denmark	Yes	Yes	Yes	Yes	Yes	Yes	Yes	7	5	..	..
Finland	Yes	Yes	Yes	Yes	Yes	Yes	No	7	8	..	100 e,f
France	Yes	Yes	Yes	Yes	Yes	Yes	Yes	13	8	77	99 e,f
Germany	Yes	Yes	Yes	Yes	Yes	Yes	Yes	13	7	66 f	..
Greece	Yes	Yes	Yes	Yes	Yes	Yes	Yes	6	2	46	..
Iceland	Yes	Yes	Yes	Yes	Yes	Yes	No	8	5	..	..
Ireland	Yes	No	No	No	No	No	No	6	3	89	100 e
Israel	Yes	Yes	Yes	Yes	Yes	No	No	12	7	..	..
Italy	Yes	Yes	Yes	Yes	Yes	Yes	Yes	10	5	41 f	..
Japan	Yes h	Yes h	No h	Yes h	No h	Yes h	No h	12	6	44	100 e,f
Liechtenstein	Yes	Yes	Yes	No	No	No	No	..	..	..	..
Luxembourg	Yes	Yes	Yes	Yes	Yes	Yes	No	6	17	..	100 e
Malta	No i	No i	No i	No i	No i	No i	No i	14	8	43 f	98 e,f
Monaco	Yes g	No g	No g	No g	No g	No g	No g	..	..	..	..
Netherlands	Yes	Yes	Yes	Yes	Yes	Yes	Yes	10	9	67	100 e,f
New Zealand	Yes	Yes	Yes	Yes	Yes	No	No	18	14	72 f	100 e,f
Norway	Yes	Yes	Yes	Yes	Yes	Yes	Yes	9	7	82	..
Portugal	Yes	Yes	Yes	Yes	Yes	Yes	Yes	15	7	63	100 e
San Marino	Yes g	No g	No g	No g	No g	No g	No g	..	..	..	..

	Legal abortion[a]							Reproductive health			
	To save the woman's life	To preserve physical health	To preserve mental health	In cases of rape or incest	In cases of foetal impairment	Economic or social reasons	On request	Maternal Mortality Ratio (per 100,000 live births)		Contraceptive use[b,d] (%)	Skilled assistance at delivery[c,d] (%)
								1990	2008	2000-2008	2000-2008
Spain	Yes	Yes	Yes	Yes	Yes	No	No	7	6	62	..
Sweden	Yes	Yes	Yes	Yes	Yes	Yes	Yes	7	5	65 f	..
Switzerland	Yes	Yes	Yes	Yes	Yes	Yes	Yes	8	10	78 f	..
United Kingdom	Yes j	Yes j	Yes j	No j	Yes j	Yes j	No j	10	12	84	99 c,f
United States of America	Yes	Yes	Yes	Yes	Yes	Yes	Yes	12	24	73	99 e,f
East Asia and the Pacific								**198 q**	**88 q**	**76 q**	**90 q**
Brunei Darussalam	Yes	No	No	No	No	No	No	28	21	..	99 e,f
Cambodia	Yes	Yes	Yes	Yes	Yes	Yes	Yes	690	290	27	44 e
China	Yes	Yes	Yes	Yes	Yes	Yes	Yes	110	38	86	98
Democratic People's Republic of Korea	Yes	Yes	Yes	Yes	Yes	Yes	Yes	270	250	58	97 e
Fiji	Yes k	Yes k	Yes k	Yes k	Yes k	No k	No k	40	26	..	99 e
Hong Kong, China (SAR)	..	..	..	..	..	..	..	..	..	75	..
Indonesia	Yes	No	No	No	No	No	No	620	240	57	79
Kiribati	Yes	No	No	No	No	No	No	..	..	31	63
Lao People's Democratic Republic	Yes	Yes	No	No	No	No	No	1200	580	29	20
Malaysia	Yes	Yes	Yes	No	No	No	No	56	31	30 f	98 e
Marshall Islands	Yes	No	No	No	No	No	No	..	..	42	86
Micronesia (Federated States of)	Yes	No	No	No	No	No	No	..	..	..	88 e
Mongolia	Yes	Yes	Yes	Yes	Yes	Yes	Yes	130	65	61	99 e
Myanmar	Yes	No	No	No	No	No	No	420	240	33	57 e
Nauru	Yes k	Yes k	Yes k	No k	No k	No k	No k	..	..	23	97
Palau	Yes	No	No	No	No	No	No	..	..	30	100 e
Papua New Guinea	Yes	Yes	Yes	No	No	No	No	340	250	20 f	53
Philippines	Yes g	No g	No g	No g	No g	No g	No g	180	94	34	62
Republic of Korea	Yes	Yes	Yes	Yes	Yes	No	No	18	18	76	100 f
Samoa	Yes k	Yes k	Yes k	No k	No k	No k	No k	..	..	23 f	100 c,f
Singapore	Yes	Yes	Yes	Yes	Yes	Yes	Yes	8	9	53 f	100 e,f
Solomon Islands	Yes	No	No	No	No	No	No	130	100	27	70
Thailand	Yes	Yes	Yes	Yes	Yes	No	No	50	48	80	97 e
Timor-Leste	Yes	No	No	No	No	No	No	650	370	7	18 e
Tonga	Yes	No	No	No	No	No	No	..	..	..	95
Tuvalu	Yes	No	No	No	No	No	No	..	..	22	98
Vanuatu	Yes	Yes	Yes	No	No	No	No	..	..	32 f	74
Viet Nam	Yes	Yes	Yes	Yes	Yes	Yes	Yes	170	56	69	88 e
Latin America and the Caribbean								**144 q**	**85 q**	**64 q**	**90 q**
Antigua and Barbuda	Yes g	No g	No g	No g	No g	No g	No g	..	..	..	100
Argentina	Yes	No	No	No	No	No	No	72	70	64	99
Bahamas	Yes	Yes	Yes	No	No	No	No	55	49	..	99
Barbados	Yes	Yes	Yes	Yes	Yes	Yes	No	120	64	..	100
Belize	Yes	Yes	Yes	No	Yes	Yes	No	72	94	31	95
Bolivia (Plurinational State of)	Yes	Yes	Yes	Yes	No	No	No	510	180	34	66
Brazil	Yes	No	No	Yes	No	No	No	120	58	70 f	97
Chile	No i	No i	No i	No i	No i	No i	No i	56	26	58	100
Colombia	Yes	Yes	Yes	Yes	Yes	No	No	140	85	68	96 e
Costa Rica	Yes	Yes	Yes	No	No	No	No	35	44	72 f	99 c
Cuba	Yes	Yes	Yes	Yes	Yes	Yes	Yes	63	53	72	100
Dominica	Yes	No	No	No	No	No	No	..	..	..	94
Dominican Republic	No	No	No	No	No	No	No	220	100	70	98
Ecuador	Yes	Yes	No	No	No	No	No	230	140	58	99 e,f
El Salvador	No i	No i	No i	No i	No i	No i	No i	200	110	66	92 e
Grenada	Yes	Yes	Yes	No	No	No	No	..	..	52 f	99
Guatemala	Yes	No	No	No	No	No	No	140	110	34	41 e
Guyana	Yes	Yes	Yes	Yes	Yes	Yes	Yes	310	270	33	83
Haiti	Yes g	No g	No g	No g	No g	No g	No g	670	300	24	26 e
Honduras	Yes l	No l	No l	No l	No l	No l	No l	210	110	56	67 e
Jamaica	Yes k	Yes k	Yes k	No k	No k	No k	No k	66	89	66	97 e

Women's reproductive health and rights

	Legal abortion[a]							Reproductive health			
	To save the woman's life	To preserve physical health	To preserve mental health	In cases of rape or incest	In cases of foetal impairment	Economic or social reasons	On request	Maternal Mortality Ratio (per 100,000 live births)		Contraceptive use[b,d] (%)	Skilled assistance at delivery[c,d] (%)
								1990	2008	2000-2008	2000-2008
Mexico	Yes m	Yes m	Yes m	Yes m	Yes m	Yes m	Yes m	93	85	67	93
Nicaragua	No i	No i	No i	No i	No i	No i	No i	190	100	69	74
Panama	Yes	Yes	No	Yes	No	No	No	86	71	..	92
Paraguay	Yes	No	No	No	No	No	No	130	95	70	82
Peru	Yes	Yes	Yes	No	No	No	No	250	98	47	71
Saint Kitts and Nevis	Yes k	Yes k	Yes k	Yes k	No k	No k	No k	..	..	..	100
Saint Lucia	Yes	Yes	Yes	Yes	No	No	No	..	..	..	98
Saint Vincent and the Grenadines	Yes	Yes	Yes	Yes	Yes	Yes	No	..	..	..	100
Suriname	Yes	No	No	No	No	No	No	84	100	45	90
Trinidad and Tobago	Yes k	Yes k	Yes k	No k	No k	No k	No k	86	55	38	98 e
Uruguay	Yes	Yes	Yes	Yes	No	No	No	39	27	75	100 e,f
Venezuela (Bolivarian Republic of)	Yes	No	No	No	No	No	No	84	68	62 f	95 e
Middle East and North Africa								**210 q**	**91 q**	**46 q**	**79 q**
Algeria	Yes	Yes	Yes	No	No	No	No	250	120	52	95 e
Bahrain	Yes	Yes	Yes	Yes	Yes	Yes	Yes	25	19	31 f	98 e,f
Egypt	Yes	No	No	No	No	No	No	220	82	58	79
Iraq	Yes	No	No	No	No	No	No	93	75	33	80
Jordan	Yes	Yes	Yes	No	Yes	No	No	110	59	41	99
Kuwait	Yes	Yes	Yes	No	Yes	No	No	10	9	39 f	98 e,f
Lebanon	Yes	No	No	No	No	No	No	52	26	34	98 e,f
Libyan Arab Jamahiriya	Yes	No	No	No	No	No	No	100	64	26 f	94 e,f
Morocco	Yes	Yes	Yes	No	No	No	No	270	110	52	63 e
Occupied Palestinian Territory	..	..	..	..	..	..	..	..	..	39	99 e
Oman	Yes	No	No	No	Yes	No	No	49	20	25	99
Qatar	Yes	No	No	No	No	No	No	15	8	32 f	99 e,f
Saudi Arabia	Yes	Yes	Yes	No	No	No	No	41	24	29 f	91 e,f
Syrian Arab Republic	Yes g	No g	No g	No g	No g	No g	No g	120	46	43	93 e
Tunisia	Yes	Yes	Yes	Yes	Yes	Yes	Yes	130	60	52	95
United Arab Emirates	Yes	No	No	No	No	No	No	28	10	24 f	99 e,f
Yemen	Yes	No	No	No	No	No	No	540	210	19	36
South Asia								**592 q**	**275 q**	**45 q**	**44 q**
Afghanistan	Yes	No	No	No	No	No	No	1700	1400	16	14 e
Bangladesh	Yes	No	No	No	No	No	No	870	340	48	18
Bhutan	Yes	No	Yes	Yes	No	No	No	940	200	31	71
India	Yes	Yes	Yes	Yes	Yes	Yes	No	570	230	49	47 e
Iran (Islamic Republic of)	Yes g	No g	No g	No g	No g	No g	No g	150	30	59	97
Maldives	Yes	Yes	No	No	No	No	No	510	37	34	84 e
Nepal	Yes	Yes	Yes	Yes	Yes	Yes	Yes	870	380	44	19 e
Pakistan	Yes n	Yes n	Yes n	No n	No n	No n	No n	490	260	19	39
Sri Lanka	Yes	No	No	No	No	No	No	91	39	53	99
Sub-Saharan Africa								**867 q**	**646 q**	**18 q**	**47 q**
Angola	Yes g	No g	No g	No g	No g	No g	No g	1000	610	5	47 e
Benin	Yes	Yes	Yes	Yes	Yes	No	No	790	410	6	74 e
Botswana	Yes	Yes	Yes	Yes	Yes	No	No	83	190	42	94 e
Burkina Faso	Yes	Yes	Yes	Yes	Yes	No	No	770	560	13	54 e
Burundi	Yes	Yes	Yes	No	No	No	No	1200	970	8	34 e
Cameroon	Yes	Yes	Yes	Yes	No	No	No	680	600	12	63 e
Cape Verde	Yes	Yes	Yes	Yes	Yes	Yes	Yes	230	94	46 f	78
Central African Republic	Yes g	No g	No g	No g	No g	No g	No g	880	850	9	53 e
Chad	Yes	Yes	No	No	Yes	No	No	1300	1200	2	14 e
Comoros	Yes	Yes	Yes	No	No	No	No	530	340	19	62 e
Congo	Yes g	No g	No g	No g	No g	No g	No g	460	580	13	83 e
Côte d'Ivoire	Yes	No	No	No	No	No	No	690	470	8	57 e
Democratic Republic of the Congo	Yes g	No g	No g	No g	No g	No g	No g	900	670	6	74
Djibouti	Yes	No	No	No	No	No	No	370	300	17	61 e
Equatorial Guinea	Yes	Yes	Yes	No	No	No	No	1000	280	6	65 e

	Legal abortion[a]							Reproductive health			
	To save the woman's life	To preserve physical health	To preserve mental health	In cases of rape or incest	In cases of foetal impairment	Economic or social reasons	On request	Maternal Mortality Ratio (per 100,000 live births)		Contraceptive use[b,d] (%)	Skilled assistance at delivery[c,d] (%)
								1990	2008	2000-2008	2000-2008
Eritrea	Yes	Yes	Yes	No	No	No	No	930	280	5	28 e
Ethiopia	Yes	Yes	Yes	Yes	Yes	No	No	990	470	14	6 e
Gabon	Yes g	No g	No g	No g	No g	No g	No g	260	260	12	86 e
Gambia	Yes k	Yes k	Yes k	No k	No k	No k	No k	750	400	13	57 e
Ghana	Yes	Yes	Yes	Yes	Yes	No	No	630	350	17	57
Guinea	Yes	Yes	Yes	Yes	Yes	No	No	1200	680	4	46
Guinea-Bissau	Yes g	No g	No g	No g	No g	No g	No g	1200	1000	6	39 e
Kenya	Yes k	Yes k	Yes k	No k	No k	No k	No k	380	530	39	44
Lesotho	Yes	No	No	No	No	No	No	370	530	35	55 e
Liberia	Yes	Yes	Yes	Yes	Yes	No	No	1100	990	10	46
Madagascar	Yes g	No g	No g	No g	No g	No g	No g	710	440	28	51 e
Malawi	Yes g	No g	No g	No g	No g	No g	No g	910	510	38	54 e
Mali	Yes g	No g	No g	Yes g	No g	No g	No g	1200	830	6	49
Mauritania	Yes g	No g	No g	No g	No g	No g	No g	780	550	8	61
Mauritius	Yes g	No g	No g	No g	No g	No g	No g	72	36	39	98 e
Mozambique	Yes	Yes	Yes	No	No	No	No	1000	550	12	55
Namibia	Yes	Yes	Yes	Yes	Yes	No	No	180	180	54	81
Niger	Yes g	No g	No g	No g	No g	No g	No g	1400	820	5	33 e
Nigeria	Yes p	Yes p	Yes p	No p	No p	No p	No p	1100	840	8	39
Rwanda	Yes	Yes	Yes	No	No	No	No	1100	540	26	52
São Tomé and Príncipe	Yes g	No g	No g	No g	No g	No g	No g	..	..	27	82
Senegal	Yes	No	No	No	No	No	No	750	410	10	52 e
Seychelles	Yes	Yes	Yes	Yes	Yes	No	No	..	..	..	..
Sierra Leone	Yes k	Yes k	Yes k	No k	No k	No k	No k	1300	970	6	42
Somalia	Yes g	No g	No g	No g	No g	No g	No g	1100	1200	1	33 e
South Africa	Yes	Yes	Yes	Yes	Yes	Yes	Yes	230	410	60	91
Sudan	Yes	No	No	Yes	No	No	No	830	750	6	49
Swaziland	Yes	Yes	Yes	No	Yes	No	No	260	420	47	69
Togo	Yes	Yes	No	Yes	Yes	No	No	650	350	11	62 e
Uganda	Yes k	Yes k	Yes k	No k	No k	No k	No k	670	430	18	42
United Republic of Tanzania	Yes k	Yes k	Yes k	No k	No k	No k	No k	880	790	20	43 e
Zambia	Yes	Yes	Yes	No	Yes	Yes	No	390	470	27	47
Zimbabwe	Yes	Yes	No	Yes	Yes	No	No	390	790	58	80 e
World								397 q	264 q	56 q	67 q

SOURCES

Columns 1-7: UN DESA 2011a.

Columns 8-9: WHO, UNICEF, UNFPA and the World Bank 2010.

Columns 10-11: UN 2010c.

NOTES

".." indicates that data are not available.

a. Data refer to specific legislation.

b. Data on contraceptive use denote the percentage of women aged 15 to 49 who are married or in a union who are using modern contraception. The figure given is produced and disseminated by the country (including data adjusted to meet international standards).

c. Skilled assistance at delivery refers to live births attended by a trained health personnel such as a doctor, nurse/midwife or community health worker.

d. Unless otherwise indicated, the data refer to the most recent year available during the period specified.

e. The figure is produced and provided by the country but adjusted to comply with internationally agreed standards, definitions and classifications.

f. Data refer to a period other than that specified.

g. The abortion laws in these countries do not expressly allow abortions to be performed to save the life of the woman, but general principles of criminal legislation allow abortions to be performed for this reason on the grounds of necessity.

h. The law contains no specific reference to abortions performed on grounds of mental health or in the case of foetal impairment. However, since the law allows abortions for economic or social reasons, mental health and foetal impairment are presumably covered by this ground.

i. The abortion laws in these countries have been amended to remove all grounds on which abortion might be performed legally. However, it is not clear whether a defence of necessity might be allowed to justify an abortion performed to save the life of the woman.

j. Refers to the abortion law of England, Wales and Scotland.

k. The abortion laws in these countries either expressly allow abortions to be performed only to save the life of the woman, or are governed by general principles of criminal legislation which allow abortions to be performed for this reason on the grounds of necessity. In addition, the British case of R v Bourne or local application of that decision apply. Under the decision, the grounds of necessity were interpreted to encompass abortion performed on physical and mental health grounds.

l. The penal code makes no exceptions to the general prohibition on the performance of abortions; the code of medical ethics, however, allows abortions to be performed for therapeutic purposes.

m. Abortion law is determined at the state level. The grounds reported refer only to those in the federal penal code. Some states allow abortions to be performed on the following grounds: to preserve physical health, to preserve mental health, in the case of foetal impairment, and for economic or social reasons.

n. The law allows abortion to be performed to save the life of the woman or to provide necessary treatment. The law does not indicate which abortions constitute necessary treatment.

p. Nigeria has two abortion laws: one for the northern states and one for the southern states. Both laws specifically allow abortions to be performed to save the life of the woman. In addition, in the southern states, the decision of R v Bourne is applied, which allows abortions to be performed for physical and mental health reasons.

q. Data are UN Women calculated population weighted averages.

Violence against women

	Violence against women laws[i]			Prevalence of intimate partner violence				Perceptions of domestic violence[v] (%)	Prevalence of other forms of violence against women		
	Domestic violence[ii]	Sexual harassment[iii]	Marital rape[iv]	Physical violence (2000-2010)		Sexual violence (2000-2010)			Female Genital Mutilation/Cutting[vi] (%) 2000-2010	Child marriage[vii] (%) 2000-2010	Child sex ratio[viii]
				Ever (%)	Last 12 months (%)	Ever (%)	Last 12 months (%)				
Central and Eastern Europe and Central Asia											
Albania	Yes	Yes	No a	8	5	3	2	..	..	10	109
Armenia	No a	Yes b	No c	9	..	3	..	..	..	10	115
Azerbaijan	No d	Yes	No b	13	10	3	2	..	..	12	117
Belarus	No d	No c	No e	..	..	..	..	..	..	7	106
Bosnia and Herzegovina	Yes	Yes	No f	..	..	..	..	..	..	6	107
Bulgaria	Yes	Yes	No f	..	..	..	..	26	..	..	106
Croatia	Yes	Yes	..	..	..	..	..	..	..	..	106
Cyprus	Yes	Yes	Yes	..	..	..	..	22	..	..	108
Czech Republic	Yes	Yes	..	35	8	11	2	..	..	..	105
Estonia	Yes	Yes	No f	..	..	..	..	..	..	..	106
Georgia	Yes	No g	No f	5	2	2	(.)	9	..	17	111
Hungary	No a	No a	No a	..	..	..	..	..	..	..	106
Kazakhstan	Yes c	No a	No b	..	..	..	..	..	..	7	106
Kyrgyzstan	Yes	No b	No h	..	..	..	..	..	..	10	104
Latvia	Yes c	Yes	No a	..	..	..	..	..	..	..	104
Lithuania	No b	Yes	No b	33	..	8	..	..	..	..	104
Montenegro	Yes	Yes f	Yes f	..	..	..	..	..	..	5	108
Poland	Yes	Yes f	No a	15	3	5	0	11	..	..	106
Republic of Moldova	Yes	Yes a	Yes f	24	14	4	3	27	..	19	106
Romania	Yes	Yes	Yes	15	..	3	..	21	..	..	106
Russian Federation	No a	Yes b	No a	21	7	..	..	18	..	..	106
Serbia	Yes	Yes j	Yes f	23 k	3 k	6 k	1 k	55	..	6	108
Slovakia	Yes	Yes f	Yes f	15	..	9	..	..	..	..	105
Slovenia	Yes	Yes	Yes	..	..	..	..	..	..	..	105
Tajikistan	No d	Yes b	No b	36 k	12 k	43 k	.. k	..	..	13	105
The former Yugoslav Republic of Macedonia	Yes	No a	Yes f	..	..	..	..	..	..	4	108
Turkey	Yes	Yes	Yes a	39	10	15	7	22	..	14	105
Turkmenistan	No b	No b	No b	..	..	..	..	..	..	7	103
Ukraine	Yes	Yes	No b	13	10	3	2	28	..	10	106
Uzbekistan	No d	No d	No a	..	..	..	..	..	..	7	104
Developed Regions											
Andorra	Yes	Yes f	No l	..	..	..	..	4	..	..	..
Australia	Yes	Yes	Yes f	25	4	8	1	9	..	..	106
Austria	Yes	Yes	..	..	..	..	..	..	..	..	105
Belgium	Yes	Yes	..	..	..	..	..	..	..	..	105
Canada	Yes	Yes	Yes f	..	..	..	..	6	..	..	105
Denmark	Yes	Yes	Yes f	20	1	6	0	..	..	..	105
Finland	Yes	Yes	..	18	6	4	2	17	..	..	104
France	Yes	Yes	Yes f	..	3	..	1	9	..	..	105
Germany	Yes	Yes	No f	23	..	7	..	28	..	..	105
Greece	Yes	Yes	Yes	..	..	..	..	..	..	..	106
Iceland	Yes	Yes	Yes f	..	..	..	..	..	..	..	106
Ireland	Yes	Yes	Yes	13	1	8	1	..	..	..	107
Israel	Yes	Yes	..	..	..	..	..	..	..	..	105
Italy	Yes	Yes	No f	12	2	6	1	9	..	..	105
Japan	Yes	No f	No a	13	3	6	1	25	..	..	106
Liechtenstein	Yes	Yes	Yes f	..	..	..	..	..	..	..	..
Luxembourg	Yes	Yes	Yes f	..	..	..	..	..	..	..	105
Malta	Yes	Yes	Yes f	..	..	..	..	..	..	..	106
Monaco	Yes f	..	No f	..	..	..	..	..	..	..	..
Netherlands	Yes	Yes	No f	21	..	..	..	11	..	..	106
New Zealand	Yes	Yes	Yes f	30	5	14	2	..	..	..	105
Norway	Yes	Yes	No f	14	..	9	1	12	..	..	105
Portugal	Yes	Yes	Yes j	..	..	..	..	..	..	..	106
San Marino	Yes	Yes	Yes f	..	..	..	..	..	..	..	..
Spain	Yes	Yes	No f	..	..	..	..	12	..	..	106

	Violence against women laws[i]			Prevalence of intimate partner violence				Perceptions of domestic violence[v] (%)	Prevalence of other forms of violence against women		Child sex ratio[viii]
	Domestic violence[ii]	Sexual harassment[iii]	Marital rape[iv]	Physical violence (2000-2010)		Sexual violence (2000-2010)			Female Genital Mutilation/Cutting[vi] (%) 2000-2010	Child marriage[vii] (%) 2000-2010	
				Ever (%)	Last 12 months (%)	Ever (%)	Last 12 months (%)				
Sweden	Yes	Yes	Yes f	18	4	..	..	8	..	..	106
Switzerland	Yes	Yes	..	9	1	3	..	19	..	..	106
United Kingdom	Yes	Yes	No f	19	3	4	(.)	12	..	..	105
United States of America	Yes	Yes	Yes m	22	1	8	(.)	15	..	..	105
East Asia and the Pacific											
Brunei Darussalam	No d	Yes n	No f	..	..	..	..	..	..	..	106
Cambodia	Yes	Yes	No f	13	8	3	2	..	..	23	104
China	Yes	Yes n	No a	15	..	..	..	25	..	..	121
Democratic People's Republic of Korea	..	..	..	..	..	..	..	..	..	..	105
Fiji	Yes	Yes b	No b	..	..	..	..	..	..	..	106
Hong Kong, China (SAR)	Yes f	Yes f	Yes a	6	1	5	1	..	..	..	108
Indonesia	Yes	No a	No f	..	..	..	..	12	..	22	104
Kiribati	No n	No n	No h	60	32	46	34	..	..	..	..
Lao People's Democratic Republic	Yes	No n	No a	..	..	..	..	..	..	..	105
Malaysia	Yes	No p	Yes c	..	..	..	..	57	..	..	106
Marshall Islands	No p	No p	No f	..	..	..	..	..	..	26	..
Micronesia (Federated States of)	No p	No p	No q	..	..	..	..	..	..	..	107
Mongolia	Yes	No a	No a	..	..	..	..	..	..	4	102
Myanmar	No p	..	No f	..	..	..	..	..	..	..	102
Nauru	No c	..	No f	..	..	..	..	..	..	27	..
Palau	No c	..	No c	..	..	..	..	..	..	..	..
Papua New Guinea	No p	Yes q	No f	..	..	..	..	..	..	21	108
Philippines	Yes	Yes	Yes f	14	8	8	5	..	..	14	105
Republic of Korea	Yes	Yes f	No a	14	0	13	10	25	..	..	110
Samoa	No d	No c	No f	41	18	20	12	..	..	..	108
Singapore	Yes f	No a	No a	..	..	..	..	..	..	..	107
Solomon Islands	No b	No b	No b	46	..	55	..	..	..	22	108
Thailand	Yes	Yes	Yes	23 k	8 k	30 k	17 k	63	..	20	108
Timor-Leste	Yes	Yes b	Yes f	34	31	3	2	..	..	..	105
Tonga	No r	..	No	..	..	..	..	..	..	..	107
Tuvalu	No p	No p	No a	..	..	..	..	..	..	..	..
Vanuatu	Yes p	No p	No b	..	..	..	..	..	..	27	106
Viet Nam	Yes	Yes p	Yes f	32	6	10	4	21	..	10	105
Latin America and the Caribbean											
Antigua and Barbuda	Yes	No s	No f	30	..	..	..	..	..	..	..
Argentina	Yes	Yes	Yes f	..	..	..	..	4	..	..	104
Bahamas	Yes	Yes	No	..	..	..	..	..	..	..	105
Barbados	Yes	No d	No	..	..	..	..	..	..	..	103
Belize	Yes	Yes	No	..	..	..	..	..	..	..	99
Bolivia (Plurinational State of)	Yes	No d	No b	..	23	..	6	..	..	26	104
Brazil	Yes	Yes	Yes f	27 k	8 k	10 k	3 k	17	..	36	104
Chile	Yes	Yes	Yes f	15	..	16	..	12	..	..	104
Colombia	Yes	Yes	Yes b	33	..	12	..	10	..	23	104
Costa Rica	Yes	Yes	Yes f	33	7	15	3	..	..	..	105
Cuba	Yes a	Yes f	Yes f	..	..	..	..	..	..	..	106
Dominica	Yes	No n	No c	..	..	..	..	..	..	..	..
Dominican Republic	Yes	Yes f	Yes	16	11	6	4	..	..	40	104
Ecuador	Yes	Yes b	No b	31	10	12	4	..	..	22	104
El Salvador	Yes	Yes a	No f	24	7	12	3	..	..	25	105
Grenada	Yes	..	No b	..	6	..	4	..	..	..	105
Guatemala	Yes	No d	No b	..	9	..	4	..	..	35	104
Guyana	Yes	Yes	Yes f	..	..	..	..	..	..	20	104
Haiti	No a	No a	No a	14	12	11	10	..	..	30	104
Honduras	Yes	Yes	Yes f	..	6	..	4	..	..	39	104
Jamaica	Yes	No d	No f	..	..	..	..	..	..	9	105
Mexico	Yes	Yes	Yes	..	..	..	..	23	..	23	104
Nicaragua	Yes a	Yes a	Yes f	27	8	13	4	..	..	41	104
Panama	Yes	Yes	No f	..	..	..	..	..	..	..	..
Paraguay	Yes	Yes	..	19	7	8	3	..	..	..	..
Peru	Yes	Yes	Yes f	31	11	8	3	..	..	..	..

ANNEX 4: Violence against women

	Violence against women laws[i]			Prevalence of intimate partner violence					Prevalence of other forms of violence against women		
	Domestic violence[ii]	Sexual harassment[iii]	Marital rape[iv]	Physical violence (2000-2010)		Sexual violence (2000-2010)		Perceptions of domestic violence[v] (%)	Female Genital Mutilation/Cutting[vi] (%) 2000-2010	Child marriage[vii] (%) 2000-2010	Child sex ratio[viii]
				Ever (%)	Last 12 months (%)	Ever (%)	Last 12 months (%)				
Saint Kitts and Nevis	Yes	No t	No f	..	..	..	..	..	..	..	..
Saint Lucia	Yes	Yes	No	..	..	..	..	..	..	..	102
Saint Vincent and the Grenadines	Yes	No c	No f	..	..	..	..	..	..	..	102
Suriname	Yes	No c	No f	..	..	..	..	..	..	19	107
Trinidad and Tobago	Yes	No f	Yes f	..	..	..	..	19	..	8	103
Uruguay	Yes	Yes	No a	..	..	..	..	20	..	..	105
Venezuela (Bolivarian Republic of)	Yes	Yes	Yes f	..	..	..	..	..	..	..	105
Middle East and North Africa											
Algeria	No a	Yes	No a	..	..	..	..	..	..	2	105
Bahrain	No a	No u	No a	..	..	..	..	..	..	..	104
Egypt	Yes	No a	No a	33	18	7	4	..	91	17	105
Iraq	No c	Yes u	No f	..	..	..	..	..	..	17	106
Jordan	Yes c	No a	No	21	12	8	6	13	..	10	105
Kuwait	No c	No u	No c	..	..	..	..	..	..	..	106
Lebanon	No d	No b	No f	..	..	..	..	..	..	11	104
Libyan Arab Jamahiriya	No a	..	No u	..	..	..	..	..	..	..	106
Morocco	Yes b	Yes	No a	6	..	7	..	33	..	16	105
Occupied Palestinian Territory	No w	No w	No b	..	..	..	..	..	..	..	105
Oman	No c	No u	No u	..	..	..	..	..	..	..	103
Qatar	No u	..	No u	..	..	..	..	..	..	..	104
Saudi Arabia	No a,d	..	No u	..	..	..	..	..	..	..	104
Syrian Arab Republic	No a	No a	No a	..	..	..	..	..	..	13	105
Tunisia	No a	Yes a	No a	..	..	..	..	..	..	10	104
United Arab Emirates	No a	..	No c	..	..	..	..	..	..	..	105
Yemen	No a	No u	No a	..	..	..	..	..	..	32	104
South Asia											
Afghanistan	No f	No n	No n	..	..	..	..	..	..	39	106
Bangladesh	Yes	Yes	No	49	18	18	11	..	..	66	104
Bhutan	No d	Yes	Yes f	..	..	..	..	..	..	..	103
India	Yes	Yes	No a	35	21	10	7	39	..	47	109
Iran (Islamic Republic of)	..	..	..	..	..	..	..	26	..	..	104
Maldives	No a	No a	No b	18	6	7	2	..	..	..	106
Nepal	Yes	No c,w	Yes f	..	..	..	..	..	..	51	105
Pakistan	No d	Yes	No c	..	..	..	..	..	..	24	104
Sri Lanka	Yes	Yes	No a	..	..	..	..	..	..	12	104
Sub-Saharan Africa											
Angola	No d	Yes f	No a	..	..	..	..	..	..	..	101
Benin	No a	Yes	No a	..	..	..	..	..	13	34	102
Botswana	Yes	Yes	No a	..	..	..	..	..	..	10	102
Burkina Faso	No a	Yes	No x	..	..	..	..	52	73	48	104
Burundi	Yes f	Yes f	Yes f	..	..	..	..	..	..	18	101
Cameroon	No a	No d	No a	39	..	14	..	..	1	36	102
Cape Verde	Yes	Yes b	Yes f	16	..	4	..	..	..	18	101
Central African Republic	Yes	Yes	No b	..	..	..	..	..	26	61	100
Chad	Yes f	No x	No n	..	..	..	..	..	45	72	101
Comoros	Yes n	Yes x	No x	..	..	..	..	..	..	30	104
Congo	No x	..	No c	..	..	..	..	..	..	..	102
Côte d'Ivoire	No x	Yes f	No y	..	..	..	..	..	36	35	101
Democratic Republic of the Congo	No b	Yes	No	57	..	35	..	..	..	39	101
Djibouti	No b	No b	No x	..	..	..	..	..	93	5	102
Equatorial Guinea	No c	Yes z	No x	..	..	..	..	..	..	..	101
Eritrea	No x	..	No c	..	..	..	..	..	89	47	103
Ethiopia	Yes x	..	No	49	29	59	44	23	74	49	102
Gabon	No x	No aa	No ab	..	..	..	..	..	..	34	102
Gambia	No c	Yes b	No x	..	..	..	..	..	78	36	102
	Yes	No b	No c	21	18	8	5	40	4	25	105
	No a	No b	No a	..	..	..	..	..	96	63	104

	Violence against women laws[i]			Prevalence of intimate partner violence				Perceptions of domestic violence[v] (%)	Prevalence of other forms of violence against women		
	Domestic violence[ii]	Sexual harassment[iii]	Marital rape[iv]	Physical violence (2000-2010)		Sexual violence (2000-2010)			Female Genital Mutilation/Cutting[vi] (%) 2000-2010	Child marriage[vii] (%) 2000-2010	Child sex ratio[viii]
				Ever (%)	Last 12 months (%)	Ever (%)	Last 12 months (%)				
Guinea-Bissau	No c	No c	..	..	..	..	..	..	45	24	101
Kenya	No d	Yes	No f	37	31	17	14	..	27	26	102
Lesotho	No d	Yes	No	..	..	..	..	..	..	23	102
Liberia	No a	No b	..	35	33	11	10	..	58	38	104
Madagascar	Yes	Yes f	No a	..	..	..	..	..	..	39	102
Malawi	Yes	No a	No a	22	12	13	11	..	..	50	102
Mali	No a	No a	No a	..	..	..	..	62	85	71	104
Mauritania	No b	No b	No b	..	..	..	..	..	72	35	104
Mauritius	Yes	Yes	No f	..	..	..	..	..	..	..	104
Mozambique	Yes c	Yes f	No a	36	15	12	6	..	..	52	101
Namibia	Yes	Yes	Yes	31	16	17	9	..	..	9	102
Niger	No x	Yes	No x	..	..	..	..	..	2	75	105
Nigeria	No d	No a	No a	18	14	4	3	..	30	39	105
Rwanda	Yes	Yes	Yes	31	..	13	..	50	..	13	100
Sao Tome and Principe	Yes c	..	..	..	27	..	8	..	..	33	102
Senegal	Yes	Yes f	No f	..	..	..	..	..	28	39	103
Seychelles	Yes	Yes f	..	..	..	..	..	..	..	..	..
Sierra Leone	Yes	No b	No d	..	..	..	..	..	91	48	99
Somalia	..	..	..	..	..	..	..	..	98	45	101
South Africa	Yes	Yes	Yes	13	6	4		37	..	6	101
Sudan	No c	..	No f	..	..	..	..	..	89	34	104
Swaziland	No d	..	No b	..	..	..	..	..	..	5	102
Togo	No a	No a	No a	..	..	..	..	..	6	24	100
Uganda	Yes	Yes	No d	48	35	36	25	..	1	46	102
United Republic of Tanzania	No a	Yes	No	33 k	15 k	23 k	13 k	..	15	38	102
Zambia	No a	Yes	No a	47	40	17	16	68	1	42	101
Zimbabwe	Yes	Yes f	Yes f	30	25	19	13	..	..	30	101

SOURCES

Columns 1-3: UN Women 2011b.

Columns 4-7: UN Women 2011a, based on García-Moreno et al. 2005; Johnson et al. 2008; Kishor and Johnson 2004; MEASURE DHS (2000–2009); CDC (2000–2009), and other population-based surveys available through 2010. The data refer to the latest year available during the period specified. For individual data sources, see UN Women 2011a.

Column 8: World Values Survey Association 2010.

Columns 9-10: UNICEF 2011.

Column 11: UN DESA 2011b.

NOTES

".." indicates that data are not available or that data sources are contradictory.

( ) indicates a value less than 1 percent.

i. The violence against women laws data refer to the existence of laws in relation to three broad categories of violence: domestic violence, sexual harassment and marital rape (see definitions below). Laws on sexual violence are not included in the annex. While acknowledging the critical importance of legislation to prohibit this form of violence, the very wide variability of laws on this issue meant that comparability across countries was difficult to ascertain. The data are based on an analysis of the latest available information from various sources. Primary data sources are: the UN Secretary-General's database on violence against women; official reports from the UN human rights system, including Universal Periodic Reviews and concluding comments by the CEDAW Committee since 2006; and UN Women's review of actual laws. In cases where a 'no' is entered, at least two corroborating sources were found. The assessment is limited to the written, codified laws of these countries and has not taken common law, case law or relevant policies, guidelines or other government or NGO initiatives into account. No assessment is made in relation to the quality of the legal provisions, or their application in practice. Although the data are based on a careful and systematic review of the various sources noted below, by definition, laws are subject to change, therefore their accuracy cannot be guaranteed as some sources may use different definitions or categories, be outdated, incomplete or conflicting. As a result, these data should be used with caution.

ii. Domestic violence 'includes a range of sexually, psychologically and physically coercive acts used against adult and adolescent women by a current or former intimate partner, without her consent' (UN General Assembly 2006, 37). The data refer to instances where domestic, family or intimate partner violence is specifically criminalized or where provisions for protection orders are in place.

iii. Sexual harassment is defined as: 'Unwelcome sexually determined behaviour, in both horizontal and vertical relationships, including in employment (including the informal employment sector), education, receipt of goods and services, sporting activities, and property transactions' (UN DESA-DAW 2009a, 28). For the purposes of this annex, the data refer to whether countries have laws in place that prohibit sexual harassment under civil or criminal law, specifically in relation to employment. Voluntary guidelines or policies are not counted.

iv. Marital rape, also called spousal rape, is non-consensual sex where the perpetrator is the victim's spouse. Although general rape laws (except where exemption of a spouse is explicitly stated) do not preclude a spouse from being prosecuted, the data refer to instances where the law explicitly criminalizes marital rape, without qualification, for example by 'providing that sexual assault provisions apply "irrespective of the nature of the relationship" between the perpetrator and complainant; or 'stating that "no marriage or other relationship shall constitute a defence to a charge of sexual assault under the legislation"' (UN DESA-DAW 2009a, 26). In other instances, a marital (or equivalent) relationship may be explicitly cited in the law as an aggravating factor.

Explicit criminalization of marital rape is recommended as best practice by, among others, the Council of Europe (Council of Europe 2009c).

v. Data refer to the percentage of women and men who think that it is sometimes or always justifiable for a man to beat his wife. The World Values Surveys ask respondents to rate on a scale from 1 to 10 the degree to which they think it is justifiable for a man to beat his wife. The data refer to the proportion who responded that it can be somewhat or always justifiable (responses 2 through 10).

vi. Data refer to the percentage of women aged 20 to 24 married before age 18. They are based on various household surveys and refer to the latest year available during the period specified. For individual data sources, see UNICEF 2011.

vii. Data refer to the percentage of women aged 15 to 49 who have undergone female genital mutilation/cutting.

viii. Data refer to the number of boys aged 0 to 4 years for every 100 girls. As noted in UN General Assembly 2006: 'Practices of son preference, expressed in manifestations such as female infanticide, prenatal sex selection and systematic neglect of girls, have resulted in adverse female-male sex ratios and high rates of female infant mortality' in some regions.

a. Data are from OHCHR 2011.

b. Information provided by UN Women regional and country offices.

c. Data are based on documents produced by Member States and the UN system for the Universal Periodic Review (UPR). The UPR is a unique process that involves a review of the human rights records of all 192 UN Member States once every four years. The UPR is a State-driven process, under the auspices of the Human Rights Council, which provides the opportunity for each State to declare what actions they have taken to improve the human rights situations in their countries and to fulfil their human rights obligations. All documents are available at: http://www.ohchr.org/en/hrbodies/upr/pages/uprmain.aspx

d. Information from the UN Secretary-General's database indicates that draft legislation is under consideration.

e. UN CEDAW 2011.

f. Data are based on UN Women review of laws, including penal codes and labour laws, as well as specific domestic violence and sexual offences laws.

g. Council of Europe 2009a.

h. UN Human Rights Council 2010d.

j. Council of Europe 2009b.

k. Data cover only part of the country.

l. Council of Europe 2007.

m. The enforcement of criminal laws in the United States is carried out through state criminal codes, only some of which explicitly criminalize marital rape.

n. Data are from US Department of State 2011.

p. Data are from UNDP 2010b.

q. Jivan and Forster 2007.

r. Roguski and Kingi 2011.

s. Pegus 2007.

t. ECLAC 2011.

u. Data are from Kelly 2010.

w. Draft legislation is under consideration, according to UN Women country or regional office.

x. ACGSD 2010.

y. UN CEDAW 2010b.

z. UN CEDAW 2004.

aa. ITUC 2007.

ab. AWRO 2009.

ANNEX 5: Convention on the Elimination of All Forms of Discrimination against Women (CEDAW)

	CEDAW status[a]	Optional Protocol[b]	Reservations to CEDAW						
			Compatibility with religious laws or traditional codes[c]	Elimination of discrimination[d]	Equality in employment[e]	Equality of nationality[f]	Equality to choose residence[g]	Equal rights in marriage and family[h]	Other concerns[i]
Central and Eastern Europe and Central Asia									
Albania	ratified	ratified							
Armenia	ratified	ratified							
Azerbaijan	ratified	ratified							
Belarus	ratified	ratified							
Bosnia and Herzegovina	ratified	ratified							
Bulgaria	ratified	ratified							
Croatia	ratified	ratified							
Cyprus	ratified	ratified							
Czech Republic	ratified	ratified							
Estonia	ratified								
Georgia	ratified	ratified							
Hungary	ratified	ratified							
Kazakhstan	ratified	ratified							
Kyrgyzstan	ratified	ratified							
Latvia	ratified								
Lithuania	ratified	ratified							
Montenegro	ratified	ratified							
Poland	ratified	ratified							
Republic of Moldova	ratified	ratified							
Romania	ratified	ratified							
Russian Federation	ratified	ratified							
Serbia	ratified	ratified							
Slovakia	ratified	ratified							
Slovenia	ratified	ratified							
Tajikistan	ratified	signature only							
The former Yugoslav Republic of Macedonia	ratified	ratified							
Turkey	ratified	ratified							
Turkmenistan	ratified	ratified							
Ukraine	ratified	ratified							
Uzbekistan	ratified								
Developed Regions									
Andorra	ratified	ratified							
Australia	ratified	ratified			reservation				reservation
Austria	ratified	ratified			reservation				
Belgium	ratified	ratified							
Canada	ratified	ratified							
Denmark	ratified	ratified							
Finland	ratified	ratified							
France	ratified	ratified				reservation		reservation	reservation
Germany	ratified	ratified							
Greece	ratified	ratified							
Iceland	ratified	ratified							
Ireland	ratified	ratified			reservation			reservation j	reservation
Israel	ratified		reservation					reservation	reservation
Italy	ratified	ratified							
Japan	ratified								
Liechtenstein	ratified	ratified							reservation
Luxembourg	ratified	ratified							
Malta	ratified				reservation			reservation	reservation
Monaco	ratified					reservation		reservation	reservation
Netherlands	ratified	ratified							
New Zealand	ratified	ratified	reservation	reservation					reservation
Norway	ratified	ratified							
Portugal	ratified	ratified							

138 | Progress of the World's Women

	CEDAW status[a]	Optional Protocol[b]	Compatibility with religious laws or traditional codes[c]	Elimination of discrimination[d]	Equality in employment[e]	Equality of nationality[f]	Equality to choose residence[g]	Equal rights in marriage and family[h]	Other concerns[i]
San Marino	ratified	ratified							
Spain	ratified	ratified							reservation l
Sweden	ratified	ratified							
Switzerland	ratified	ratified						reservation	reservation
United Kingdom	ratified	ratified			reservation	reservation		reservation k	reservation
United States of America	signed but not ratified		—	—	—	—	—	—	—
East Asia and the Pacific									
Brunei Darussalam	ratified		reservation			reservation			
Cambodia	ratified	ratified							
China	ratified								
Democratic People's Republic of Korea	ratified			reservation		reservation			
Fiji	ratified								
Hong Kong, China (SAR)	—	—	—	—	—	—	—	—	—
Indonesia	ratified	signature only							
Kiribati	ratified								
Lao People's Democratic Republic	ratified								
Malaysia	ratified		reservation			reservation		reservation	reservation
Marshall Islands	ratified								
Micronesia (Federated States of)	ratified			reservation	reservation			reservation	reservation
Mongolia	ratified	ratified							
Myanmar	ratified								
Nauru	not signed or ratified		—	—	—	—	—	—	—
Palau	not signed or ratified		—	—	—	—	—	—	—
Papua New Guinea	ratified								
Philippines	ratified	ratified							
Republic of Korea	ratified	ratified				reservation		reservation	
Samoa	ratified								
Singapore	ratified		reservation	reservation	reservation			reservation	
Solomon Islands	ratified	ratified							
Thailand	ratified	ratified						reservation	
Timor-Leste	ratified	ratified							
Tonga	not signed or ratified		—	—	—	—	—	—	—
Tuvalu	ratified								
Vanuatu	ratified	ratified							
Viet Nam	ratified								
Latin America and the Caribbean									
Antigua and Barbuda	ratified	ratified							
Argentina	ratified	ratified							
Bahamas	ratified			reservation		reservation			
Barbados	ratified								
Belize	ratified	ratified							
Bolivia (Plurinational State of)	ratified	ratified							
Brazil	ratified	ratified							
Chile	ratified	signature only							
Colombia	ratified	ratified							
Costa Rica	ratified	ratified							
Cuba	ratified	signature only							
Dominica	ratified								
Dominican Republic	ratified	ratified							
Ecuador	ratified	ratified							
El Salvador	ratified	signature only							
Grenada	ratified								
Guatemala	ratified	ratified							
Guyana	ratified								
Haiti	ratified								

Convention on the Elimination of All Forms of Discrimination against Women (CEDAW)

| | CEDAW status[a] | Optional Protocol[b] | Reservations to CEDAW | | | | | | |
			Compatibility with religious laws or traditional codes[c]	Elimination of discrimination[d]	Equality in employment[e]	Equality of nationality[f]	Equality to choose residence[g]	Equal rights in marriage and family[h]	Other concerns[i]
Honduras	ratified								
Jamaica	ratified								
Mexico	ratified	ratified							reservation ❙
Nicaragua	ratified								
Panama	ratified	ratified							
Paraguay	ratified	ratified							
Peru	ratified	ratified							
Saint Kitts and Nevis	ratified	ratified							
Saint Lucia	ratified								
Saint Vincent and the Grenadines	ratified								
Suriname	ratified								
Trinidad and Tobago	ratified								
Uruguay	ratified	ratified							
Venezuela (Bolivarian Republic of)	ratified	ratified							
Middle East and North Africa									
Algeria	ratified			reservation			reservation	reservation	
Bahrain	ratified		reservation	reservation		reservation	reservation	reservation	
Egypt	ratified		reservation	reservation				reservation	
Iraq	ratified		reservation	reservation		reservation		reservation	
Jordan	ratified					reservation		reservation	
Kuwait	ratified		reservation			reservation		reservation	
Lebanon	ratified					reservation		reservation	
Libyan Arab Jamahiriya	ratified	ratified	reservation	reservation				reservation	
Morocco	ratified		reservation ❙	reservation ❙		reservation ❙	reservation ❙	reservation ❙	reservation ❙
Occupied Palestinian Territory	—	—	—	—	—	—	—	—	—
Oman	ratified		reservation			reservation	reservation	reservation	
Qatar	ratified		reservation ❙	reservation		reservation	reservation	reservation	reservation
Saudi Arabia	ratified		reservation			reservation			
Syrian Arab Republic	ratified		reservation	reservation		reservation	reservation	reservation	
Tunisia	ratified	ratified				reservation	reservation	reservation	
United Arab Emirates	ratified		reservation	reservation		reservation		reservation	reservation
Yemen	ratified								
South Asia									
Afghanistan	ratified								
Bangladesh	ratified	ratified	reservation	reservation				reservation	
Bhutan	ratified								
India	ratified		reservation ❙					reservation ❙	reservation ❙
Iran (Islamic Republic of)	not signed or ratified		—	—	—	—	—	—	—
Maldives	ratified	ratified	reservation					reservation	
Nepal	ratified	ratified							
Pakistan	ratified								
Sri Lanka	ratified	ratified							
Sub-Saharan Africa									
Angola	ratified	ratified							
Benin	ratified	signature only							
Botswana	ratified	ratified							
Burkina Faso	ratified	ratified							
Burundi	ratified	signature only							
Cameroon	ratified	ratified							
Cape Verde	ratified								
Central African Republic	ratified								
Chad	ratified								
Comoros	ratified								
Congo	ratified	signature only							
Côte d'Ivoire	ratified								

	CEDAW status[a]	Optional Protocol[b]	Compatibility with religious laws or traditional codes[c]	Elimination of discrimination[d]	Equality in employment[e]	Equality of nationality[f]	Equality to choose residence[g]	Equal rights in marriage and family[h]	Other concerns[i]
Democratic Republic of the Congo	ratified								
Djibouti	ratified								
Equatorial Guinea	ratified	ratified							
Eritrea	ratified								
Ethiopia	ratified								
Gabon	ratified	ratified							
Gambia	ratified								
Ghana	ratified	ratified							
Guinea	ratified								
Guinea-Bissau	ratified	ratified							
Kenya	ratified								
Lesotho	ratified	ratified	reservation	reservation					
Liberia	ratified	signature only							
Madagascar	ratified	signature only							
Malawi	ratified	signature only							
Mali	ratified	ratified							
Mauritania	ratified		reservation						
Mauritius	ratified	ratified							
Mozambique	ratified	ratified							
Namibia	ratified	ratified							
Niger	ratified	ratified	reservation	reservation			reservation	reservation	reservation
Nigeria	ratified	ratified							
Rwanda	ratified	ratified							
São Tomé and Príncipe	ratified	signature only							
Senegal	ratified	ratified							
Seychelles	ratified	ratified							
Sierra Leone	ratified	signature only							
Somalia	not signed or ratified		—	—	—	—	—	—	—
South Africa	ratified	ratified							
Sudan	not signed or ratified		—	—	—	—	—	—	—
Swaziland	ratified								
Togo	ratified								
Uganda	ratified								
United Republic of Tanzania	ratified	ratified							
Zambia	ratified	signature only							
Zimbabwe	ratified								

SOURCE

Column 1-10: UN Women systemization based on data from UN 2011c, as of April 2011.

NOTES

" " indicates where information on CEDAW status and/ or CEDAW reservations are not applicable.

a. The Convention on the Elimination of All Forms of Discrimination against Women was adopted in 1979 by the United Nations General Assembly in its resolution A/RES/34/180. It came into force on 3 September 1981.

b. The Optional Protocol to the Convention on the Elimination of All Forms of Discrimination against Women was adopted by the United Nations General Assembly on 6 October 1999 in its resolution A/RES/54/4 and came into force on 22 December 2000. Article 2 of the Protocol states that: 'Communications may be submitted by or on behalf of individuals or groups of individuals, under the jurisdiction of a State party, claiming to be victims of a violation of any of the rights set forth in the Convention by that State party. Where a communication is submitted on behalf of individuals or groups of individuals, this shall be with their consent unless the author can justify acting on their behalf without such consent'.

c. 'Compatibility with religious laws or traditional codes' indicates that a State finds some provisions of CEDAW incompatible with laws based on ethnic or religious identity, which the State cannot or will not change.

d. 'Elimination of discrimination' indicates reservations to the commitments to condemn discrimination against women in 'all its forms' contained in article 2. The CEDAW Committee has identified these rights as central to the object and purpose of the Convention.

e. 'Equality of employment' indicates reservations to article 11 of CEDAW, on equality in employment.

f. 'Equality of nationality' refers to reservations concerning article 9, which ensures equal nationality and citizenship rights, including the transmission of citizenship from mother to child.

g. 'Equality to choose residence' reflects a country's reservation to article 15(4), which accords to women and men the same legal rights with regard to their movement and the freedom to choose their residence and domicile.

h. 'Equal rights in marriage and family' encapsulates reservations from countries to CEDAW's provisions on rights relating to marital and family issues, including the obligation to ensure women and men equal rights to marry; to exercise free and full consent; to dissolve marriage; to make parental decisions; to decide on the number and spacing of children; to act as guardian to their children; to choose a profession; and to own and manage property. Most of these relate to article 16. The CEDAW Committee has identified these rights as central to the object and purpose of the Convention.

i. 'Other concerns' encompasses States that make a variety of different types of reservations to CEDAW, such as those relating to social security payments or royal titles.

j. The text of the reservation reads: 'Articles 16, 1 (d) and (f): Ireland is of the view that the attainment in Ireland of the objectives of the Convention does not necessitate the extension to men of rights identical to those accorded by law to women in respect of the guardianship, adoption and custody of children born out of wedlock and reserves the right to implement the Convention subject to that understanding'.

k. The text of the reservation reads: 'As regards sub-paragraph 1 (f) of article 16, the United Kingdom does not regard the reference to the paramountcy of the interests of the children as being directly relevant to the elimination of discrimination against women, and declares in this connection that the legislation of the United Kingdom regulating adoption, while giving a principal position to the promotion of the children's welfare, does not give to the child's interests the same paramount place as in issues concerning custody over children'.

l. This reservation is expressed in the form of a Declaration.

Selected global resolutions, conventions and agreements on women's rights

Year	Document	Significance
1948	Resolution on the Universal Declaration of Human Rights	A comprehensive statement of universal human rights, believed to be the world's most translated document.
1949	Convention for the Suppression of the Traffic in Persons and of the Exploitation of the Prostitution of Others	Commits States parties to take steps to prevent and punish the trafficking of women for sexual exploitation.
1951	ILO Convention Concerning Equal Remuneration for Men and Women Workers for Work of Equal Value	Commits States parties to ensure the application of the principle of equal remuneration for women and men for work of equal value.
1957	Convention on the Nationality of Married Women	States parties must guarantee women's right to choose their nationality upon marriage.
1958	ILO Convention Concerning Discrimination in Respect of Employment and Occupation	States parties are required to formulate national policies, legislation and agreements for the prevention of discrimination in employment and occupation.
1962	Convention on Consent to Marriage, Minimum Age for Marriage and Registration of Marriages	Obligates States parties to specify a minimum age for marriage, officially register all marriages and prohibit marriages entered into without free and full consent of both parties.
1979	Convention on the Elimination of All Forms of Discrimination against Women (CEDAW)	The pivotal women's rights convention outlining international legal obligations on States parties to prevent discrimination against women.
1981	ILO Convention Concerning Equal Opportunities and Equal Treatment for Men and Women Workers: Workers with family responsibilities	Compels States parties to take all possible measures to enable persons with family responsibilities to exercise their right to engage in employment without being subject to discrimination.
1982 – 2009 (12)*	General Assembly Resolution on Improvement of the Situation of Women in Rural Areas	States urged to recognize rural women's unpaid work and to improve the situation of rural women in their development strategies, including through legislation to ensure full and equal rights to own land, inheritance rights and the right to microcredit.
1993	Vienna Declaration and Programme of Action	The World Conference on Human Rights reaffirmed that the human rights of women and of the girl child are an inalienable, integral and indivisible part of universal human rights.
1993 – 2009 (9)*	General Assembly Resolution on Violence against Women Migrant Workers	Encourages governments to implement measures to protect the human rights of migrant women workers (including domestic workers), regardless of immigration status, to prevent economic exploitation, discrimination, sexual harassment and abuse in the workplace.
1994 – 2010 (9)*	General Assembly Resolution on Trafficking in Women and Girls	Urges governments to eliminate the demand for trafficked women and girls and calls upon them to criminalize all forms of trafficking and to condemn and penalize offenders.
1994	International Conference on Population and Development Programme of Action	Places women's rights, health and empowerment at the centre of efforts to achieve human rights and sustainable development; recognizes that reproductive rights are human rights and urges States to take steps to address the reproductive health needs of women.
1995	Beijing Declaration and Platform for Action	The Beijing Declaration was adopted by consensus by governments at the Fourth World Conference on Women. The Platform for Action outlines international commitments to equality for women and to gender mainstreaming in all development and political processes.
1997 – 2001 (4)*	General Assembly Resolution on Traditional or Customary Practices Affecting the Health of Women and Girls	Calls upon States to implement legislation to prosecute those who violate the health of women and girls by practising harmful traditional or customary practices.
1997 – 2009 (7)*	General Assembly Resolution on Women in Development	Reaffirms that gender equality is of fundamental importance to achieving sustained economic growth and sustainable development, and urges governments to consider and include women in all development strategies, laws and policies.
2000	ILO Convention Concerning the Revision of the Maternity Protection Convention (Revised), 1952	The Convention commits States parties to ensure a minimum of 14 weeks maternity leave, with cash and medical benefits, breastfeeding breaks and freedom from discrimination in employment.

2000	United Nations Millennium Declaration	Sets out a visionary international development agenda. The Millennium Development Goals, signed by 189 countries, include Goal 3 to promote gender equality and women's empowerment.
2000	Security Council Resolution 1325	Landmark Security Council resolution that addresses the impact of war on women and their contribution to conflict resolution and sustainable peace.
2000 – 2004 (3)*	General Assembly Resolution on the Elimination of All Forms of Violence against Women	Urges Member States to strengthen awareness and preventative measures for the elimination of all forms of violence against women.
2000 – 2004 (3)*	General Assembly Resolution on Working towards the Elimination of Crimes against Women Committed in the Name of Honour	Calls upon States to intensify efforts to prevent and prosecute crimes against women committed in the name of honour and to provide support services for victims.
2000	Protocol to Prevent, Suppress and Punish Trafficking in Persons Especially Women and Children, Supplementing the United Nations Convention against Transnational Organized Crime	The first universal instrument on all aspects of human trafficking.
2001	General Assembly Declaration of Commitment on HIV/AIDS	Urges Member States to address HIV/AIDS, recognizing that women and girls are disproportionately affected and that empowering women is an essential part of efforts to address the pandemic.
2003	General Assembly Resolution on Women and Political Participation	Urges Member States to promote and protect women's right to participate in election processes and in all levels of government.
2006 – 2010 (5)*	General Assembly Resolution on the Intensification of Efforts to Eliminate All Forms of Violence against Women	Strongly condemns violence against women and girls perpetrated by the State, private persons or non-state actors and encourages international institutions and States to intensify their efforts and support for activities to eliminate it.
2007	General Assembly Resolution on the Protection of and Assistance to Internally Displaced Persons	Expresses concern at the grave problems faced by many internally displaced women and children and encourages governments to provide protection and assistance.
2008	Security Council Resolution 1820	The first Security Council resolution to recognize conflict-related sexual violence as a matter of international peace and security.
2009	Human Rights Council Resolution on Preventable Maternal Mortality and Morbidity and Human Rights	Recognizes that the prevention of maternal mortality and morbidity requires the promotion and protection of the human rights of women and girls.
2009	ILO Resolution Concerning Gender Equality at the Heart of Decent Work	Promotes gender equality as a basic human right, as intrinsic to the goals of decent work and poverty alleviation, and as an instrument for more inclusive globalization.
2009	Security Council Resolution 1888	Calls for the inclusion of sexual violence in peace negotiations and the development of approaches to address the effects of sexual violence.
2009 – 2010 (2)*	Human Rights Council Resolution on the Elimination of Discrimination against Women	Calls upon States to revoke laws that discriminate on the basis of sex, remove gender bias in the administration of justice and ensure full representation and participation of women in political, social and economic decision-making.
2009	Security Council Resolution 1889	Addresses obstacles to women's participation in peace processes and peacebuilding, as prescribed in Security Council resolution 1325.
2010	Economic and Social Council Ministerial Declaration on Implementing the Internationally Agreed Goals and Commitments in Regard to Gender Equality and Empowerment of Women	Reaffirms that States must take all appropriate measures to ensure gender equality and women's empowerment, recognizing the importance of the eradication of poverty and the achievement of the Millennium Development Goals.
2010	Human Rights Council Resolution on Accelerating Efforts to Eliminate All Forms of Violence against Women: Ensuring due diligence in prevention	Stresses that States have an obligation to exercise 'due diligence' to prevent, investigate, prosecute and punish the perpetrators of violence against women.
2010	Security Council Resolution 1960	Calls for a monitoring and reporting framework to track sexual violence in conflict.

NOTES

* Indicates that the same (or similar) resolution was passed in multiple years. The range of years indicates the first and most recent year the resolution was passed. The figure in parentheses indicates the number of times the resolution was passed over this time period.

Regional groupings

Central and Eastern Europe and Central Asia

Albania	Croatia	Kazakhstan	Republic of Moldova	Tajikistan
Armenia	Cyprus	Kyrgyzstan	Romania	The former Yugoslav Republic
Azerbaijan	Czech Republic	Latvia	Russian Federation	of Macedonia
Belarus	Estonia	Lithuania	Serbia	Turkey
Bosnia and Herzegovina	Georgia	Montenegro	Slovakia	Turkmenistan
Bulgaria	Hungary	Poland	Slovenia	Ukraine
				Uzbekistan

Developed Regions

Andorra	Finland	Israel	Monaco	Spain
Australia	France	Italy	Netherlands	Sweden
Austria	Germany	Japan	New Zealand	Switzerland
Belgium	Greece	Liechtenstein	Norway	United Kingdom of Great
Canada	Iceland	Luxembourg	Portugal	Britain and Northern Ireland
Denmark	Ireland	Malta	San Marino	United States of America

East Asia and the Pacific

Brunei Darussalam	Hong Kong, China (Special	Marshall Islands	Palau	Solomon Islands
Cambodia	Administrative Region)	Micronesia	Papua New Guinea	Thailand
China	Indonesia	(Federated States of)	Philippines	Timor-Leste
Democratic People's Republic	Kiribati	Mongolia	Republic of Korea	Tonga
of Korea	Lao People's	Myanmar	Samoa	Tuvalu
Fiji	Democratic Republic	Nauru	Singapore	Vanuatu
	Malaysia			Viet Nam

Latin America and the Carribbean

Antigua and Barbuda	Chile	El Salvador	Mexico	Saint Vincent and
Argentina	Colombia	Grenada	Nicaragua	the Grenadines
Bahamas	Costa Rica	Guatemala	Panama	Suriname
Barbados	Cuba	Guyana	Paraguay	Trinidad and Tobago
Belize	Dominica	Haiti	Peru	Uruguay
Bolivia (Plurinational State of)	Dominican Republic	Honduras	Saint Kitts and Nevis	Venezuela
Brazil	Ecuador	Jamaica	Saint Lucia	(Bolivarian Republic of)

Middle East and North Africa

Algeria	Jordan	Morocco	Qatar	United Arab Emirates
Bahrain	Kuwait	Occupied Palestinian	Saudi Arabia	Yemen
Egypt	Lebanon	Territory	Syrian Arab Republic	
Iraq	Libyan Arab Jamahiriya	Oman	Tunisia	

South Asia

Afghanistan	Bhutan	Iran (Islamic Republic of)	Nepal	Sri Lanka
Bangladesh	India	Maldives	Pakistan	

Sub-Saharan Africa

Angola	Congo	Ghana	Mauritius	Somalia
Benin	Côte d'Ivoire	Guinea	Mozambique	South Africa
Botswana	Democratic Republic	Guinea-Bissau	Namibia	Sudan
Burkina Faso	of the Congo	Kenya	Niger	Swaziland
Burundi	Djibouti	Lesotho	Nigeria	Togo
Cameroon	Equatorial Guinea	Liberia	Rwanda	Uganda
Cape Verde	Eritrea	Madagascar	São Tomé and Príncipe	United Republic of Tanzania
Central African Republic	Ethiopia	Malawi	Senegal	Zambia
Chad	Gabon	Mali	Seychelles	Zimbabwe
Comoros	Gambia	Mauritania	Sierra Leone	

Endnotes

Introduction

1. See Annex 1.

2. Christensen 2010; UN Women calculation based on data in Annex 1. The number of countries that have reached or surpassed the 30 percent mark refers to women's representation in upper and lower houses.

3. See Annex 5. UN 2011c.

4. UN Women calculation using data from ILO 2010b. 'Vulnerable employment', as defined by the ILO, is the sum of own account (self-employment with no employees) and contributing family workers (unpaid family workers) as a proportion of total employment.

5. UNICEF 2009.

6. UN Women 2010f and 2011a.

7. UN Women analysis of data from World Bank 2010c. Data as of January 2011.

8. UN General Assembly 1979.

9. The Republic of Uganda 2000, 67.

10. Kathrynp 2010; Gentleman 2009.

11. Nowrojee 2005, 24.

12. Ministry of Planning and International Co-Operation, Hashemite Kingdom of Jordan, UNDP Jordan and the Jordanian Hashemite Fund for Human Development/ Queen Zein Al Sharaf Institute for Development 2004, 112.

13. UN Security Council 2004.

14. Irving 2008.

15. Chirayath et al. 2005.

16. Tripp et al. 2009.

17. The OECD-DAC is made up of major bilateral and multilateral donors. UN Women analysis defined justice aid as the total amount in two categories: legal and judicial development, and human rights. To avoid double counting some projects, the analysis is restricted to bilateral donors and the EU.

18. The OECD-DAC has a gender marker system, which donors are requested to use to classify their spending. As indicated in OECD 2007 (114), the gender equality marker system includes three categories: principal or primary, which indicates that gender equality is fundamental to the design and impact of the activity and is an explicit objective of the activity; significant or secondary, which indicates that, although gender equality is an important policy objective, it is not one of the principal reasons for undertaking the activity; not targeted, which means that the activity has been assessed, but was found not be targeted to gender equality. The United States, the single largest justice aid donor, does not currently use the gender marker system. As a result, out of the total $4.2 billion allocated to justice in 2009, $2.5 billion was not assessed for gender equality. However, the OECD anticipates that the United States will begin using it in 2011.

19. The World Bank project database (World Bank 2010e) contains data on World Bank lending projects from 1947 to the present. UN Women analysis included grants and loans that were started and/or finished between 2000 and 2010, which was determined using the approval year (or the date that the Board of Directors voted to approve a loan or credit) and the closing year (or the date that all financial activities related to the project stopped). This produced a dataset of 6,382 projects. The World Bank project database categorizes projects by major sectors and major themes. There are 11 major sectors, of which public administration, law and justice is one, and 11 major themes, including the rule of law, and social development, gender and inclusion. Each project can have up to five major sectors and five major themes. Each project includes information on what proportion is allocated to each of the five major sectors; therefore, in order to calculate what was spent on the public administration, law and justice major sector, all the projects that included public administration, law and justice as a major sector were identified and the total amount that was allocated to it was calculated. The analysis is based on the amounts of money allocated to grants and loans at the project approval stage, not the amount that was actually spent. For more information on this analysis, see Minaya 2011.

20. The 21 projects were in Latin America (10 projects), East Asia (3 projects), sub-Saharan Africa (3 projects), Central and Eastern Europe and Central Asia (2 projects), South Asia (2 projects) and the Middle East (1 project). In order to identify these 21 projects, 87 project documents were analysed: 51 of these had both rule of law, and social development, gender and inclusion as major themes. The remaining 36 projects had access to law and justice as at least one major theme. Although these projects did not have social development, gender and inclusion as a major theme, since this report is about access to justice, it was decided to include them in the dataset. Of these 87 projects, 21 specifically mentioned gender or women in the project documents. Of the remaining 66 projects, 46 were related to the rule of law or access to law and justice, but had no mention of gender or women in the project documents (in some cases these projects were related to other aspects of social development and inclusion, but not gender equality specifically); 8 were only related to gender equality and had no rule of law component; and for 12 projects, the documents were not available. Note that there may be other rule of law grants and loans that address gender equality, but they do not have social development, gender and inclusion as a major sector, so they were not included in the analysis. Also note that the World Bank's publicly available projects database (World Bank 2010e) does not include the World Bank's analytical and technical assistance work, including activities of relevance to women's access to justice, such as work by the Justice for the Poor programme, which is therefore not included in this analysis.

21. World Bank 2010b and 2010h.

Balancing the Scales

1. *Dhungana on behalf of FWLD v HMG, Ministry of Parliamentary Affairs, Council of Ministers, Ministry of Law and Justice, Parliament.*

2. Ibid.

3. Pradhan Malla 2010.

4. *Vishaka and others v State of Rajasthan and others.*

5. The Protection of Women Against Sexual Harassment at Workplace Bill.

6. *Bangladesh National Women Lawyers Association v Government of Bangladesh.*

7. Iqbal 2010.

8. *Şahide Goekce (deceased) v Austria; Fatma Yildirim v Austria.*

9. *Şahide Goekce (deceased) v Austria.*

10. UNIFEM (now part of UN Women) 2009a.

11. *Maria da Penha Maia Fernandes v Brazil.*

12. *Maria da Penha Law.*

13. *Sandra Lovelace v Canada.*

14. Bill C-31: An Act to Amend the Indian Act.

15. See *McIvor and others v Registrar, Indian and Northern Affairs Canada and others.*

16. *Bhe and others v Khayelitsha Magistrate and others,* para 92.

17. Ibid.

18. Dow 1995, 31.

19. *The Attorney General of the Republic of Botswana v Unity Dow.*

20. UN Women calculation based on Manby 2009.

21. Women's Link Worldwide 2007.

22. Decree No. 4444 on the Regulation of Certain Reproductive Health Services; see also Technical Norms on Care for Voluntary Termination of Pregnancy.

23. UN Human Rights Committee 2010.

24. *Prosecutor v Delalic*, ICTY, No. IT-96-21-T; *Prosecutor v Furundžija*, No. IT-95-17/1-T; *Prosecutor v Krstic*, ICTY, No. IT-98-33-T; *Prosecutor v Kunarac et al.*, No. IT-96-23-T & IT-96-23/1-T; *Prosecutor v Kunarac et al.*, No. IT-96-23 & IT-96-23/1-A; ; *Prosecutor v Tadić*, No. IT-94-1-T; *Prosecutor v Tadić*, No. IT-94-1-A.

25. *Prosecutor v Akayesu*, No. ICTR-96-4-A; *Prosecutor v Akayesu*, No. ICTR-96-4-T.

26. Copelon 2000; *Prosecutor v Akayesu*, No. ICTR-96-4-1.

27. *González and others ('Cotton Field') v Mexico.*

28. See also United Nations Human Rights Council 2010c.

Endnotes

Chapter 1: Legal Frameworks

1. *Meera Dhungana on behalf of FWLD vs. HMG, Ministry of Law and Justice.*

2. Pandey 2002.

3. Domestic Violence (Crime Punishment) Act 2066.

4. Baskota 2010.

5. The Government of Nepal, Ministry of Finance 2010.

6. CBS, NPC and HMG 2002; Dhital 2010.

7. Ipas 2008.

8. Center for Reproductive Rights 2010.

9. Lamsal 2010.

10. In the 1999 elections, women held just 6 percent of the seats. UNDP Nepal 2011; Election Commission, Nepal 2008.

11. Pradhan Malla 2011.

12. See Annex 4; UN Women analysis of data from World Bank 2010c, 2010f and 2010g.

13. Waldorf 2010.

14. Irving 2008; Waylen 2006.

15. UN CEDAW 2009e.

16. EIU 2010a.

17. EIU 2010b.

18. Europa 2010.

19. See UN General Assembly 1957, 1962, 1966a, and 1966b.

20. *Uganda Association of Women Lawyers and others v the Attorney General* as cited in Banda 2008.

21. UN Statistics Division 2010b.

22. This figure excludes China. UNICEF 2009 as cited in UNICEF 2010a.

23. UNICEF 2010a.

24. Note that the statistical definition of child marriage is the proportion of women aged 20 to 24 years who report being married by age 18, but recent data are not available for this indicator, therefore these data are used as a proxy indicator. UN DESA 2004; UN CEDAW 2010a.

25. Kelly 2010.

26. *The Attorney General of the Republic of Botswana v Unity Dow.*

27. UN Women calculation based on Manby 2009.

28. *Toonen v Australia.* Other bodies have also found that sexual orientation is a 'protected ground'. See UN Committee on Economic, Social and Cultural Rights 2003; UN Committee on Economic, Social and Cultural Rights 2000; UN Committee on the Rights of the Child 2003a; UN Committee on the Rights of the Child 2003b; UN Commission on Human Rights 2003b.

29. UN CEDAW 2010c and 2010d, para 18.

30. See for example, UN CEDAW 1999.

31. UN Commission on Human Rights 1997; UN Commission on Human Rights 1999; UN Commission on Human Rights 2002b, para 102; UN Commission on Human Rights 2005, para 27.

32. UN Human Rights Council 2010b.

33. Bruce-Jones and Itaborahy 2011.

34. Cosar and Onbaşi 2008; Ilkkaracan 2007; Anil et al. 2005.

35. UN DPI 2007.

36. See UN General Assembly 1948, 1966a, and 1998; Organization of American States 1994; Council of Europe 2002; African Union 2003; ASEAN 2004.

37. *R v R.*

38. See UN DESA-DAW (now part of UN Women) 2009a and UN Women 2011c.

39. African Union 2003, article 5.

40. UN Women 2010b.

41. Organic Act 1/2004 of 28 December on Integrated Protection Measures Against Gender Violence.

42. UNDP Cambodia 2009.

43. ILO 2009a.

44. ILO 2004.

45. ILC 2010.

46. Perera 2010; Omelaniuk 2005.

47. Human Rights Watch 2006.

48. HomeNet South Asia 2007.

49. HomeWorkers Worldwide 2010.

50. ILO 2010a.

51. UN CEDAW 2008; UN CMW 2011.

52. Human Rights Watch 2010a.

53. Law Number 23 of Year 2004 Regarding Elimination of Violence in Household.

54. OHCHR 2009b.

55. See Annex 4; UN Women analysis of data from World Bank 2010g.

56. The Labour Code of the Socialist Republic Of Viet Nam and Implementation Documents, article 11.

57. ILO 2010b.

58. UNDP 2010b.

59. ILO 2008.

60. Glenn et al. 2009.

61. *Velez and others v Novartis Pharmaceuticals, Novartis Corporation, and Ebeling.*

62. Bray 2010.

63. Office for National Statistics 2010.

64. *Wilson and Ors v North Cumbria Acute NHS Trust.*

65. UNISON 2005.

66. UNISON 2006.

67. Albanesi and Olivetti 2006.

68. Chichilnisky and Hermann Frederiksen 2008; ILC 2009.

69. Correll et al. 2007.

70. World Bank 2010g.

71. Johansson 2010.

72. Glenn et al. 2009.

73. UN Women analysis of information from World Bank 2010f.

74. Villarreal 2006.

75. Nyamu-Musembi 2005.

76. Deininger et al. 2010.

77. Waldorf 2010.

78. IANWGE 2009.

79. This box is adapted from Powley 2006.

80. See Annex 1.

81. Daley et al. 2010.

82. Dore-Weeks and Arnesen 2007; Daley et al. 2010.

83. UN 1994.

84. UN 1995.

85. UN General Assembly 1979.

86. See article 43(1)(a), the Constitution of the Republic of Kenya.

87. Grimes et al. 2006.

88. See for example, UN CEDAW 2006a and 2009b.

89. Center for Reproductive Rights 2010.

90. *A, B and C v Ireland.*

91. *Karen Noelia Llantoy Huamán v Peru; Paulina del Carmen Ramírez Jacinto v Mexico.*

92. OHCHR 2009a.

93. *A. S. v Hungary,* Communication No. 4/2004.

94. UN General Assembly 1979, article 12(2); UN General Assembly 1979, article 16 (1)(e).

95. ERRC 2009.

96. Stefiszyn 2010.

97. Bernard 2010; NAM 2010; GNP+ 2010.

98. Pearshouse 2007; Stefiszyn 2010; IPPF, GNP+ and ICW 2008.

99. UN Human Rights Council 2010b.

100. Stefiszyn 2010.

101. UNAIDS 2008.

102. UN Human Rights Council 2010e; UN 1995; UN General Assembly 2000.

Display. See Annex 1 for the share of women in parliament and quotas; see Annex 5 for UN CEDAW and UN CEDAW reservations. For references for specific sources regarding laws see Harvard School of Public Health 2010. For Macedonia, see also UN CEDAW 2006b; for Tanzania, UN CEDAW 2009d and FAO 2010; for Spain, UN CEDAW 2009a; for Rwanda, Daley, et al. 2010; and for Nepal, UN CEDAW 2004. Information on quotas includes only countries with constitutional or election law quotas at the national parliamentary level.

Chapter 2: The Justice Chain

1. Council of Europe 1950.
2. Abdel Monem 2009.
3. *Bevacqua and S. v Bulgaria.*
4. Protection Against Domestic Violence Act.
5. Makeva 2008 as cited in The Advocates for Human Rights and The Bulgarian Gender Research Foundation 2008.
6. Examples of organizations working to improve the coordinated community response to domestic violence, police structures and response and funding for NGOs include the Bulgarian Gender Research Foundation, Demetra and The Bulgarian Fund for Women as cited in The Advocates for Human Rights and The Bulgarian Gender Research Foundation 2008.
7. UN 2009
8. UN General Assembly 1979.
9. World Values Survey Association 2010.
10. Goldstein 2010; UN Human Rights Council 2008a.
11. The rate of 14 percent was calculated based on a simple average of conviction data for Austria (18 percent), Belgium (4 percent), England (7 percent), Germany (23 percent), Hungary (34 percent), Ireland (8 percent), Portugal (16 percent), Scotland (16 percent), and Sweden (10 percent). Lovett and Kelly 2009.
12. The Asia Foundation 2008.
13. Lanthier 2008.
14. Benradi and Ounnir 2010.
15. DuMont and White 2007; Maru 2006.
16. Amnesty International 2007b.
17. Harrington and Chopra 2010.
18. Telephone interview with Sabin Shrestha, Forum for Women, Law and Development, July 2010, quoted in Bailey 2010.
19. Yrigoyen et al. 2007.
20. Chêne et al. 2010; Goldstein 2010.
21. Balchin 2010b.
22. UN General Assembly 1966a; Skinnider 1999; Smith 2003.
23. Bailey 2010.
24. Morris et al. 2007.
25. Judicial Service of Ghana et al. 2008.
26. UNODC 2006.
27. In response to this, in 2010, the Government of Morocco passed a new law establishing a family assistance fund for indigent women divorcees and their children. Benradi and Ounnir 2010.
28. Sieder and Sierra 2010.
29. Khan et al. 2008.
30. UNAMA 2009.
31. See for example, articles 74, 75, and 76 of the Penal Code of the Islamic Republic of Iran quoted in Equality Now 2004; Sisters of Islam Questionnaire, as cited in Banda 2008.
32. Dyer 2001.
33. UN General Assembly 2001; Crenshaw 2000.
34. *Vertido v The Philippines.*
35. Ateneo Human Rights Center 2010.
36. UN Women 2011b.
37. Criminal Law Amendment Act
38. Promulgation of Combating of Domestic Violence Act.
39. Sexual Offences Act.
40. Ministry of Public Health & Sanitation and Ministry of Medical Services 2009.
41. Population Reference Bureau 2010; National Statistical Committee of the Kyrgyz Republic 2002.
42. UNIFEM (now part of UN Women) 2010.
43. Littel 2001.
44. Campbell 2006.
45. Karanjawala and Chugh 2009.
46. Lawyers Collective Women's Rights Initiative 2008.
47. USAID 2010.
48. UN 2011b.
49. UNIFEM (now part of UN Women) 2009b.
50. DEMI 2007; Sieder and Sierra 2010.
51. Murshed 1998; BRAC 2010.
52. Fiji Women's Crisis Centre 2009; Telephone interview with Edwina Kotuisuva, Fiji Women's Crisis Centre, July 2010, as cited in Bailey 2010.
53. Sardenberg et al. 2010; Jubb et al. 2008.
54. Somaliland is not recognized as a United Nations Member State. UNDP 2007.
55. UN DESA-DAW (now part of UN Women) 2009a recommends laws 'provide for the creation of specialized courts or special court proceedings guaranteeing timely and efficient handling of cases of violence against women.' (Sec. 3.2.5).
56. Cornell University Law School 2011; Valente 2010.
57. Benradi and Ounnir 2010.
58. Welch and Mason 2007.
59. Jenkins and Goetz 2010.
60. Jubb et al. 2008.
61. Peresie 2005, as cited in Feenan 2009.
62. Sakshi 1998; Kapur 2010.
63. Gainsborough 2008.
64. Fair 2009; Kruttschnitt 2010; Caulfield 2010; Bastick et al. 2008.
65. Walmsley 2005; Lemgruber 2000; WHO Europe and UNODC 2009.
66. Townhead 2007.
67. Bastick et al. 2008; Stone 2010.
68. UN DPI 2010.
69. UN 1955.
70. UN General Assembly 2010b.
71. European Parliament 2008; Fair 2009.
72. Munro 2010; UNDEF 2009; Goldstein 2010.
73. WATCH 2008.

Display. UN Women elaboration of data from Vetten et al. 2008.

Chapter 3: Legal Pluralism and Justice for Women

1. CONAMU is a Government body that was created in October 1999 in response to the commitments acquired by the Ecuadorian government at the 1995 Beijing Conference. In May 2009 a new official institution, the Transitional Commission towards the National Commission for Gender Equality (Comisión de Transición hacia el Consejo Nacional para la Igualdad de Género) replaced CONAMU.
2. Sieder and Sierra 2010.
3. See for example, Tamanaha 2008, von Benda-Beckmann 2002 and Merry 1988.
4. Chirayath et al. 2005.
5. UN General Assembly 2007b.
6. ICHRP 2009; Danish Institute for Human Rights forthcoming 2011.
7. Sezgin 2010.
8. Balchin 2010b.
9. ILO 1989.

Endnotes

10. The 11 States are: Argentina, Belize, Brazil, Colombia, Ecuador, Guatemala, Guyana, Mexico, Nicaragua, Paraguay, and the Bolivarian Republic of Venezuela. Based on UN Women's review of legislative sources using Georgetown University 2010.

11. UN General Assembly 2007b.

12. ICHRP 2009.

13. Arbitration Act.

14. UN CEDAW 2009f.

15. Ibid.

16. Coalition Equality Without Reservation 2010.

17. Musawah 2009.

18. See for example, Galanter and Jayanth 2004; World Bank 2011a; Maru 2009.

19. Macaulay 2006; Hein de Campos 2001; Hein de Campos 2003.

20. Balchin 2010a.

21. Balchin 2010b.

22. Chirayath et al. 2005.

23. Case law on the matter was only settled with *Abeysundere v Abeysundere and Attorney General.* See Balchin 2010b.

24. Amnesty International 2007a.

25. Amnesty International 2010.

26. These include Botswana, Burundi, Gambia, Ghana, Lesotho, Malawi, Mauritius, Nigeria, Sierra Leone, Zambia and Zimbabwe.

27. Article 24 (4), the Constitution of the Republic of Kenya.

28. Faundez 2003.

29. Balchin 2010b.

30. Weilenmann 2007; Malzbender et al. 2005; Höhne 2007; Lastarria-Cornhiel 2005; Buur and Kyed 2006; von Benda-Beckmann et al. 2003.

31. Golub 2010.

32. Maru 2007.

33. Warraich 2010.

34. UNICEF Papua New Guinea 2009; Grandjean 2010.

35. The information in this box is from PEKKA and AusAID 2010.

36. CALS 2002; Meer and Sever 2004.

37. CALS 2002.

38. See CEWLA 2006.

39. BAOBAB for Women's Human Rights 2003.

40. Imam 2010.

41. WLUML 1996.

42. Golub 2003.

43. UN Women Burundi 2010.

44. Warraich 2010.

45. Kodikara 2003.

46. Chopra 2007.

47. Nassali 2010.

48. Terven 2008; Sieder and Sierra 2010.

Chapter 4: Justice for Women During and After Conflict

1. UN Women 2010e.

2. Although there is very little available research, it is estimated that men comprise around 10 percent of victims of sexual violence in conflict. See Baaz and Stern 2010. However, in some cases men identify as victims themselves where their female relatives have been attacked, or report on their behalf. Vinck 2010.

3. UNIFEM (now part of UN Women) et al. 2010; Meertens and Zambrano 2010.

4. UN Commission on Human Rights 1996b, para 16.

5. UN Security Council 1993a; UN Security Council 1994a.

6. UN Security Council 2009a, 5.

7. CPC Initiative 2008.

8. Harvard Humanitarian Initiative 2010.

9. Martin and Tirman 2009.

10. Meertens and Zambrano 2010.

11. Defensoría del Pueblo 2008.

12. UNICEF and UNFPA 2005; UNIFEM (now part of UN Women) et al. 2010.

13. Pham et al. 2010.

14. Rubio-Marín 2006.

15. Sex disaggregated statistics not available. Vinck et al. 2008.

16. The Republic of Kenya 2008.

17. Ibid.

18. International Criminal Court 2010a.

19. Sellers 2007.

20. ICRC 1929, article 3; Sellers 2007.

21. UN 1945; UN 1946, article 6.

22. Sellers 2007.

23. Moyo and Reddi 2008.

24. Ungváry 2004; Balthazar 2006.

25. ICRC 1949, article 27; Sellers 2007; ICRC 1977, articles 75 and 76.

26. UN Security Council 1993c, article 5(g); UN Security Council 1994b, article 3.

27. *Prosecutor v Akayesu*, No. ICTR-96-4-T; *Prosecutor v Akayesu* No. ICTR-96-4-A; MacKinnon 2006.

28. *Prosecutor v Anto Furundžija; Prosecutor v Delalic.*

29. *Prosecutor v Krstic;* McHenry 2002.

30. *Prosecutor v Brima, et al.;* Gong-Gershowitz 2009.

31. *Prosecutor v Sylvestre Gacumbitsi; Sylvestre Gacumbitsi v The Prosecutor,* para 155.

32. *Sylvestre Gacumbitsi v The Prosecutor,* para 153 as cited in Sellers 2007.

33. UN General Assembly 1998; International Criminal Court 2010b.

34. International Criminal Court 2011.

35. UN Security Council 2000.

36. UN Security Council 1820.

37. UN Security Council 2009b.

38. UN Security Council 2009c.

39. UN Security Council 2010.

40. Nowrojee 2004.

41. Ibid.

42. Henry 2009.

43. Nowrojee 2004.

44. Horn et al. 2009.

45. Mertus 2004.

46. Scanlon and Muddell 2009.

47. UN Security Council 2002, article 16.

48. Horn et al. 2009.

49. Women's Initiatives for Gender Justice 2009; The Trust Fund for Victims 2010.

50. Women's Initiatives for Gender Justice 2009.

51. Askin 2010; Women's Initiatives for Gender Justice 2009.

52. UN Security Council 2008, article 13.

53. Vinck et al. 2008.

54. UNDP and UNIFEM (now part of UN Women) 2009.

55. UNDP 2010a.

56. Askin 2011a, 2011b and 2011c; American Bar Association Rule of Law Initiative 2009.

57. Adriko 2008.

58. OHCHR 2008a.

59. See for example, the Special Court for Sierra Leone 2010; ECCC 2009.

60. The Democratic Republic of the Congo, Ministry of Justice and Human Rights 2010.

61. IRIN 2009.

62. Human Rights Watch 2010b.

63. Campbell-Nelson 2011.

64. Sierra Leone Truth and Reconciliation Commission 2004.

65. Nesiah et al. 2006.

66. CVR 2003.

67. UN Women 2010c.

68. Nesiah et al. 2006.

69. Ibid.

70. Graybill 2002.

71. International Organising Committee for the Women's International War Crimes Tribunal 2001, articles 874, 875, 883, 888.

72. UN CEDAW 2009c, para 38.

73. UN General Assembly 2007a.

74. Women's League of Burma and the Nobel Women's Initiative 2010.

75. Impunity Watch 2010.

76. Commission for Historical Clarification 2000; Impunity Watch 2010.

77. LACWHN 2010; Tribunal de conciencia contra la violencia sexual hacia las mujeres durante el conflicto armado interno en Guatemala 2010.

78. UN Women 2010a.

79. OHCHR 2008b.

80. UN Human Rights Council 2010c.

81. Rubio-Marín 2006.

82. Duggan et al. 2008.

83. UN Human Rights Council 2010c.

84. UN Human Rights Council 2010c; Chinkin 2008.

85. Duggan et al. 2008.

86. Meertens and Zambrano 2010.

87. OHCHR 2010a.

88. OHCHR 2010b.

89. UN Women et al. 2010; Awareness Times Sierra Leone 2011.

90. UN 2010a; Coalition for Women's Human Rights in Conflict Situations 2007.

91. Bell and O'Rourke 2010; Chinkin 2003.

92. Bell and O'Rourke 2010.

93. Tripp et al. 2009.

Display. We use conflict data from the Uppsala Conflict Data Program (UCDP) and the Centre for the Study of Civil Wars, International Peace Research Institute, Oslo (PRIO) version 4 (2009). Based on case law of the ICTY, ICTR and SCSL, the UN Secretary-General has stated that 'widespread' refers to the large-scale nature of the attack and the number of victims, while 'systematic' refers to the organized nature of the acts of violence and the improbability of their random occurrence; UN Security Council 2009a. For the Hague Conventions, see International Conferences (The Hague) 1907, sec. III, article 46. For the Geneva Convention (1929), see ICRC 1929, article 3. For Second World War, see UN Commission on Human Rights 1996a and UN Commission on Human Rights 2000b, as well as Yoshiaki 2000,

79–80. For the Nuremberg and Tokyo Tribunals, see UN 1945 and 1946, as well as Moyo and Reddi 2008. For the Geneva Convention (1949), see ICRC 1949, article 27. For Protocol I and II to the Geneva Conventions (1977) see, ICRC 1977a, articles 75 and 76; ICRC 1977b, article 4. For the establishment of the International Criminal Court (ICC), see International Criminal Court 2011. For the establishment of the Special Court for Sierra Leone, see *Prosecutor v Brima, et al.*, For Jean-Pierre Bemba case opens as the ICC, see Askin 2010. For Colombia, see United Nations Human Rights Council 2010a, UN Commission on Human Rights 2002b, para 42 and Casa de la Mujer 2011. For Timor-Leste, see UN General Assembly 1999, para 48; for cases, see also paras 50 and 51; see also UN Commission on Human Rights 2000a, paras 35 and 36. For Bosnia and Herzegovina, see UN Security Council 1993b and UN Security Council 1992, as well as UN Security Council 1993a and UN Security Council 1994a. For Rwanda, see UN Commission on Human Rights 1996b, para 16 and the AVEGA study as cited in Amnesty International 2004. For Darfur, see International Commission of Inquiry on Darfur 2005, para 353 and UN Human Rights Council 2008b. For Security Council resolution 1820 see, UN Security Council 2008.

Gender Justice and the Millennium Development Goals

1. For example, see UN DESA-DAW (now part of UN Women) 2009c; UNDG 2009; Millennium Project 2006.

2. UN 2011a.

3. ILO 2011.

4. De Schutter 2010.

5. WFP and FAO 2010.

6. FAO 2011.

7. ECLAC 2004.

8. UN Statistics Division 2010a.

9. Fälth and Blackden 2009.

10. UN 1995.

11. Stiglitz et al. 2009.

12. Rihani et al. 2006.

13. UN 2011a.

14. UNESCO 2010a.

15. Contreras and Talavera Simoni 2003.

16. ILO 2011.

17. UN 2011a.

18. ILO 2009a.

19. UN 2011a.

20. Schurmann 2009; Erulkar and Muthengi 2007.

21. See UN 1995 and UN General Assembly 1979.

22. Countries with constitutional, electoral and/or voluntary party quotas at the national parliamentary level are included in the list of 23. Andorra, Cuba, Belarus, Denmark and New Zealand do not have quotas. International IDEA, Stockholm University and IPU 2010.

23. UN 2011a.

24. UNICEF 2010a.

25. Lawn et al. 2006; UNICEF 2008; WHO 2005; UNESCO 2010b.

26. Sen 2003; UNDP 2010c.

27. OHCHR et al. forthcoming.

28. 2008 estimates. WHO 2010.

29. OHCHR et al. forthcoming.

30. Ibid.

31. Chung and Das Gupta 2007; Sang-Hun 2007.

32. The 14 countries that have achieved 5.5 percent average annual reductions in maternal deaths are: Bhutan, Bolivia (Plurinational State of), China, Egypt, Equatorial Guinea, Eritrea, Estonia, Iran (Islamic Republic of), Latvia, Maldives, Poland, Romania, Turkey and Viet Nam. WHO et al. 2010.

33. UNFPA n.d.

34. Singh et al. 2009.

35. UN 2010d.

36. Batungwanayo and Reyntjens 2006; Marriott et al. 2009.

37. Skilled birth attendance in Indonesia increased from 37 percent in 1994 to 73 percent in 2007. See Harttgen and Klasen 2010.

38. Save the Children 2010.

39. UNAIDS 2010b; UN 2010b; UNAIDS 2010a.

40. US Census Bureau 2010; CDC 2008.

41. UNAIDS 2009; UNAIDS 2010a.

42. Dunkle et al. 2004.

43. UNGASS 2007.

44. London School of Hygiene & Tropical Medicine 2006.

45. Agarwal and Panda 2007; Strickland 2004.

46. UNFPA 2009.

47. Lambrou and Paina 2006.

48. See Adapta Sertão 2009.

49. OECD 2010a.

50. OECD 2010b.

51. This figure refers to the proportion of sector allocable aid from 14 OECD-DAC donors. UN 2010c.

52. World Bank 2010a.

References

Abdel-Monem, T. 2009. "Opuz v Turkey: Europe's Landmark Judgment on Violence Against Women." *Human Rights Brief* 17, no. 1: 29–33.

ACGSD (African Centre for Gender and Social Development). 2010. *Violence Against Women in Africa: A Situational Analysis.* United Nations Economic Commission for Africa.

Adapta Sertão. 2009. "The Adapta Sertão project." http://pintadas-solar.org/default.aspx. Accessed 7 December 2010.

ADFM (Women's Democratic Association of Morocco). 2010. "Home". http://www.adfm.ma. Accessed 15 January 2011.

Adriko, M.J. 2008. "The Domestication of the Rome Statute in Africa: Challenges and Prospects." Background paper prepared for the Obligations of State Parties Under the Rome Statute Workshop organized by the Uganda Coalition on the International Criminal Court, 5–6 September 2008, Entebbe, Uganda.

The Advocates for Human Rights and the Bulgarian Gender Research Foundation. 2008. "Implementation of the Bulgarian Law on Protection against Domestic Violence." *Women's Human Rights Report Series: Bulgaria.* The Advocates for Human Rights, Minneapolis.

African Union. 2003. *Protocol to the African Charter on Human and People's Rights on the Rights of Women in Africa.* 11 July 2003.

Agarwal, B. and Panda, P. 2007. "Toward Freedom from Domestic Violence: The Neglected Obvious." *Journal of Human Development* 8, no. 3: 359–388.

Albanesi, S. and C. Olivetti. 2006. "Home Production, Market Production and the Gender Wage Gap: Incentives and Expectations." Working Paper 12212, National Bureau of Economic Research Working Paper Series. NBER, Cambridge, Massachusetts.

American Bar Association Rule of Law Initiative. 2009. "DRC's Mobile Courts Strike a Blow Against Rape and Related Crimes." November 2009. http://apps.americanbar.org/rol/news/news_drc_mobile_courts_strike_blow%20against_crimes_1109.shtml. Accessed 13 December 2010.

Amnesty International. 2004. *Rwanda: "Marked for Death", rape survivors living with HIV/AIDS in Rwanda.* London: Amnesty International.

——. 2007a. *Maze of Injustice: The Failure to Protect Indigenous Women from Sexual Violence in the USA.* New York: Amnesty International.

——. 2007b. *Uganda: Doubly Traumatised: The lack of access to justice for female victims of sexual and gender-based violence in Northern Uganda.* London: Amnesty International.

——. 2010. "Amnesty International Applauds Passage of Landmark Legislation Addressing Sexual Violence Against Native Women." 21 July 2010. http://www.amnestyusa.org/document.php?id=ENGUSA20100721002&lang=e. Accessed 5 November 2010.

Anil, E., C. Arın, A. B. Hacımirzaoğlu, M. Bingöllü, P. İlkkaracan, and L. E. Amado. 2005. *Turkish Civil and Penal Code Reforms from a Gender Perspective: The Success of Two Nationwide Campaigns.* Istanbul: Women for Women's Human Rights – New Ways.

ASEAN (Association of Southeast Asian Nations). 2004. *Declaration on the Elimination of Violence Against Women in the ASEAN Region.* http://www.aseansec.org/16189.htm. Accessed 21 March 2011.

The Asia Foundation. 2008. *Law and Justice in Timor-Leste: A Survey of Citizen Awareness and Attitudes Regarding Law and Justice.* Timor-Leste: The Asia Foundation; USAID; The Justice Facility; AusAid.

Askin, K. 2010. "Bemba Trial: The International Criminal Court Takes on Gender Crimes." *The Guardian.* 24 November 2010. http://www.guardian.co.uk/law/2010/nov/24/international-criminal-court-international-criminal-justice. Accessed 15 December 2010.

——.2011a. E-mail communication with authors. February 2011.

——. 2011b. "Fizi Diary: Guilty." *Open Society Foundations Blogs.* 22 February 2011. http://blog.soros.org/2011/02/fizi-diary-guilty/. Accessed 16 March 2011.

——. 2011c. "Fizi Diary: Mobile Court Tries Landmark Rape Case." *Open Society Foundations Blogs.* 17 February 2011. http://blog.soros.org/2011/02/fizi-diary-mobile-court-tries-landmark-rape-case/. Accessed 16 March 2011.

Ateneo Human Rights Center. 2010. "CEDAW Interactive Benchbook." http://www.cedawbenchbook.org/. Accessed 15 March 2011.

Awareness Times Sierra Leone. 2011. "In Sierra Leone, NaCSA Certifies Female War Victims." *Local News.* 17 March 2011. http://news.sl/drwebsite/publish/article_200517525.shtml. Accessed 21 March 2011.

AWRO (Observatoire des droits de la femme africaine). 2009. Questionnaire adressé aux États membres.

Ayuko, B. and T. Chopra. 2008. "The Illusion of Inclusion: Women's Access to Rights in Northern Kenya." Justice for the Poor and Legal Resources Foundation Trust, Nairobi.

Baaz, M.E. and M. Stern. 2010. *The Complexity of Violence: A critical analysis of sexual violence in the Democratic Republic of Congo (DRC).* Sida Working Paper on Gender-based Violence. Uppsala: Swedish International Development Cooperation Agency (Sida).

Bailey, S. 2010. "Legal Aid and Women's Access to Justice." Background paper for *Progress of the World's Women 2011–2012.* UN Women, New York.

Balchin, C. 2010a. "Sitting in Judgment: For Men Only?" *openDemocracy.* 2 August 2010. http://www.opendemocracy.net/5050/cassandra-balchin/sitting-in-judgement-for-men-only#. Accessed 5 December 2010.

——. 2010b. "Women's Access to Justice in Plural Legal Orders: Reframing Debates in the Light of Women's Experiences." Background paper for *Progress of the World's Women 2011–2012.* UN Women, New York.

Balthazar, S. 2006. "Gender Crimes and the International Criminal Tribunals." *Gonzaga Journal of International Law* 10, no. 1.

Banda, F. 2008. "Project on a Mechanism to Address Laws that Discriminate Against Women." Women's Rights and Gender Unit, OHCHR, Geneva.

BAOBAB for Women's Human Rights. 2003. *Sharia Implementation in Nigeria: The Journey So Far.* Lagos, Nigeria: BAOBAB.

Baskota, K. H. 2010. "Gender Responsive Budget: the Nepalese Experience." *UN Women, Gender Responsive Budgeting.* http://www.gender-budgets.org/index.php?option=com_content&view=article&id=719:gender-responsive-budget-the-nepalese-experience&catid=51:news&Itemid=642. Accessed 8 December 2010.

Bastick, M., L. Townhead and R. Brett. 2008. *Women in Prison. A Commentary on the UN Standard Minimum Rules for the Treatment of Prisoners.* Human Rights and Refugees Publications. Geneva: Quaker United Nations Office.

Batungwanayo, C. and L. Reyntjens. 2006. "Impact of the Presidential Decree for Free Care on the qf Health Care in Burundi." Ministry of Public Health, Government of Burundi.

Bell, C. and C. O'Rourke. 2010. "Peace agreements or pieces of paper? The impact of UNSC resolution 1325 on peace processes and other agreements." *International and Comparative Law Quarterly*, 59: 941–980.

Benetech. 2010. "The Sierra Leone Truth and Reconciliation Commission data." http://hrdag.org/about/sierra_leone.shtml. Accessed January 2011.

Benradi, M. and A. Ounnir. 2010. "L'acces des Femmes Victimes de Violences a la Justice." Background paper for *Progress of the World's Women 2011–2012.* UN Women, New York.

Bernard, E.J. 2010. "'Where HIV is a crime, not just a virus: a global ranking of prosecutions for HIV non-disclosure, exposure and transmission." Presentation at the XVIII International AIDS Conference, 18–23 July 2010, Vienna, Austria.

Blue Diamond Society. 2007. "Supreme Court Decision – summary note." 21 December 2007. http://www.bds.org.np/decision.html. Accessed 11 February 2011.

Boyenge, J. S. 2007. "ILO Database on Export Processing Zones (Revised)." Sectoral Activities Programme Working Paper (WP.251). ILO, Geneva.

BRAC (Bangladesh Rural Advancement Committee). 2010. "About Human Rights & Legal Aid Services." http://www.brac.net/content/what-we-do-human-rights-legal-aid-services. Accessed 3 December 2010.

Bray, C. 2010. "Novartis Unit Settles Gender Suit for About $175 Million." *The Wall Street Journal.* 14 July 2010. http://online.wsj.com/article/SB10001424052748703394204575367530777045418.html. Accessed 16 February 2011.

Bruce-Jones, E. and L.P. Itaborahy. 2011. *State-sponsored Homophobia: A world survey of laws criminalising same-sex sexual acts between consenting adults.* Brussels: International Lesbian, Gay, Bisexual, Trans and Intersex Association.

Buur, L. and H.M. Kyed. 2006. "State Recognition of Traditional Authority in Mozambique: The Legible Space between State and Community." DIIS Working Paper 36. Danish Institute for International Studies, Copenhagen.

CALS (Centre for Applied Legal Studies). 2002. *Gender, Citizenship and Governance Project.* Amsterdam: Royal Tropical Institute.

Campbell, R. 2006. "Rape Survivors' Experiences with the Legal and Medical Systems." *Violence Against Women* 12, no 1: 30–45.

Campbell-Nelson, K. March 2011. E-mail communication with authors.

Casa de la Mujer 2011. *First Survey on the Prevalence of Sexual Violence against Women in the Context of the Colombian Armed Conflict 2001–2009 Executive Summary.* Campaign Rape and other Violence: Leave my Body Out of War. Bogotá, Oxfam; Ministry of Foreign Affairs; the Netherlands MDG 3 Fund; and Violaciones y Otras Violencias.

Caulfield, L. 2010. "Rethinking the Assessment of Female Offenders." *The Howard Journal of Criminal Justice,* 49, no 4: 315–327

CAVR (Commission for Reception, Truth, and Reconciliation Timor-Leste). 2005. "Chega! The Report of the Commission for Reception, Truth, and Reconciliation Timor-Leste." CAVR, Dili.

CBS (Central Bureau of Statistics), NPC (National Planning Commission) and HMG (His Majesty's Government), the Federal Democratic Republic of Nepal. 2002. "Population Census 2001." National Report in Collaboration with UNFPA Nepal.

CDC (Centers for Disease Control and Prevention). 2000–2009. "International Reproductive Health Surveys: Reports, Publications, and Datasets." http://www.cdc.gov/reproductivehealth/surveys/SurveyCountries.htm. Accessed January 2011.

——. 2001. *HIV/AIDS Surveillance Report.* Atlanta: CDC.

——. 2008. "Subpopulation Estimates from the HIV Incidence Surveillance System – United States, 2006." Morbidity and Mortality Weekly Reports, 57, no. 36: 985–989.

Center for Reproductive Rights. 2010. "A Ten-Year Retrospective: Reproductive Rights at the Start of the 21st Century: Global Progress, Yet Backpedaling on Gains in U.S." Center for Reproductive Rights, New York.

CEWLA (The Centre for Egyptian Women's Legal Assistance). 2006. http://www.cewla.org/. Accessed 24 February 2011.

Chávez, C. 2008. "Del deber ser a la Praxis: Los jueces de paz en el renovado Campo Judicial de Cuetzalan ¿Hacia un Fortalecimiento de la Jurisdicción Indígena?" MA Thesis in Social Anthropology. Centro de Investigaciones y Estudios Superiores en Antropología Social, Mexico City.

Chêne, M., B. Clench, and C. Fagan. 2010. "Corruption and Gender in Service Delivery: The Unequal Impacts." Working Paper #02/2010. Transparency International, Berlin.

Chichilnisky, G. and E. Hermann Frederiksen. 2008. "An Equilibrium Analysis of the Gender Wage Gap." *International Labour Review* 147, no. 4: 297–320.

Chinkin, C. 2003. "Peace Agreements as a Means for Promoting Gender Equality and Ensuring Participation of Women." Background paper prepared for the UN DESA-DAW (now part of UN Women) Expert Group Meeting on Peace agreements as a means for promoting gender equality and ensuring participation of women – A framework of model provisions EGM/PEACE/2003/BP.1, 10–13 November 2003, Ottawa, Canada.

——. 2008. "The Protection of Economic, Social and Cultural Rights Post-Conflict." Women's Human Rights and Gender Section, OHCHR, Geneva.

Chirayath, L., C. Sage, and M. Woolcock. 2005. "Customary Law and Policy Reform: Engaging with the Plurality of Justice Systems." Background paper for the *World Development Report 2006: Equity and Development.* World Bank, Washington, DC.

Chopra, T. 2007. "Promoting Women's Rights by Indigenous Means: An Innovative Project in Kenya." *Justice for the Poor Briefing Note* 1, no. 2 . World Bank, Washington, DC.

Christensen, M. 2010. "Worldwide Guide to Women in Leadership." http://www.guide2womenleaders.com/index.html. Accessed 30 November 2010.

Chung, W. and M. Das Gupta. 2007. "Why is Son Preference Declining in South Korea? The Role of Development and Public Policy, and the Implications for China and India." Policy Research Working Paper 4373. Development Research Group, Human Development and Public Services Team, World Bank, Washington, DC.

Coalition Equality Without Reservation. 2010. "Home." http://cedaw.wordpress.com/. Accessed 2 February 2011.

Coalition for Women's Human Rights in Conflict Situations. 2007. "Nairobi Declaration on Women's and Girls' Right to a Remedy and Reparation." International Meeting on Women's and Girls' Right to Remedy and Reparation, 19–21 March 2007, Nairobi, Kenya.

CODHES (Consultoría para los Derechos Humanos y el Desplazamiento). 2010. "Salto estratégico o salto al vacío?" CODHES, Bogotá.

Commission for Historical Clarification. 2000. *Guatemala: Memory of Silence: Report of the Commission for Historical Clarification,* http://shr.aaas.org/guatemala/ceh/report/english/toc.html. Accessed 16 March 2011.

Contreras, M. and M. Talavera Simoni. 2003. "The Bolivian Education Reform 1992–2002: Case Studies in Large Scale Education Reform." *Education Reform and Management Publication Series* 2, no. 2.

Copelon, R. 2000. "Gender Crimes as War Crimes: Integrating Crimes against Women into International Criminal Law." *McGill Law Journal* 46, no. 1: 217–240.

Cornell University Law School. 2011. "Gender Justice in the Argentine Context: Justice Highton de Nolasco Shares her Views." *Women and Justice.* http://www.lawschool.cornell.edu/womenandjustice/features/details.cfm?id=169585. Accessed January 2011.

Correll, S., S. Benard, and I. Paik. 2007. "Getting a Job: Is there a Motherhood Penalty?" *American Journal of Sociology* 112, no. 5: 1297–1338.

Cosar, S. and F. G. Onbaşi. 2008. "Women's Movement in Turkey at a Crossroads: From Women's Rights Advocacy to Feminism." *South European Society and Politics* 13, no. 3: 325–344.

Council of Europe. 1950. *European Convention for the Protection of Human Rights and Fundamental Freedoms.* 4 November 1950. ETS 5.

——. 2002. *Recommendation Rec(2002)5 of the Committee of Ministers to Member States on the Protection of Women Against Violence.* 30 April 2002.

References

——. 2007. *Legislation in the Member States of the Council of Europe in the Field of Violence Against Women. Volume I: Albania to Ireland.* Strasbourg: France.

——. 2009a. *Legislation in the Member States of the Council of Europe in the Field of Violence Against Women. Volume I: Armenia to Lithuania.* September 2009. Strasbourg: France.

——. 2009b. *Legislation in the Member States of the Council of Europe in the Field of Violence Against Women. Volume II: Moldova to United Kingdom.* Strasbourg: France.

——. 2009c. *Rape of women, including marital rape.* Doc. 12013. http://assembly.coe.int/Main.asp?link=/Documents/WorkingDocs/Doc09/EDOC12013.htm. Accessed January 2011.

CPC Initiative (Care and Protection of Children (CPC) in Crisis Affected Countries initiative). 2008. *Care and Protection of Children in Crisis Affected Countries: A Good Practice–Policy Change Initiative.* New York: Program on Forced Migration and Health, Mailman School of Public Health, Columbia University.

Crenshaw, K. 2000. "Gender-Related Aspects of Race Discrimination." Background paper for the United Nations Expert Group Meeting on Gender and Racial Discrimination, 21–24 November 2000, Zagreb, Croatia.

CVR (Comisión de la Verdad y Reconciliación). 2003. "Report of the Peru Truth and Reconciliation Commission." 28 August 2003. http://www.cverdad.org.pe/ingles/pagina01.php. Accessed 14 January 2011.

Daley, E., R. Dore-Weeks, and C. Umuhoza. 2010. "Ahead of the Game: Land Tenure Reform in Rwanda and the Process of Securing Women's Land Rights." *Journal of Eastern African Studies* 4, no. 1: 131–152.

Danish Institute for Human Rights. Forthcoming 2011. *Study on Informal Justice Systems: Access to Justice and Human Rights.* Copenhagen: Danish Institute for Human Rights.

De Schutter, O. 2010. "Food Commodities Speculation and Food Price Crises: Regulation to Reduce the Risks of Price Volatility." Briefing Note 02 – September 2010. United Nations Human Rights Council, New York.

Defensoría del Pueblo. 2008. *Promoción y Monitoreo de los Derechos Sexuales y Reproductivos de Mujeres Víctimas de Desplazamiento Forzado con Énfasis en Violencias Intrafamiliar y Sexual.* Bogota: Defensoría del Pueblo, USAID and International Organization for Migration.

Deininger, K., A. Goyal and H. Nagarajan. 2010. "Inheritance Law Reform and Women's Access to Capital: Evidence from India's Hindu Succession Act." Policy Research Working Paper 5338. World Bank, Washington DC.

DEMI (Defensoría de la Mujer Indígena). 2007. *El Acceso de las Mujeres Indígenas al Sistema de Justicia Oficial de Guatemala: Segundo Informe.* Guatemala: DEMI.

The Democratic Republic of the Congo, Ministry of Justice and Human Rights. 2010. "Press Release Of His Excellency, the Minister of Justice and Human Rights." Grand Hotel Kinshasa, 2 October 2010. http://www.justice.gov.cd/j/index.php?option=com_docman&task=cat_view&gid=19&dir=DESC&order=name&Itemid=54&limit=5&limitstart=15 (filed under "Discours sur le Rapport du projet mapping"). Accessed 22 March 2011.

Dhital, M. 2010. "Gender Issues in Agriculture and Land." *Land First, Journal of Land and Agrarian Reforms*, 10: 14–19.

Dore-Weeks, R. and K. Arnesen. 2007. *Facilitating a Shift to Gender Equitable Land Distribution: Legal Frameworks, Inheritance Patterns and the Gap between Policy and Practice.* African Rights, Kigali.

Dow, U. (Ed.) 1995. *The Citizenship Case: The Attorney General of the Republic of Botswana vs. Unity Dow, Court Documents, Judgements, Cases and Material.* Gaborone: Lentswe la Lesedi.

Du Mont, J. and D. White. 2007. *The uses and impacts of medico-legal evidence in sexual assault cases: A global review.* Sexual Violence Research Initiative. Geneva: World Health Organization.

Duggan, C., C. Paz y Paz Bailey, and J. Guillerot. 2008. "Reparations for Sexual and Reproductive Violence: Prospects for Achieving Gender Justice in Guatemala and Peru." *The International Journal of Transitional Justice* 2, no. 7: 192–213.

Dunkle, K., R. Jewkes, H. Brown, G. Gray, J. McIntryre, and S. Harlow. 2004. "Gender-Based Violence, Relationship Power, and Risk of HIV Infection in Women Attending Antenatal Clinics in South Africa." *The Lancet* 363, no. 9419: 1415–1421.

Dyer, C. 2001. "Lords rule rape shield law unfair." *The Guardian.* 18 May 2001. http://www.guardian.co.uk/uk/2001/may/18/lords.politics. Accessed 3 December 2010.

ECCC (Extraordinary Chambers in the Courts of Cambodia). 2009. "Extraordinary Chambers in the Courts of Cambodia." http://www.eccc.gov.kh/english/. Accessed 13 December 2010.

ECLAC (Economic Commission for Latin America and the Caribbean). 2004. "Poverty and Inequality from a Gender Perspective." *Social Panorama of Latin America, 2002–2003.* Santiago: ECLAC.

ECLAC Subregional Headquarters for the Caribbean. May 2011. E-mail communication with authors.

EIU (Economist Intelligence Unit). 2010a. "New study spotlights opportunities and barriers for working women worldwide." *Women's economic opportunity Index.* http://www.eiu.com/sponsor/weo. Accessed 10 March 2011.

——. 2010b. *Women's economic opportunity: A new pilot index and global ranking from the Economist Intelligence Unit.* London: EIU.

Election Commission, Nepal. 2008. "Constituent Assembly 2064, List of Winning Candidates." http://www.election.gov.np/EN/. Accessed 16 February 2011.

ELLN (European Labour Law Network). 2010. "New law on non-discrimination on the grounds of gender (28-04-2010)." *Legislative developments.* http://www.labourlawnetwork.eu/national_labour_law/legislative_developments/prm/109/v__detail/ses_id__5c8c37dc222e711184d541bea86c42af/id__1041/category__4/size__1/index.html. Accessed 15 March 2011.

EMACE (Environment & Science, Manpower & Skills, Adult & Parenthood Development Assistance, Childcare & Women's Rights, Education & Culture). 2010. EMACE Sri Lanka. http://www.emacesrilanka.com. Accessed 30 December 2010.

Equality Now. 2004. *Words and Deeds: Holding Governments Accountable in the Beijing + 10 Review Process.* New York: Equality Now.

ERRC (European Roma Rights Centre). 2009. "Hungary provides compensation to coercively sterilised Romani Woman." http://www.errc.org/cikk.php?cikk=3011. Accessed 9 March 2011.

Erulkar, A. and E. Muthengi. 2007. *Evaluation of Berhane Hewan: A Pilot Program to Promote Education & Delay Marriage in Rural Ethiopia.* New York: The Population Council.

Europa. 2010. "Equality: Commission welcomes end of discriminatory pension ages in Greece and Italy; closes infringement cases." *Press Releases.* 24 November 2010. http://europa.eu/rapid/pressReleasesAction.do?reference=IP/10/1553&type=HTML. Accessed 15 March 2011.

European Parliament. 2008. *Report on the situation of women in prison and the impact of the imprisonment of parents on social and family life (2007/2116(INI)).* A6-0033/2008

Fair, H. 2009. "International review of women's prisons." *Prison Service Journal*, 184.

Fälth, A. and M. Blackden. 2009. "Unpaid Care Work." Policy Brief: Gender Equality and Poverty Reduction, Issue 01. UNDP, New York.

FAO (Food and Agriculture Organization of the United Nations). 2010. "Gender and Land Rights Database." http://www.fao.org/gender/landrights. Accessed 30 November 2010.

———. 2011. *The State of Food and Agriculture: Women in Agriculture: closing the gender gap for development.* Rome: FAO.

Faundez, J. 2003. "Non-State Justice Systems in Latin America Case Studies: Peru and Colombia." Prepared for the Workshop on Working with Non-State Justice Systems. UK Department for International Development, London.

Feenan, D. 2009. "Editorial Introduction: Women and Judging." *Feminist Legal Studies* 17, no. 1: 1–9.

Fiji Women's Crisis Centre. 2009. "National Research on Domestic Violence and Sexual Assault." http://www.fijiwomen.com/index.php?option=com_content&view=article&id=99&Itemid=80. Accessed 3 December 2010.

Gainsborough, J. 2008. "Women In Prison: International Problems and Human Rights Based Approaches to Reform." *William and Mary Journal of Women and the Law,* 14: 271.

Galanter, M. and K. Jayanth. 2004. "Bread for the Poor: Access to Justice and the Rights of the Needy in India." *Hastings Law Journal* 55, no. 4: 789–834.

García-Moreno, C., H. Jansen, M. Ellsberg, L. Heise, and C. Watts. 2005. *WHO Multi-country Study on Women's Health and Domestic Violence against Women: Initial results on prevalence, health outcomes and women's responses.* Geneva: WHO.

Gentleman, A. 2009. "Who is worth more to society, a classroom assistant or a gravedigger?" *Guardian.* 16 March 2009. http://www.guardian.co.uk/world/2009/mar/16/equal-pay-claims-gender%20-. Accessed 20 December 2010.

Georgetown University. 2010. "Political Database of the Americas." http://pdba.georgetown.edu. Accessed 30 December 2010.

Glenn, S., S. Melis, and L. Withers. 2009. *Gender (in)equality in the labour market: an overview of global trends and developments.* Brussels: International Trade Union Confederation and Income Data Services.

Global Barometer Surveys. 2010. "Global Barometer Database." http://www.globalbarometer.net/. Accessed October 2010.

GNP+ (Global Network of People Living with HIV/AIDS). 2010. *The Global Criminalisation Scan Report 2010: Documenting trends, presenting evidence.* Amsterdam: GNP+.

Goldstein, A. 2010. "Functioning of Courts and Women's Access to Justice." Background paper for *Progress of the World's Women 2011–2012.* UN Women, New York.

Golub, S. 2003. "Non-state Justice Systems in Bangladesh and the Philippines." Prepared for the Workshop on Working with Non-State Justice Systems. UK Department for International Development, London.

———. 2010. "Legal Empowerment: Practitioners' Perspectives." Legal and Governance Reform: Lessons Learned, No. 2. Rome: International Development Law Organization.

Gong-Gershowitz, J. 2009. "Forced Marriage: A 'New' Crime Against Humanity?" *Northwestern Journal of International Human Rights,* 8, no. 1: 53–76.

The Government of Nepal, Ministry of Finance. 2010. "Public Statement on Income and Expenditure of Fiscal Year 2010–11." Available at http://mof.gov.np/publication/speech/2010_1/pdf/budgetspeech_english.pdf.

Grandjean, A. 2010. "No Rights Without Accountability: Promoting Access to Justice for Children." Legal Empowerment Working Paper No. 10. International Development Law Organization, Rome.

Graybill, L. 2002. *Truth and Reconciliation in South Africa: Miracle or Model?* Boulder: Lynne Rienner Publishers, Inc.

Grimes, D.A., J. Benson, S. Singh, M. Romero, B. Ganatra, F.E. Okonofua, and I.H. Shah. 2006. "Unsafe abortion: the preventable pandemic." *The Lancet* 368, no. 9550: 1908–1919.

Harrington, A. and T. Chopra. 2010. "Arguing Traditions: Denying Kenya's Women Access to Land Rights." Justice for the Poor Research Report No. 2. World Bank, Washington, DC.

Harttgen, K. and S. Klasen. 2010. Computation of Statistics using DHS Surveys (ICF Macro) Prepared for *Progress of the World's Women 2011–2012.* UN Women, New York.

Harvard Humanitarian Initiative. 2010. "Now, the World is Without Me: An Investigation of Sexual Violence in Eastern Democratic Republic of Congo." A Report by the Harvard Humanitarian Initiative with Support from Oxfam America. Harvard Humanitarian Initiative, Cambridge, Massachusetts.

Harvard School of Public Health. 2010. "Annual Review of Population Law Database." http://www.hsph.harvard.edu/population/annual_review.htm. Accessed 30 December 2010.

Hein de Campos, C. 2001. "Violência Doméstica no Espaço da lei." In *Tempos e Lugares de Gênero.* C. Bruschini and C. Pinto (Eds.). Sao Paulo: Fundaçao Carlos Chagas. 301–323.

———. 2003. "Juizados Especiais Criminais e seu Déficit Téorico." *Revista Estudos Feministas* 11, no. 1: 155–170.

Henry, N. 2009. "Witness to Rape: The Limits and Potential of International War Crimes Trials for Victims of Wartime Sexual Violence." *International Journal of Transitional Justice* 3, no. 1: 114–134.

Höhne, M. 2007. "From Pastoral to State Politics: Traditional Authorities in Northern Somalia." In *State Recognition and Democratization in Sub-Saharan Africa: A New Dawn for Traditional Authorities?* L. Buur and H. Kyed (Eds.). New York: Palgrave Macmillan.

HomeNet South Asia. 2007. "About Us." *HomeNet South Asia.* http://www.homenetsouthasia.org/index.php. Accessed 8 December 2010.

HomeWorkers Worldwide. 2010. "About Us/What is Homework?" http://www.homeworkersww.org.uk/about-us/what-is-homework. Accessed 20 October 2010.

Horn, R., S. Charters and S. Vahidy. 2009. "Testifying in an International War Crimes Tribunal: The Experience of Witnesses in the Special Court for Sierra Leone." *International Journal of Transitional Justice* 3, no. 1: 135–149.

Human Rights Watch. 2006. *Swept Under the Rug: Abuses Against Domestic Workers Around the World.* New York: Human Rights Watch.

———. 2010a. *Slow Reform: Protection of Migrant Domestic Workers in Asia and the Middle East.* New York: Human Rights Watch.

———. 2010b. *World Report 2010.* New York: Human Rights Watch.

Hunter, R. 2008. "Can Feminist Judges Make a Difference?" *International Journal of the Legal Profession* 15, no. 1–2: 7–36.

IANWGE (United Nations Inter-Agency Network on Women and Gender Equality). 2009. "CEDAW Success Stories." *30 Years: United Nations Convention on the Elimination of All Forms of Discrimination against Women.* http://www.unifem.org/cedaw30/success_stories/#kyrgyzstan2. Accessed 19 August 2010.

ICHRP (International Council on Human Rights Policy). 2009. *When Legal Worlds Overlap: Human Rights, State and Non-State Law.* Versoix: ICHRP.

ICRC (International Committee of the Red Cross). 1929. *Geneva Convention Relative to the Treatment of Prisoners of War.* 27 July 1929. http://www.icrc.org/ihl.nsf/full/305?opendocument. Accessed 5 May 2011.

References

———. 1949. *Geneva Convention Relative to the Protection of Civilian Persons in Time of War (Fourth Geneva Convention).* 12 August 1949. 75 UNTS 287.

———.1977a. *Protocol Additional to the Geneva Conventions of 12 August 1949, and Relating to the Protection of Victims of International Armed Conflicts (Protocol I).* 8 June 1977. 1125 UNTS 3.

———. 1977b. *Protocol Additional to the Geneva Conventions of 12 August 1949, and relating to the Protection of Victims of Non-International Armed Conflicts (Protocol II).* 8 June 1977. 1125 UNTS 609.

ICVS (The International Crime Victim Survey). Latest available. "The 2004/05 International Crime Victims Survey." http://rechten.uvt.nl/icvs/index.htm. Accessed February 2011.

ILC (International Labour Conference). 2009. *Gender Equality at the Heart of Decent Work.* 98th session, Sixth item on the agenda, Report VI. ILO, Geneva.

———. 2010. *Decent Work for Domestic Workers.* 99th session, Fourth item on the agenda, Report IV(1). ILO, Geneva.

Ilkkaracan, P. 2007. "Reforming the Penal Code in Turkey: The Campaign for the Reform of the Turkish Penal Code from a Gender Perspective." Prepared for the project on Citizen Engagement and National Policy Change. Institute of Development Studies, Brighton, UK.

ILO (International Labour Organization). 1989. *Indigenous and Tribal Peoples Convention, C169.* 27 June 1989.

———. 2004. "Work-family reconciliation: What trade unions are doing." Information Sheet No. WF-8. ILO, Geneva.

———. 2008. *Global Wage Report 2008/09: Minimum wages and collective bargaining, Towards policy coherence.* Geneva: ILO.

———. 2009a. *Global Employment Trends for Women: March 2009.* Geneva: ILO.

———. 2009b. *Key Indicators of the Labor Market* (6th Edition). Geneva: ILO.

———. 2010a. "Domestic Workers." http://www.ilo.org/travail/areasofwork/lang--en/WCMS_DOC_TRA_ARE_DOM_EN/index.htm. Accessed 3 November 2010.

———. 2010b. *Women in labour markets: Measuring progress and identifying challenges.* Geneva: ILO.

———. 2011. *Global Employment Trends 2011: The challenge of a jobs recovery.* Geneva: ILO.

Imam, A. September 2010. E-mail communication with authors.

Impunity Watch. 2010. "Guatemalan women hold Tribunal of Conscience." *News.* 8 April 2010. http://www.impunitywatch.org/en/publication/67. Accessed 16 March 2011.

International Commission of Inquiry on Darfur. 2005. *Report of the International Commission of Inquiry on Darfur to the United Nations Secretary-General: Pursuant to Security Council resolution 1564 of 18 September 2004.* Geneva: International Commission of Inquiry on Darfur.

International Conferences (The Hague). 1907. *Hague Convention (IV) Respecting the Laws and Customs of War on Land and Its Annex: Regulations Concerning the Laws and Customs of War on Land.* 18 October 1907.

International Criminal Court. 2010a. "ICC judges grant the Prosecutor's request to launch an investigation on crimes against humanity with regard to the situation in Kenya." *Press Releases (2010).* 31 March 2010. http://www.icc-cpi.int/Menus/Go?id=e808c0b7-e0f8-4 d56-9ced-3c724c0df81f&lan=en-GB. Accessed 16 March 2011.

———. 2010b. "The States Parties to the Rome Statute." http://www.icc-cpi.int/menus/asp/states%20parties/the%20states%20parties%20to%20the%20rome%20statute?lan=en-GB. Accessed 15 October 2010.

———. 2011. "Situations and cases." http://www.icc-cpi.int/Menus/ICC/Situations+and+Cases/. Accessed April 2011.

International Criminal Tribunal for Rwanda. 1998. "Handbook for Journalists." *International Criminal Tribunal for Rwanda.* http://www.unictr.org/News/HandbookforJournalists/tabid/68/Default.aspx. Accessed 14 January 2011.

International IDEA (Institute for Democracy and Electoral Assistance), Stockholm University, and IPU (Inter-Parliamentary Union). 2010. "Global Database of Quotas for Women." http://www.quotaproject.org/. Accessed 7 December 2010.

International Organising Committee for the Women's International War Crimes Tribunal. 2001. *Judgement on the Common Indictment and the Application for Restitution and Reparation (Case No. PT-2000-1-T).* The Women's International War Crimes Tribunal for the Trial of Japan's Military Sexual Slavery, The Hague.

Ipas. 2008. "Medical abortion increasing safe abortion access in Nepal." 9 June 2008. http://www.ipas.org/Library/News/News_Items/Medical_abortion_increasing_safe_abortion_access_in_Nepal.aspx. Accessed 24 February 2011.

IPPF (International Planned Parenthood Federation), GNP+ (Global Network of People Living with HIV/AIDS), and ICW (International Community of Women Living with HIV/AIDS. 2008. *HIV: Verdict on a Virus: Public Health, Human Rights and Criminal Law.* London: IPPF, GNP+ and ICW.

IPU (Inter-Parliamentary Union). 2010a. "Women in national parliaments: Statistical archive." http://www.ipu.org/wmn-e/world.htm. Accessed 30 November 2010.

———. 2010b. "Women in Parliament in 2009: The Year in Perspective." IPU, Geneva.

———. 2010c. "Women in Politics: 2010." http://www.ipu.org/pdf/publications/wmnmap10_en.pdf. Accessed 3 January 2011.

———. 2010d. "Women's Suffrage." http://www.ipu.org/wmn-e/suffrage.htm. Accessed 4 January 2011.

———. 2011a. "Women in national parliaments" http://www.ipu.org/wmn-e/classif.htm. Accessed 1 February 2011.

———. 2011b. "Women Speakers of National Parliaments: History and the Present." http://www.ipu.org/wmn-e/speakers.htm. Accessed 4 January 2011.

Iqbal, F. 27 October 2010. E-mail communication with authors.

IRC (International Rescue Committee). 2009. "Congo Crisis." IRC, New York.

IRIN. 2009. "Rwanda: Jury still out on effectiveness of 'Gacaca' courts," 23 June 2009. http://www.irinnews.org/report.aspx?ReportID=84954. Accessed 3 December 2010.

Irving, H. 2008. *Gender and the Constitution: Equity and Agency in Comparative Constitutional Design.* New York: Cambridge University Press.

ITUC (International Trade Union Confederation). 2007. *Internationally-Recognised Core Labour Standards in Gabon and Cameroon.* Report for the WTO General Council Review of the Trade Policies of Gabon and Cameroon, 2 and 4 October 2007.

Jenkins, R. and A. Goetz. 2010. "Addressing Sexual Violence in Internationally Mediated Peace Negotiations." *International Peacekeeping* 17, no. 2: 261–277.

Jivan V. and C. Forster. 2007. *Translating CEDAW into Law: CEDAW Legislative Compliance in Nine Pacific Island Countries.* Suva, Fiji: UNDP Pacific Centre and UNIFEM Pacific Regional Office.

Johansson, E. 2010. "The Effect of Own and Spousal Parental Leave on Earnings." Working Paper 2010: 4. The Institute for Labour Market Policy Evaluation, Uppsala, Sweden.

Johnson, H., N. Ollus, and S. Nevala. 2008. *Violence Against Women: An International Perspective.* New York: Springer.

Jubb, N., G. Camacho, A. D'Angela, G. Yáñez De la Borda, K. Hernández, I. Macassi León, C. MacDowell Santos, Y. Molina, and W. Pasinato. 2008. *Regional Mapping Study of Women's Police Stations in Latin America.* Access to Justice for Women in Situations of Violence: A Comparative Study of Women's Police Stations in Latin America. Quito, Ecuador and Ottawa. Centro de Planificación y Estudios Sociales and International Development Research Centre.

Judicial Service of Ghana, UNDP (United Nations Development Programme), UNIFEM (United Nations Development Fund for Women, now part of UN Women), ILAC (International Legal Assistance Consortium), IAWJ (International Association of Women Judges), and International Center for Ethics, Justice and Public Life, Brandeis University. 2008. "The Role of the Judiciary in Promoting Gender Justice in Africa." *Report of the Partners for Gender Justice Conference hosted by the Judicial Service of Ghana.* 19–21 November 2008, Accra, Ghana.

Kapur, N. 8 December 2010. E-mail communication with authors.

Karanjawala, T., and S. Chugh. 2009. "The Legal Battle against Domestic Violence in India: Evolution and Analysis." *International Journal of Law, Policy and the Family* 23, no. 3: 289–308.

Kathrynp. 2010. "Jackie Gilchrist, Teaching Assistant and Equal Pay Claimant." *Sheblogs.* http://www.sheblogs.co.uk/2010/07/19/jackie-gilchrist-teaching-assistant-and-equal-pay-claimant/. Accessed 13 December 2010.

Kelly, S. and J. Breslin (Eds.). 2010. *Women's Rights in the Middle East and North Africa: Progress Amid Resistance.* New York: Freedom House; Lanham, Maryland: Rowman & Littlefield.

Khan, M.E., I. Bhuiya, A. Bhattacharya, and A. Bansal. 2008. "A Situation Analysis of Care and Support for Rape Survivors at First Point of Contact in India and Bangladesh." Population Council and USAID, New Delhi.

Kishor, S. and K. Johnson. 2004. *Profiling domestic violence: A multi-country study.* Calverton, Maryland: ORC Macro.

Kodikara, C. 2003. "Engaging with Muslim Personal Law in Sri Lanka: The Experience of MWRAF." *Lines Magazine.* August 2003.

Kruttschnitt, C. 2010. "The paradox of women's imprisonment." *Daedalus,* 139, no. 3: 5–7.

LACWHN (Latin American and Caribbean Women's Health Network). 2010. "Tribunal of Conscience Against Sexual Violence in Guatemala." *News.* 20 March 2010. http://www.reddesalud.org/news/act1_int.php?id=82. Accessed 11 March 2011.

Lambrou, Y. and G. Paina. 2006. *Gender: The Missing Component of the Response to Climate Change.* Rome: FAO.

Lamsal, N. R. 2010. "Measuring Maternal Mortality Rate in Nepal: Initiatives and Efforts." ESA/STAT/AC.219/18. Presentation at the Global Forum on Gender Statistics, 11–13 October 2010. Manila, Philippines.

Lanthier, S. 2008. *Documenting Women's Experiences with the Toronto Police Services in Domestic Violence Situations.* Toronto: Women Abuse Council of Toronto.

Lastarria-Cornhiel, S. 2005. "Gender and Property Rights within Postconflict Situations." Issue Paper No. 12. USAID, Washington, DC.

Lawn, J., J. Zupan, G. Begkoyian, and R. Knippenberg. 2006. "Newborn Survival." In *Disease Control Priorities in Developing Countries.* D. Jamison, J. Breman, A. Measham, G. Alleyne et al. (Eds.). Washington, DC: World Bank

Lawyers Collective Women's Rights Initiative. 2008. *Staying Alive: Second Monitoring and Evaluation Report 2008 on the Protection of Women from Domestic Violence Act, 2005.* New Delhi: Lawyers Collective.

Lemgruber, J. 2000. "Women in the Criminal Justice System" In *Women in the Criminal Justice System: International Examples & National Responses.* N. Ollus and S. Nevala (Eds.). Proceedings of the workshop held at the Tenth United Nations Congress on the Prevention of Crime and the Treatment of Offenders, 10–17 April 2000, Vienna, Austria.

Littel, K. 2001. "Sexual Assault Nurse Examiner (SANE) Programs: Improving the Community Response to Sexual Assault Victims." OVC Bulletin. US Department of Justice, Washington, DC.

London School of Hygiene & Tropical Medicine. 2006. "HIV trial in South Africa cuts domestic violence rates by 55%." *2006 Press Releases.* http://www.lshtm.ac.uk/news/2006/imagetrial.html. Accessed 25 February 2011.

Lovett, J. and L. Kelly. 2009. *Different systems, similar outcomes? Tracking attrition in reported rape cases across Europe.* London: Child and Women Abuse Studies Unit, London Metropolitan University.

Macaulay, F. 2006. "Judicialising and (De)criminalising Domestic Violence in Latin America." *Social Policy and Society* 5, no. 1: 103–114.

MacKinnon, C. 2006. "Defining Rape Internationally: A Comment on *Akayesu.*" *Columbia Journal of Transnational Law,* 44, no. 3: 940–58

Makeva, B. 2008. "Initiatives of the Ministry of Interior and the National Police Service for Prevention and Counteraction to Domestic Violence, Undertaken in Fulfillment of the Law for Protection Against Domestic Violence, at 3." Unpublished manuscript. The Advocates for Human Rights, New York.

Malzbender, D., J. Goldin, A. Turton, and A. Earle. 2005. "Traditional Water Governance and South Africa's 'National Water Act' – Tension or Cooperation?" International Workshop on African Water Laws: Plural Legislative Frameworks for Rural Water Management in Africa, 26–28 January 2005, Johannesburg, South Africa.

Manby, B. 2009. *Citizenship Law in Africa: A Comparative Study.* New York: Africa Governance Monitoring and Advocacy Project and Open Society Justice Initiative.

Marriott, A., B. Goodey, and C. Green. 2009. *Your Money or Your Life: Will leaders act now to save lives and make health care free in poor countries?* London: Oxfam International.

Martin, S. and Tirman, J. 2009. *Women, Migration, and Conflict: Breaking a Deadly Cycle.* New York: Springer.

Maru, V. 2006. "Between Law and Society: Paralegals and the Provision of Primary Justice Services in Sierra Leone and Worldwide." *The Yale Journal of International Law* 31, no. 427: 428–476.

———. 2007. "Timap for Justice: A Paralegal Approach for Justice Services in Sierra Leone." In *Access to Justice in Africa and Beyond: Making the Rule of Law a Reality.* Penal Reform International (PRI) and Bluhm Legal Clinic of the Northwestern University School of Law (Eds.). Chicago: PRI and Bluhm Legal Clinic of the Northwestern University School of Law.

———. 2009. "Access to Justice and Legal Empowerment: A Review of World Bank Practice." Justice & Development Working Paper 51843. World Bank, Washington DC.

McHenry, J.R. 2002. "The Prosecution of Rape Under International Law: Justice That Is Long Overdue." *Vanderbilt Journal of Transnational Law,* 35: 1269–1311

MEASURE DHS. 2000–2009. "Domestic Violence Module Country Reports." http://www.measuredhs.com/topics/gender/dv_surveys.cfm.

———. Latest available (2004–2009). "Demographic and Health Surveys." http://www.measuredhs.com/accesssurveys/. Accessed January 2011.

———. 2010. "STATCompiler." http://www.statcompiler.com/start.cfm?action=new_table&userid=309121&usertabid=333815&CFID=7589885&CFTOKEN=36776915. Accessed 30 November 2010.

References

Meer, S. and C. Sever. 2004. *Gender and Citizenship: Overview Report*. BRIDGE Cutting Edge Pack. Brighton: Institute of Development Studies.

Meertens, D. and M. Zambrano. 2010. "Citizenship Deferred: The Politics of Victimhood, Land Restitution and Gender Justice in the Colombian (Post?) Conflict." *International Journal of Transitional Justice* 42, no. 2: 189–206.

Merry, S. 1988. "Legal Pluralism." *Law & Society Review* 22, no. 5: 869–896.

Mertus, J. 2004. "Women's Participation in the International Criminal Tribunal for the Former Yugoslavia (ICTY): Transitional Justice for Bosnia and Herzegovina." Women Waging Peace and Policy Commission. Hunter Alternatives Fund, Cambridge, MA.

Millennium Project. 2006. "Education and Gender Equality." http://www. unmillenniumproject.org/reports/tf_gender.htm. Accessed 7 December 2010.

Miller, N. 2004. "Domestic Violence: A Review of State Legislation Defining Police and Prosecution Duties and Powers." Institute for Law and Justice, Alexandria, Virginia.

Minaya, V. 2011. "An assessment of World Bank funding for the rule of law and gender equality." Background paper for *Progress of the World's Women 2011–2012*. UN Women, New York.

Ministry of Planning and International Co-Operation, Hasemite Kingdom of Jordan, UNDP Jordan (United Nations Development Programme, Jordan) and the Jordanian Hashemite Fund for Human Development/Queen Zein Al Sharaf Institute for Development. 2004. *Jordan Human Development Report 2004: Building Sustainable Livelihoods*. Ministry of Planning and International Co-Operation, Hasemite Kingdom of Jordan, UNDP Jordan, Amman.

Ministry of Public Health & Sanitation and Ministry of Medical Services. 2009. *National Guidelines on Management of Sexual Violence in Kenya, 2nd edition*. Ministry of Public Health & Sanitation and Ministry of Medical Services: Nairobi.

Mischkowski, G. and G. Mlinarevic. 2009. *"…and that it does not happen to anyone anywhere in the world:" The Trouble with Rape Trials – Views of Witnesses, Prosecutors and Judges on Prosecuting Sexualised Violence during the War in the former Yugoslavia*. Cologne: medica mondiale.

Morris, C., N. Rashid, S. Charlé, and R. Diprose. 2007. *Justice For All?: An Assessment of Access to Justice in Five Provinces of Indonesia*. Jakarta: National Development Planning Agency, Government of Indonesia, the Centre for Rural and Regional Development Studies at Gadjah Mada University and UNDP Indonesia.

Moyo, W. P., and M. Reddi. 2008. "Prosecuting Gender-Based International Crimes: An Appraisal of the Ad Hoc Tribunals' Jurisprudence." *Journal for Juridical Science* 33, no. 2: 128–144.

Munuo, Justice Eusebia. 17 August 2010. Telephone interview with authors.

Murshed, R. 1998. "Gender Intervention as Applied in BRAC's Organisation and Programmes." Women in Agriculture and Modern Communication Technology– Proceedings of a Workshop, 30 March–3 April 1998, Denmark.

Musawah. 2009. *Musawah Framework for Action*. Selangor, Malaysia: Sisters in Islam

NAM. 2010. "Where HIV is a crime, not just a virus." *HIV treatment update*. Issue 199, August/September 2010. NAM, London.

Nassali, M. 2010. "Engaging Cultural Institutions to Expand Access to Justice for Women's Rights." Background paper for *Progress of the World's Women 2011–2012*. UN Women, New York.

National Statistical Committee of the Kyrgyz Republic. 2002. "First Agricultural Census of the Kyrgyz Republic of 2002." National Statistical Committee of the Kyrgyz Republic, Agricultural Census Division, Bishkek City.

Nesiah, V. et al. 2006. "Truth Commissions and Gender: Principles, Policies and Procedures." Gender Justice Series. New York: International Center for Transitional Justice.

Nowrojee, B. 2004. "We Can Do Better Investigating and Prosecuting International Crimes of Sexual Violence." Paper presented at the Colloquium of Prosecutors of International Criminal Tribunals, 25–27 November 2004, Arusha, Tanzania.

——. 2005. "Your Justice is too Slow: Will the ICTR Fail Rwanda's Rape Victims?" UNRISD, Geneva.

Nyamu-Musembi, C. 2005. "For or Against Gender Equality? Evaluating the Post-Cold War 'Rule of Law' Reforms in Sub-Saharan Africa." Occasional Paper 7 for *Gender Equality: Striving for Justice in an Unequal World*. UNRISD, Geneva.

OAU (Organization of African Unity). 1990. *African Charter on the Rights and Welfare of the Child*. CAB/LEG/24.9/49.

OECD (Organisation for Economic Co-operation and Development). 2007. *Reporting Directives for the Creditor Reporting System* (No. DCD/DAC(2007)39). Paris: OECD-DAC.

——. 2010a. "50 years of official development assistance." *Aid Statistics*. http://www. oecd.org/document/41/0,3746,en_2649_34447_46195625_1_1_1_1,00.html. Accessed 11 January 2011.

——. 2010b. "Aid Statistics, Donor Aid Charts." *Aid Statistics*. http://www.oecd.org/co untrylist/0,3349,en_2649_34447_1783495_1_1_1_1,00.html. Accessed 11 January 2011.

——. 2010c. "Social Institutions and Gender Index." http://genderindex.org. Accessed 15 July 2010.

——. 2011. "OECD Aid Statistics 2010". Personal communication with authors.

Office for National Statistics, United Kingdom. 2010. "Earnings: Full-time gender pay gap narrows." *Labour Market*. 8 December 2010. http://www.statistics.gov.uk/cci/ nugget.asp?id=167. Accessed 3 March 2011.

OHCHR (Office of the United Nations High Commissioner for Human Rights). 2008a. *Rule-of-law tools for post-conflict States: Maximizing the legacy of hybrid courts*. New York and Geneva: United Nations.

——. 2008b. *Rule-of-law Tools for Post-Conflict States: Reparations programmes*. New York and Geneva: United Nations.

——. 2009a. "Report of the Working Group on the Universal Periodic Review: Mexico. Addendum: Views on conclusions and/or recommendations, voluntary commitments and replies presented by the state under review." Geneva, OHCHR.

——. 2009b. "The story of Creuza Oliveira." *News and Events*. April 2009. http:// www.ohchr.org/EN/NEWSEVENTS/Pages/DRCCreuzaOliveira.aspx. Accessed 19 November 2010.

——. 2010a. "Democratic Republic of Congo, 1993–2003: Report of the Mapping Exercise documenting the most serious violations of human rights and international humanitarian law committed within the territory of the Democratic Republic of the Congo between March 1993 and June 2003." Geneva, OHCHR.

——. 2010b. "UN panel urges support for sexual violence victims in DR Congo." *News and Events*. 13 October 2010. http://www.ohchr.org/SP/NewsEvents/Pages/ DisplayNews.aspx?NewsID=10436&LangID=E. Accessed 13 December 2010.

——. 2011. "Universal Human Rights Index of United Nations Documents." http://www. universalhumanrightsindex.org. Accessed February 2011.

OHCHR (Office of the United Nations High Commissioner for Human Rights), UNFPA (United Nations Population Fund), UNICEF (United Nations Children's Fund), UN Women (United Nations Entity for Gender Equality and the Empowerment of Women), and WHO (World Health Organization). Forthcoming. *Preventing Gender-Biased Sex Selection: An Interagency Statement*. New York: United Nations.

Omelaniuk, I. 2005. *Gender, Poverty Reduction and Migration*. Washington, DC: World Bank.

Organization of American States. 1994. *Inter-American Convention on the Prevention, Punishment and Eradication of Violence against Women ("Convention of Belem do Para")*. 9 June 1994.

Pandey, B. 2002. "Women's Property Rights Movement in Nepal." *Workers News,* 32. March 2002. Kathmandu, GEFONT (General Federation of Nepalese Trade Unions).

Parliament of Canada. 2010. "Women's Right to Vote in Canada." http://www2.parl.gc.ca/Parlinfo/compilations/ProvinceTerritory/ProvincialWomenRightToVote.aspx. Accessed 15 October 2010.

Pearshouse, R. 2007. "Legislation Contagion: The Spread of Problematic New HIV Laws in Western Africa." *HIV/AIDS Policy & Law Review* 12, no. 2/3.

Pegus, C. 2007. "Review and Analysis of Compliance of the National Labour Legislation of Antigua and Barbuda with CARICOM Model Labour Laws."

PEKKA (Pemberdayaan Perempuan Kepala Keluarga) and AusAID (Australian Agency for International Development). 2010. *Access to Justice: Empowering female heads of household in Indonesia.* PEKKA and AusAID.

Perera, A. 2010. "Sri Lankan Maids Become Victims in Saudi Arabia." *Time Magazine,* 16 November 2010. http://www.time.com/time/world/article/0,8599,2031351,00.html. Accessed 30 November 2010.

Peresie, J. 2005. "Female Judges Matter: Gender and Collegial Decisionmaking in the Federal Appellate Courts." *The Yale Law Journal* 114: 1759–1790.

Pham, P., P. Vinck, M. Balthazard, S. Hean, and E. Stover. 2010. *So We Will Never Forget: A Population-Based Survey on Attitudes about Social Reconstruction and the Extraordinary Chambers in the Courts of Cambodia.* Berkeley: Human Rights Center, University of California Berkeley.

Pillay, A. 2001. "Violence against Women in the Aftermath." In *The Aftermath: Women in Post-Conflict Transformation.* S. Meintjes, M. Turshen, and A. Pillay (Eds.). London: Zed Books. 35–45.

Population Reference Bureau. 2010. "2009 World Population Data Sheet." http://www.prb.org/Publications/Datasheets/2009/2009wpds.aspx. Accessed 8 December 2010.

Powley, E. 2006. "Rwanda: The Impact of Women Legislators on Policy Outcomes Affecting Children and Families." Background paper for the *State of the World's Children 2007.* UNICEF, New York.

Pradhan Malla, S. 2010. "Upholding Women's Right through Litigation." Interactive Expert Panel Commemorating 30 years of CEDAW. United Nations Commission on the Status of Women, Fifty-fourth session, New York.

———. February 2011. E-mail communication with authors.

The Republic of Kenya. 2008. *Commission of Inquiry into the Post Election Violence (CIPEV) Final Report.* Nairobi: Office of Public Communications, the Republic of Kenya.

The Republic of Sierra Leone. 2007. *Justice Sector Reform Strategy and Investment Plan: 2008–2011.* November 2007.

The Republic of Uganda. 2000. *Uganda Participatory Poverty Assessment Report.* Kampala: Ministry of Finance, Planning and Economic Development, the Republic of Uganda.

Rihani, M., L. Kays, and S. Psaki. 2006. *Keeping the Promise: Five Benefits of Girls' Secondary Education.* Washington DC: Academy of Educational Development.

Roguski, M. and V. Kingi. 2011. "Update of Baseline In-Country Review: Tonga Report." *Pacific Prevention of Domestic Violence Programme.* Prepared for the New Zealand Police.

Rubio-Marín, R. 2006. *What Happened to the Women? Gender and Reparations for Human Rights Violations.* New York: Social Science Research Council.

Sakshi. 1998. *Gender and Judges: A Judicial Point of View.* New Delhi: Sakshi.

Sang-Hun, C. 2007. "Where Boys Were Kings, a Shift Toward Baby Girls." *The New York Times.* 23 December 2007. http://www.nytimes.com/2007/12/23/world/asia/23skorea.html. Accessed 15 December 2010.

Sardenberg, C., M.Gomes, W. Pasinato, and M. Tavares 2010. "Domestic Violence and Women's Access to Justice in Brazil." Background paper for *Progress of the World's Women 2011–2012.* UN Women, New York.

Save the Children. 2010. *Women on the Front Lines of Health Care: State of the World's Mothers 2010.* Westport, Connecticut: Save the Children.

Scanlon, H. and K. Muddell. 2009. "Gender and Transitional Justice in Africa: Progress and Prospects." *African Journal on Conflict Resolution* 9, no. 2: 9–28.

Schurmann, A. 2009. "Review of the Bangladesh Female Secondary School Stipend Project Using a Social Exclusion Framework." *Journal of Health, Population and Nutrition* 27, no. 4: 505–517.

Scribner, D. and P. Lambert. 2010. "Constitutionalizing Difference: A Case Study Analysis of Gender Provisions in Botswana and South Africa." *Politics & Gender* 6: 37–61.

Seck, P. and G. Azcona. 2010. "Women and the Millennium Development Goals: A Focus on Inequality." Background paper for *Progress of the World's Women 2011–2012.* UN Women, New York.

Sellers, P. 2007. "The Prosecution of Sexual Violence in Conflict: The Importance of Human Rights as Means of Interpretation." Women's Human Rights and Gender Unit, Office of the United Nations High Commissioner for Human Rights, Geneva.

Sen, A. 2003. "Missing Women Revisited." *British Medical Journal* 327, no. 7427: 1297–98.

Sezgin, Y. 2010. "Women's Rights under Religious Law." Background paper for *Progress of the World's Women 2011–2012.* UN Women, New York.

Sieder, R. and M. Sierra. 2010. "Indigenous Women's Access to Justice in Latin America." Background paper for *Progress of the World's Women 2011–2012.* UN Women, New York. Available at: http://www.cmi.no/publications/file/3880-indigenous-womens-access-to-justice-in-latin.pdf.

Sierra Leone Truth and Reconciliation Commission. 2004. *Witness to Truth: Report of the Sierra Leone Truth and Reconciliation Commission.* Available at http://www.sierra-leone.org/TRCDocuments.html.

Singh S., J.E. Darroch, L.S. Ashford, and M. Vlassoff. 2009. *Adding It Up: The Costs and Benefits of Investing in Family Planning and Maternal and Newborn Health.* New York: Guttmacher Institute and UNFPA.

Skinnider, E. 1999. *The Responsibility of States to Provide Legal Aid.* Paper prepared for the Legal Aid Conference, Beijing, China, March 1999.The International Centre for Criminal Law Reform and Criminal Justice Policy, Vancouver.

Smith, R. 2003. "Criminal Legal Aid: International Law and Practice." Paper produced for a roundtable discussion in Bishkek, Kyrgyzstan.

The Special Court for Sierra Leone. 2010 . "Essential Court Documents." http://www.sc-sl.org/DOCUMENTS/tabid/176/Default.aspx. Accessed 13 December 2010.

Stapleton, A. 2010. "Empowering the Poor to Access Criminal Justice. A Grassroots Perspective." In *Legal and Governance Reform: Lessons Learned.* S. Golub (Ed.). Rome: International Development Law Organization.

Stefiszyn, K. 2010. "HIV and Women's Access to Justice." Background paper for *Progress of the World's Women 2011–2012.* UN Women, New York.

Stiglitz, S., A. Sen, and J.P. Fitoussi. 2009. "Report by the Commission on the Measurement of Economic Performance and Social Progress." Commission on the Measurement of Economic Performance and Social Progress, Paris.

References

Stone, L. 2010. "Number of women in prison up 50 per cent: 'Troubling trend' over past decade may only get worse with push toward harsher laws, experts say." *The Vancouver Sun*. 10 May 2010. http://www.vancouversun.com/health/Number+wo men+prison+cent/3008161/story.html. Accessed 14 January 2011.

Strickland, R. 2004. "To Have and To Hold: Women's Property and Inheritance Rights in the Context of HIV/AIDS in Sub-Saharan Africa." Working paper. International Center for Research on Women and The Global Coalition on Women and AIDS, Washington, DC.

Tamanaha, B. 2008. "Understanding Legal Pluralism: Past to Present, Local to Global." *Sydney Law Review* 30: 375–411.

Terven, A. 2008. "Justicia Indígena en Tiempos Multiculturales. Hacia la Conformación de un Proyecto Colectivo Propio: La Experiencia Organizativa de Cuetzalan." PhD thesis in Social Anthropology. Mexico City: Centro de Investigaciones y Estudios Superiores en Antropología Social.

Townhead, L. 2007. "Pre-Trial Detention of Women: And its impact on their children." *Women in Prison and Children of Imprisoned Mothers Series*. Quaker United Nations Office, Geneva.

Tribunal de conciencia contra la violencia sexual hacia las mujeres durante el conflicto armado interno en Guatemala. 2010. *Pronunciamiento final*. Available at: http://www.repem.org.uy/files/Pronunciamiento%20Final%20T.Conciencia.pdf.

Tripp, A., I. Casimiro, J. Kwesiga, and A. Mungwa. 2009. *African Women's Movements: Transforming Political Landscapes*. New York: Cambridge University Press.

The Trust Fund for Victims. 2010. *Learning from the TFV's second mandate: From implementing rehabilitation assistance to reparations. Fall 2010 Programme Progress Report*. The Hague, International Criminal Court.

Tsanga, A.S., J. Osterhaus, and I. Kipfer-Didavi. 2004. "Facilitating Justice: The Work of Paralegals." *Strengthening Women's Rights*. Eschborn, Germany: Deutsche Gesellschaft für Technische Zusammenarbeit (GTZ).

UN (United Nations). 1945. *Charter of the International Military Tribunal – Annex to the Agreement for the Prosecution and Punishment of the Major War Criminals of the European Axis ("London Agreement")*. 8 August 1945.

——. 1946. *Charter of the International Military Tribunal for the Far East*. 19 January 1946.

——. 1955. *Standard Minimum Rules for the Treatment of Prisoners*. 30 August 1955.

——. 1994. *International Conference on Population and Development (ICPD '94): Summary of the Programme of Action*. Adopted at the ICPD, Cairo.

——. 1995. *Beijing Declaration and Platform for Action*. Adopted at the 16th plenary meeting. Fourth World Conference on Women, Beijing.

——. 2009. "Guidance Note of the Secretary-General on Democracy." United Nations, New York.

——. 2010a. "Guidance Note of the Secretary-General: United Nations Approach to Transitional Justice." March 2010. United Nations, New York.

——. 2010b. "Millennium Development Goals: Gender Equality and Women's Empowerment: Progress Chart 2010." United Nations, New York.

——. 2010c. "Millennium Development Goals Indicators." http://unstats.un.org/unsd/mdg/Default.aspx. Accessed 20 December 2010.

——. 2010d. *The Millennium Development Goals Report 2010*. New York: United Nations.

——. 2011a. *The Millennium Development Goals Report 2011*. New York: United Nations.

——. 2011b. "Statement by H.E. Ms. Lulu Xingwana, Minister of Women, Children and People with Disabilities of the Republic of South Africa, to the 55th Session of the Commission on the Status of Women." United Nations Headquarters, New York. 24 February 2011.

——. 2011c. "United Nations Treaty Collection Database: Convention on the Elimination of All Forms of Discrimination against Women Reservations and Declarations." http://treaties.un.org/. Accessed April 2011.

UN CEDAW (United Nations Committee on the Elimination of Discrimination against Women). 1992. *General Recommendations No. 19 on Violence against Women*. A/47/38.

——. 1999. *Concluding Observations of the Committee on the Elimination of Discrimination Against Women: Kyrgyzstan*. A/54/38.

——. 2004. *Report of the Committee on the Elimination of Discrimination against Women: Fifty-Ninth Session*. A/59/38(SUPP).

——. 2006a. *Concluding Comments of the Committee on the Elimination of Discrimination against Women: Philippines*. CEDAW/C/PHI/CO/6.

——. 2006b. *Concluding Comments of the Committee on the Elimination of Discrimination against Women: The Former Yugoslav Republic of Macedonia*. CEDAW/C/MKD/CO/3.

——. 2008. *General Recommendation No. 26 on women migrant workers*. CEDAW/C/2009/WP.1/R.

——. 2009a. *Concluding Observations of the Committee on the Elimination of Discrimination against Women: Spain*. CEDAW/C/ESP/CO/6.

——. 2009b. *Concluding Observations of the Committee on the Elimination of Discrimination against Women: Guatemala*. CEDAW/C/GUA/CO/7.

——. 2009c. *Concluding Observations of the Committee on the Elimination of Discrimination against Women: Japan*. CEDAW/C/JPN/CO/6.

——. 2009d. *Concluding Observations of the Committee on the Elimination of Discrimination against Women: United Republic of Tanzania*. CEDAW/C/TZA/CO/6.

——. 2009e. *Consideration of reports submitted by States parties under article 18 of the Convention on the Elimination of All Forms of Discrimination against Women: Combined fourth, fifth, sixth and seventh periodic report of States parties: Uganda*. CEDAW/C/UGA/7.

——. 2009f. *General Recommendation on Economic Consequences of Marriage and its Dissolution: Concept Note*. CEDAW/C/2009/II/WP.2/R.

——. 2010a. *Concluding Observations of the Committee on the Elimination of Discrimination against Women: Tunisia*. CEDAW/C/TUN/CO/6.

——. 2010b. *Consideration of reports submitted by States parties under article 18 of the Convention on the Elimination of All Forms of Discrimination against Women. Combined initial to third periodic reports of States parties: Côte d'Ivoire*. CEDAW/C/CIV/1-3.

——. 2010c. *General Recommendation No. 27 on Older Women and Protection of their Human Rights*. CEDAW/C/2010/47/GC.1.

——. 2010d. *General Recommendation No. 28 on the Core Obligations of States Parties under Article 2 of the Convention on the Elimination of All Forms of Discrimination against Women*. CEDAW/C/2010/47/GC.2.

——. 2011. *Concluding Observations of the Committee on the Elimination of Discrimination Against Women: Belarus*. CEDAW/C/BLR/CO/7.

UN CMW (United Nations Committee on the Protection of the Rights of all Migrant Workers and Members of Their Families). 2011. *General Comment No. 1 on migrant domestic workers*. CMW/C/GC/1.

UN Commission on Human Rights (United Nations Commission on Human Rights). 1996a. *Contemporary Forms of Slavery: Preliminary report of the Special Rapporteur on the* situation of systematic rape, sexual slavery and slavery-like practices during periods of armed conflict, Ms. Linda Chavez. E/CN.4/Sub.2/1996/26.

——.1996b. Question of the Violation of Human Rights and Fundamental Freedoms in any Part of the World, with Particular Reference to Colonial and Other Dependent Countries and Territories: Report on the situation of human rights in Rwanda submitted by Mr. René Degni-Ségui, Special Rapporteur of the Commission on Human Rights, under paragraph 20 of resolution S-3/1 of 25 May 1994. E/CN.4/1996/68.

——. 1997. Report of the Special Rapporteur on violence against women, its causes and consequences, Ms. Radhika Coomaraswamy. E/CN.4/1997/47.

——. 1999. Report of the Special Rapporteur on violence against women, its causes and consequences, Ms. Radhika Coomaraswamy, submitted in accordance with Commission on Human Rights resolution 1995/85. E/CN.4/1999/68.

——. 2000a. "Annex: Report of the High Commissioner for Human Rights on the situation of human rights in East Timor submitted to the Commission on Human Rights at its fourth special session." Question of the violation of Human Rights and fundamental freedoms in any part of the world: Situation of human rights in East Timor, note by the secretariat. E/CN.4/2000/44.

——. 2000b. Contemporary Forms of Slavery: Systematic rape, sexual slavery and slavery-like practices during armed conflict: Update to the final report submitted by Ms. Gay J. McDougall, Special Rapporteur. E/CN.4/Sub.2/2000/21.

——. 2001. Integration of the Human Rights of Women and the Gender Perspective: Report of the Special Rapporteur on violence against women, its causes and consequences, Ms. Radhika Coomaraswamy, submitted in accordance with Commission on Human Rights resolution 2000/45: Violence against women perpetrated and/or condoned by the State during times of armed conflict (1997–2000). E/CN.4/2001/73.

——. 2002a. Report of the Special Rapporteur on violence against women, its causes and consequences, Ms. Radhika Coomaraswamy, submitted in accordance with Commission on Human Rights resolution 2001/49. E/CN.4/2002/83.

——. 2002b. Report of the Special Rapporteur on violence against women, its causes and consequences, Ms. Radhika Coomaraswamy, submitted in accordance with Commission on Human Rights resolution 2001/49, Addendum: Integration of the human rights of women and the gender perspective, violence against women. E/CN.4/2002/83/Add.3.

——. 2003a. Integration of the Human Rights of Women and the Gender Perspective: Violence Against Women: Report of the Special Rapporteur on violence against women, its causes and consequences, Ms. Radhika Coomaraswamy, submitted in accordance with Commission on Human Rights resolution 2002/52. E/CN.4/2003/75.

——. 2003b. Report of the Working Group on Arbitrary Detention. E/CN.4/2004/3.

——. 2005. Report of the Special Rapporteur on violence against women, its causes and consequences, Yakin Erturk. E/CN.4/2005/72.

UN Committee on Economic, Social and Cultural Rights (United Nations Committee on Economic, Social and Cultural Rights). 2000. General Comment No. 14 (2000). E/C.12/2000/4.

——. 2003. General Comment No. 15 (2002), E/C.12/2002/11.

UN Committee on the Rights of the Child (United Nations Committee on the Rights of the Child). 2003a. General Comment No. 3 (2003). CRC/GC/2003/3.

——. 2003b. General Comment No. 4 (2003). CRC/GC/2003/4.

UN DESA (United Nations Department of Economic and Social Affairs). 2004. World Fertility Report: 2003. ESA/P/WP/189.

——. 2009a. "World Fertility Patterns 2009." United Nations, New York.

——. 2009b. "World Population Prospects: The 2008 Revision." Population Database. http://esa.un.org/UNPP/. Accessed 15 December 2010.

——. 2011a. "World Abortion Policies 2011." United Nations, New York.

——. 2011b. "World Population Prospects: The 2010 Revision." Population Database. http://esa.un.org/unpd/wpp/index.htm. Accessed 5 May 2011.

UN DESA-DAW (United Nations Department of Economic and Social Affairs, Division for the Advancement of Women, now part of UN Women). 2009a. Handbook for Legislation on Violence Against Women. New York: United Nations.

——. 2009b. 2009 World Survey on the Role of Women in Development: Women's Control over Economic Resources and Access to Financial Resources, including Microfinance. New York: United Nations.

——. 2009c. "Expert Group Meeting: The Impact of the Implementation of the Beijing Declaration and Platform for Action on the Achievement of the Millennium Development Goals." http://www.un.org/womenwatch/daw/egm/impact_bdpfa/index.html. Accessed 7 December 2010.

UN DPI (United Nations Department of Public Information). 2007. "United Nations Must be at Forefront of Efforts to Curb Violence Against Women, Says Secretary-General at Observance of International Day." United Nations Secretary-General SG/SM/10903 OBV/610 WOM/1620. 8 March 2007.

——. 2010. "General Assembly Adopts 52 Resolutions, 6 Decisions Recommended by Third Committee on Broad Range of Human Rights, Social, Cultural Issues. UN Women, 'Bangkok Rules' for Women Prisoners, Rights of the Child, Extrajudicial Executions, Death Penalty Moratorium among Issues Addressed." United Nations General Assembly GA/11041. 21 December 2010.

UN General Assembly (United Nations General Assembly). 1948. Universal Declaration of Human Rights. 217 A(III).

——. 1957. Convention on the Nationality of Married Women. Treaty Series, Vol. 309, No. 4468.

——. 1962. Convention on Consent to Marriage, Minimum Age for Marriage and Registration of Marriages. Treaty Series, Vol. 521, No. 7525.

——. 1966a. International Covenant on Civil and Political Rights. Treaty Series, Vol. 999 and Vol. 1057, No. 14468.

——. 1966b. International Covenant on Economic, Social and Cultural Rights. Treaty Series, Vol. 993, No. 14531.

——. 1979. Convention on the Elimination of All Forms of Discrimination against Women. Treaty Series, Vol. 1249, No. 20378.

——. 1998. Rome Statute of the International Criminal Court. A/CONF. 183/9.

——. 1999. Situation of human rights in East Timor. Note by the Secretary-General. A/54/660.

——. 2000. Resolution adopted by the General Assembly [on the report of the Ad Hoc Committee of the Whole of the Twenty-third Special Session of the General Assembly (A/S-23/10/Rev.1)]. A/RES/S-23/3.

——. 2001. "Review of reports, studies and other documentation for the preparatory Committee and the World Conference." World Conference Against Racism, Racial Discrimination, Xenophobia and Related Intolerance. A/CONF.189/PC.2/1/Add.1.

——. 2006. In-depth study on all forms of violence against women. Report of the Secretary-General. A/61/122/Add.1.

——. 2007a. Resolution adopted by the General Assembly: Situation of human rights in Myanmar. A/RES/61/232.

——. 2007b. United Nations Declaration on the Rights of Indigenous Peoples. UN General Assembly resolution 61/295.

References

——. 2010a. *Keeping the Promise: United to achieve the Millennium Development Goals.* A/65/L.1.

——. 2010b. *United Nations Rules for the Treatment of Women Prisoners and Non-custodial Measures for Women Offenders (the Bangkok Rules).* A/C.3/65/L.5.

UN General Assembly (United Nations General Assembly) and UN Security Council (United Nations Security Council). 2000. *Identical letters dated 31 January 2000 from the Secretary-General addressed to the President of the General Assembly, the President of the Security Council and the Chairperson of the Commission on Human Rights.* A/54/726 and S/2000/59.

UN Human Rights Committee (United Nations Human Rights Committee). 2010. *Consideration of Reports Submitted by States Parties under article 40 of the Covenant: Concluding Observations of the Human Rights Committee.* CCPR/C/CAN/CO/5.

UN Human Rights Council (United Nations Human Rights Council). 2008a. *Promotion and Protection of All Human Rights, Civil, Political, Economic, Social and Cultural, including the Right to Development.* Report of the Special Rapporteur on violence against women its causes and consequences, Yakin Ertürk. A/HRC/7/6.

——. 2008b. *Report prepared by the Special Rapporteur on the situation of human rights in the Sudan on the status of implementation of the recommendations compiled by the Group of Experts mandated by the Human Rights Council in resolution 4/8 to the Government of the Sudan for the implementation of Human Rights Council resolution 4/8 pursuant to Human Rights Council resolution 6/34.* A/HRC/9/13/Add.1.

——. 2008c. *Resolution 8/7: Mandate of the Special Representative of the Secretary-General on the issue of human rights and transnational corporations and other business enterprises.* 28th meeting, 18 June 2008.

——. 2010a. *Report of the Special Rapporteur on extrajudicial, summary or arbitrary executions, Philip Alston: Addendum: Mission to Colombia.* A/HRC/14/24/Add.2

——. 2010b. *Report of the Special Rapporteur on the right of everyone to the enjoyment of the highest attainable standard of physical and mental health, Anand Grover.* A/HRC/14/20.

——. 2010c. *Report of the Special Rapporteur on violence against women, its causes and consequences, Rashida Manjoo.* A/HRC/14/22.

——. 2010d. *Report of the Special Rapporteur on violence against women, its causes and consequences, Rashida Manjoo: Addendum, Mission to Kyrgyzstan.* A/HRC/14/22/Add.2.

——. 2010e. *Resolution 15/23 on Elimination of discrimination against women.* /HRC/RES/15/23.

UN Security Council (United Nations Security Council). 1992. *Security Council resolution 798.* S/RES/798 (1992).

——. 1993a. "Annex I: European Community investigative mission into the treatment of Muslim women in the former Yugoslavia." *Letter dated 2 February 1993 from the Permanent Representative of Denmark to the United Nations addressed to the Secretary-General.* S/25240.

——. 1993b. *Letter Dated 9 February 1993 from the Secretary-General addressed to the President of the Security Council.* S/25274.

——. 1993c. *Report of the Secretary-General Pursuant to Paragraph 2 of Security Council resolution 808 (1993) [Contains text of the Statute of the International Tribunal for the Prosecution of Persons Responsible for Serious Violations of International Humanitarian Law Committed in the Territory of the Former Yugoslavia since 1991] Resolution 820 (1993) Adopted by the Security Council at its 3200th meeting, on 17 April 1993.* S/RES/820 (1993).

——. 1994a. *Letter dated 24 May 1994 from the Secretary-General to the President of the Security Council.* S/1994/674.

——. 1994b. *Statute of the International Criminal Tribunal for Rwanda (as last amended on 13 October 2006).* 8 November 1994.

——. 2000. *Security Council resolution 1325.* S/RES/1325 (2009).

——. 2002. *Statute of the Special Court for Sierra Leone.*

——. 2004. *The rule of law and transitional justice in conflict and post-conflict societies: Report of the Secretary-General.* S/2004/616.

——. 2008. *Security Council resolution 1820.* S/RES/1820 (2008).

——. 2009a. *Report of the Secretary-General pursuant to Security Council resolution 1820.* S/2009/362.

——. 2009b. *Security Council resolution 1888.* S/RES/1888 (2009).

——. 2009c. *Security Council resolution 1889.* S/RES/1889 (2009).

——. 2010. *Security Council resolution 1960.* S/RES/1960 (2010).

UN Statistics Division (United Nations Statistics Division). 2010a. *The World's Women 2010: Trends and Statistics.* New York: United Nations.

——. 2010b. "UNdata." http://data.un.org/. Accessed 8 December 2010.

UN Women (United Nations Entity for Gender Equality and the Empowerment of Women). 2010a. *A Window of Opportunity? Making Transitional Justice Work for Women.* New York: UN Women.

——. 2010b. "Act on the Punishment of Sexual Violence and Protection of Victims." *The UN Secretary-General's database on violence against women.* http://webapps01.un.org/vawdatabase/searchDetail.action?measureId=10585. Accessed 21 October 2010.

——. 2010c. *Gender and Transitional Justice Programming: A Review of Peru, Sierra Leone and Rwanda.* New York: UN Women.

——. 2010d. *Gender Justice: Key to Achieving the Millennium Development Goals.* New York: UN Women.

——. 2010e. "Project Liberia log frame." From the programme: *From communities to global security institutions: Engaging women in building peace and security.* UN Women, New York.

——. 2010f. "The Facts: Violence against Women & Millennium Development Goals." UN Women, New York.

——. 2011a. "Matrix of Violence against Women Prevalence Surveys, by Country."

——. 2011b. "The UN Secretary-General's database on violence against women." http://webapps01.un.org/vawdatabase/home.action. Accessed April 2011.

——. 2011c. "Virtual Knowledge Centre to End Violence Against Women and Girls." Information compiled by Advocates for Human Rights. http://www.endvawnow.org. Accessed 2 February 2011.

UN Women Burundi. 5 August 2010. E-mail communication with authors.

UN Women (United Nations Entity for Gender Equality and the Empowerment of Women), UN Trust Fund (UN Trust Fund in Support of Actions to Eliminate Violence against Women) and UNiTE (United Nations Secretary-General's Campaign to End Violence against Women). 2010. *The United Nations Trust Fund to End Violence against Women: Annual Report 2010.* New York: UN Women.

UNAIDS (Joint United Nations Programme on HIV/AIDS). 2008. "Policy Brief: Criminalization of HIV Transmission." UNAIDS, Geneva.

——. 2009. *HIV Transmission in Intimate Partner Relationships in Asia.* Geneva: UNAIDS.

——. 2010a. *Global Report: UNAIDS Report on the Global AIDS Epidemic 2010.* Geneva: UNAIDS.

——. 2010b. *UNAIDS Outlook Report 2010*. Geneva: UNAIDS.

UNAIDS (Joint United Nations Programme on HIV/AIDS), Marie Stopes International China, and Institute of Social Development Research. 2009. *The China Stigma Index Report*. Geneva: UNAIDS and Partners.

UNAMA (United Nations Assistance Mission in Afghanistan). 2009. *Arbitrary Detention in Afghanistan: A Call for Action, Volume I – Overview and Recommendations*. Kabul. UNAMA.

UNDEF (United Nations Democracy Fund). 2009. "News from the Field: Women build jurisprudence on the ground to address AIDS in Tanzania." 6 November 2009. http://www.un.org/democracyfund/XNewsTanzania.htm. Accessed 30 November 2010.

UNDG (United Nations Development Group). 2009. "About the MDG Task Force." http://www.undg.org/index.cfm?P=1294. Accessed 7 December 2010.

UNDP (United Nations Development Programme). 2007. *Strengthening the Rule of Law in Conflict- and Post-Conflict Situations. A Global UNDP Programme for Justice and Security 2008–2011*. New York: UNDP.

——. 2009. *Overcoming barriers: Human mobility and development. Human Development Report 2009*. New York: Palgrave Macmillan.

——. 2010a. "Concept Note: Strengthening Women's Security and Access to Justice Implementing UNDP's Eight-Point Agenda for Women's Empowerment and Gender Equality in Crisis Prevention and Recovery." UNDP, New York.

——. 2010b. *Power, Voice and Rights: A Turning Point for Gender Equality in Asia and the Pacific. Asia-Pacific Human Development Report*. Colombo: Macmillan.

——. 2010c. *The Real Wealth of Nations: Pathways to Human Development. Human Development Report 2010*. New York: Palgrave Macmillan.

UNDP (United Nations Development Programme) Cambodia. 2009. "Domestic Violence in Cambodia: What has changed between 2005 and 2009?" Available at: http://www.un.org.kh/undp/~docs/Violence_Against_Women_2009_Follow-Up_Survey-Leaflet.pdf.

UNDP (United Nations Development Programme) Nepal. 2011. "Advancing gender equality and social inclusion." *Gender and Social Development*. http://www.undp.org.np/gender/index.php. Accessed 3 March 2011.

UNDP (United Nations Development Programme) and UNIFEM (United Nations Development Fund for Women, now part of UN Women). 2009. "Case Studies of Gender Sensitive Police Reform in Rwanda and Timor-Leste." UNDP and UNIFEM (now part of UN Women), New York.

UNESCO (United Nations Educational, Scientific and Cultural Organization). 2010a. "Deprivation and Marginalization in Education (DME)." *EFA Global Monitoring Report 2010: Reaching the marginalized*. http://www.unesco.org/new/en/education/themes/leading-the-international-agenda/efareport/dme/. Accessed 3 January 2011.

——. 2010b. *EFA Global Monitoring Report 2010: Reaching the marginalized*. Paris: UNESCO.

UNESCO Institute of Statistics. 2011. "Statistics database." http://stats.uis.unesco.org. Accessed 5 May 2011.

UNFCCC (United Nations Framework Convention on Climate Change). 2008. "National Adaptation Programmes of Action (NAPAs)." http://unfccc.int/national_reports/napa/items/2719.php. Accessed 30 October 2010.

UNFPA (United Nations Population Fund). n.d. "Giving Birth Should Not be a Matter of Life and Death." UNFPA, New York.

——. 2009. *State of World Population 2009: Facing a changing world: Women, population and climate*. New York: UNFPA.

UNGASS (United Nations General Assembly Special Session (on AIDS)). 2007. *UNGASS Country Progress Report: P.R. China*. Geneva: UNAIDS.

Ungváry, K. 2004. *Battle for Budapest: One Hundred Days in World War II*. London: I. B. Tauris.

UNICEF (United Nations Children's Fund). 2008. *State of the World's Children 2009*. New York: UNICEF.

——. 2009 *Progress for Children: A Report Card on Child Protection, Number 8, September 2009*. New York: UNICEF.

——. 2010a. *Beijing + 15: Bringing Girls into Focus*. New York: Gender, Rights and Civic Engagement, Division of Policy and Practice, UNICEF.

——. 2010b. *Progress for Children: Achieving the MDGs with Equity, Number 9, September 2010*. New York: UNICEF.

——. 2011. "Childinfo: Monitoring the Situation of Children and Women." http://www.childinfo.org/. Accessed 24 March 2011.

UNICEF (United Nations Children's Fund) Papua New Guinea. 2009. *Evaluation of the Village Courts: Women and Children's Access to Community Justice (Child Protection) Programme (Terms of Reference)*. Port Moresby: UNICEF.

UNICEF (United Nations Children's Fund) and UNFPA (United Nations Population Fund). 2005. *The Effects of Conflict on Health and Well-being of Women and Girls in Darfur: Situational Analysis Report: Conversations with the Community*. New York: UNICEF and UNFPA.

UNIFEM (United Nations Development Fund for Women, now part of UN Women). 2009a. "Background Notes CEDAW Anniversary." Unpublished paper. UNIFEM (now part of UN Women): New York.

——. 2009b. *Domestic Violence Legislation and its Implementation. An Analysis for ASEAN Countries Based on International Standards and Good Practices*. Bangkok: UNIFEM (now part of UN Women) East and Southeast Asia Regional Office.

——. 2010. *Women's Rights to Land: Kyrgyzstan and Tajikistan*. New York: UNIFEM (now part of UN Women).

UNIFEM (United Nations Development Fund for Women, now part of UN Women), UN DPKO (United Nations Department of Peacekeeping Operations) and UN Action against Sexual Violence in Conflict. 2010. *Addressing Conflict-Related Sexual Violence: An Analytical Inventory of Peacekeeping Practice*. New York: United Nations.

UNISON. 2005. "UNISON wins historic equal pay award." *Latest News*. http://www.unison.org.uk/news/news_view.asp?did=1933. Accessed 8 March 2011.

——. 2006. *Agenda for change and private contractor staff – England: A UNISON guide*. London: UNISON.

University of Richmond. 2010. "Constitution Finder." http://confinder.richmond.edu. Accessed 30 December 2010.

UNODC (United Nations Office on Drugs and Crime). 2006. *Assessment of the Integrity and Capacity of the Justice System in Three Nigerian States: Technical Assessment Report*. Vienna: UNODC.

——. 2009. "The Tenth United Nations Survey of Crime Trends and Operations of Criminal Justice Systems, covering the period 2005–2006." Report generated on 27 January 2009. http://www.unodc.org/documents/data-and-analysis/CTS10%20replies%20by%20section.pdf. Accessed 30 December 2010.

Uppsala University and International Peace Research Institute. 2009. "UCDP/PRIO Armed Conflict Dataset (Version 4)." Accessed 1 May 2011.

References

US Census Bureau. 2010. "Table POV02: People in Families by Family Structure, Age, and Sex, Iterated by Income-to-Poverty Ratio and Race: 2009, Below 100% of Poverty, Black Alone." *Current Population Survey (CPS), Annual Social and Economic Supplement (ASEC) Supplement.* http://www.census.gov/hhes/www/cpstables/032010/pov/new02_100_06.htm. Accessed 11 January 2011.

US Department of State. 2011. "2010 Country Reports on Human Rights Practices." http://www.state.gov/g/drl/rls/hrrpt/2010/. Accessed April 2011.

USAID (United States Agency for International Development). 2010. "Project: Thuthuzela Care Centers (TCC)." USAID, Pretoria, South Africa.

Valente, M. 2010. "Pioneer in Mainstreaming Gender Perspective in Justice System." 22 September 2010. http://ipsnews.net/news.asp?idnews=52930. Accessed 11 January 2011.

Varga, C. 2006. *A Network Approach to Women's Property and Inheritance Rights in the Context of HIV/AIDS: The Case of the Justice for Widows and Orphans Project in Zambia.* Lusaka: Justice for Widows and Orphans Project and the International Center for Research on Women.

Vetten, L., R. Jewkes, R. Sigsworth, N. Christofides, L. Loots, and O. Dunseith. 2008. *Tracking Justice: The Attrition of Rape Cases through the Criminal Justice System in Gauteng.* Johannesburg: Tshwaranang Legal Advocacy Centre to End Violence against Women (TLAC), the South African Medical Research Council (MRC) and the Centre for the Study of Violence and Reconciliation (CSVR).

Villarreal, M. 2006. "Changing customary land rights and gender relations in the context of HIV/AIDS in Africa." In *Colloque International "Les Frontières de la Question Foncière – At the Frontier of Land Issues."* Montpellier.

Vinck, P. December 2010. E-mail communication with authors.

Vinck, P. and P. Pham. 2010a. *Building Peace, Seeking Justice: A Population-Based Survey on Attitudes about Accountability and Social Reconstruction in the Central African Republic.* Berkeley: Human Rights Center, University of California Berkeley.

——. 2010b. "Outreach Evaluation: The International Criminal Court in the Central African Republic." *International Journal of Transitional Justice* 4, no. 3: 421–442.

Vinck, P., P. Pham, S. Baldo, and R. Shigekane. 2008. *Living with Fear: A Population-Based Survey on Attitudes about Peace, Justice, and Social Reconstruction in Eastern Democratic Republic of the Congo.* Berkeley and New York: Human Rights Center, University of California Berkeley, Payson Center for International Development and the International Center for Transitional Justice.

von Benda-Beckmann, F. 2002. "Who's Afraid of Legal Pluralism?" *Journal of Legal Pluralism* 47: 37–82.

von Benda-Beckmann, F., K. von Benda-Beckmann, J. Eckert, F. Pirie, and B. Turner. 2003. "Vitality and revitalisation of tradition in law: Going back into the past or future-oriented development?" In *Max Planck Institute for Social Anthropology Report 2002–2003.* Max Planck Institute for Social Anthropology (Ed.). Halle/Saale: Max Planck Institute for Social Anthropology: 296–306.

Wakabi, W. 2008. "Sexual Violence Increasing in Democratic Republic of Congo." *The Lancet* 371, no. 9606: 15–16.

Waldorf, L. 2010. "Constitutional and Legal Reform." Background paper for *Progress of the World's Women 2011–2012.* UN Women, New York.

Walmsley, R. 2005. "World Female Imprisonment List." King's College London: International Centre for Prison Studies.

Warraich, S. 2010. "Shirkat Gah Women's Resource Centre, Lahore (Pakistan). Legal Consciousness Training and Experience of Trainings of Marriage Registrars." Background note for *Progress of the World's Women 2011–2012.* UN Women, New York.

WATCH. 2008. *WATCH Report: Impact of Court Monitoring on Hennepin County, Minnesota.* Minneapolis, Minnesota: WATCH.

Waylen, G. 2006. "Constitutional Engineering: What Opportunities for the Enhancement of Gender Rights?" *Third World Quarterly* 27, no. 7: 1209–1221.

Weilenmann, M. 2007. "Legal Pluralism: A New Challenge for Development Agencies." In *Access to Justice in Africa and Beyond: Making the Rule of Law a Reality.* PRI (Penal Reform International) and Bluhm Legal Clinic of the Northwestern University School of Law (Eds.). Chicago: PRI.

Welch, J. and F. Mason. 2007. "Rape and Sexual Assault." *British Medical Journal* 334, no. 7604: 1154–1158.

WFP (World Food Programme) and FAO (Food and Agriculture Organization). 2010. *The State of Food Insecurity in the World: Addressing food insecurity in protracted crises.* Rome: FAO.

WHO (World Health Organization). 2002. *World report on violence and health.* Geneva: WHO.

——. 2005. *The World Health Report 2005: Make every mother and child count.* Geneva: WHO.

——. 2007. *Unsafe Abortion: Global and regional estimates of the incidence of unsafe abortion and associated mortality in 2003, Fifth edition.* Geneva: WHO.

——. 2010. "Global Health Observatory Database." http://www.who.int/gho/en/. Accessed 30 November 2010.

WHO Europe (World Health Organization Regional Office for Europe) and UNODC (United Nations Office on Drugs and Crime). 2009. *Women's health in prison: Correcting gender inequity in prison health.* Copenhagen: WHO.

WHO (World Health Organization), UNICEF (United Nations Children's Fund), UNFPA (United Nations Population Fund) and the World Bank. 2010. *Trends in Maternal Mortality: 1990 to 2008.* Geneva: WHO.

WID Tech (Women in Development Technical Assistance Project). 2003. "Women's Property and Inheritance Rights: Improving Lives in Changing Times." Final Synthesis and Conference Proceedings Paper. WID Tech, Washington, DC.

WLUML (Women Living Under Muslim Laws). 1996. *Fatwas Against Women in Bangladesh.* Readers and Compilations Series. London: WLUML.

——. 2006. *Knowing Our Rights: Women, family, laws and customs in the Muslim world.* London: WLUML.

Women's Initiatives for Gender Justice. 2009. *Gender Report Card 2009 on the International Criminal Court.* The Hague: Women's Initiatives for Gender Justice.

Women's League of Burma and the Nobel Women's Initiative. 2010. *International Tribunal on Crimes Against Women on Burma.* 2 March 2010, New York.

Women's Link Worldwide. 2007. "C-355/2006. Excerpts of The Constitutional Court's Ruling That Liberalized Abortion in Colombia." Women's Link Worldwide.

World Bank. n.d. "Concept Note: Women's Legal Empowerment Project." Unpublished.

——. 2005. *Gender Issues and Best Practices in Land Administration Projects: A Synthesis Report.* Washington, DC: World Bank.

——. 2010a. "Accra Agenda for Action." 3rd High Level Forum on Aid Effectiveness, 2–4 September 2008, Accra, Ghana.

——. 2010b. "Gender – A Special Theme for IDA 16." *Gender Equality as Smart Economics.* October 2010. World Bank, Washington, DC.

——. 2010c. "GenderStats." http://genderstats.worldbank.org. Accessed 8 December 2010.

——. 2010d. "PovcalNet Online Poverty Analysis Tool." http://iresearch.worldbank.org/PovcalNet. Accessed 3 January 2011.

——. 2010e. "Project Database." http://go.worldbank.org/IAHNQIVK30. Accessed October 2010.

——. 2010f. "Women, Business and the Law Database." http://wbl.worldbank.org/. Accessed 10 March 2011.

——. 2010g. *Women, Business and the Law: Measuring Legal Gender Parity for Entrepreneurs and Workers in 128 Economies.* Washington DC: World Bank.

——. 2010h. "World Bank's Fund for the Poorest Receives Almost $50 Billion in Record Funding." *News.* 15 December 2010. http://go.worldbank.org/F5A0QOJ8K0. Accessed 15 March 2011.

——. 2010i. "World Development Indicators Databank." http://data.worldbank.org/data-catalog/world-development-indicators. Accessed 3 January 2011.

——. 2011a. "Access to Justice – Topic Brief." http://go.worldbank.org/ZELBVA60W0. Accessed 24 February 2011.

——. 2011b. "Increasing Access to Justice for Women, the Poor, and Those Living in Remote Areas: An Indonesian Case Study." Justice for the Poor Briefing Note: Volume 6, Issue 2. March 2011. World Bank, Washington, DC.

World Values Survey Association. 2010. "World Values Survey" http://www.worldvaluessurvey.org. Accessed October 2010.

Yoshiaki, Y. 2000. *Comfort Women: Sexual Slavery in the Japanese Military During World War II.* Trans. S. O'Brien. New York: Columbia University Press.

Yrigoyen Fajardo, R., R. Kong, and S. Phan. 2007. *Pathways to Justice: Access to Justice with a Focus on Poor, Women and Indigenous Peoples.* Phnom Penh: Ministry of Justice and UNDP Cambodia.

Court Cases

A. S. v Hungary, Communication No. 4/2004, CEDAW Comm., CEDAW/C/36/D/4/2004 (2006).

A. T. v Hungary, Communication No. 2/2003, CEDAW Comm., CEDAW/C/32/D/2/2003 (2005).

Abeysundere v Abeysundere and Attorney General, S.C. Appeal No. 70/96 (1996).

The Attorney General of The Republic of Botswana v Unity Dow, App. Ct. of Botswana, [1992] LRC (Const) 628 (1992).

Bangladesh National Women Lawyers Association v Government of Bangladesh. W.P. No. 5916 of 2008 (2009).

Bevacqua and S. v Bulgaria, App. No. 71127/01, Eur. Ct. H.R. (12 June 2008).

Bhe and others v Khayelitsha Magistrate and others, 2005 (1) BCLR 1 C.C. (15 Oct. 2004).

Fatma Yildirim v Austria, Communication No. 6 /2005, CEDAW Comm., CEDAW/C/39/D/6/2005 (2007).

González and others ("Cotton Field") v Mexico, Preliminary Objection, Merits, Reparations, and Costs, Inter-Am. C.H.R., Series C No. 205 (16 November 2009).

Karen Noelia Llantoy Huamán v Peru, Communication No. 1153/2003, CEDAW Comm., CCPR/C/85/D/1153/2003 (2005).

Maria da Penha Maia Fernandes v Brazil, Case 12.051, Report No. 54/01, OEA/Ser.L/V/II.111 Doc. 20 rev. at 704 (2000).

McIvor and others v Registrar, Indian and Northern Affairs Canada and others. 2007 B.C.S.C. 827 (2007).

McIvor v Canada Registrar, Indian and Northern Affairs, 2009 B.C.C.A. 153 (2009).

Meera Dhungana on behalf of FWLD v HMG, Ministry of Law and Justice, Writ No. 3392, 2052, Decision No. 6013/2059, NKP 2059 Vol. 6, p. 462 (1995).

Meera Dhungana on behalf of FWLD v HMG, Ministry of Parliamentary Affairs, Council of Ministers, Ministry of Law and Justice, Parliament, Writ No. 55/2058, Supreme Court Bulletin 2058 (2002), Vol.5, p. 129 (2001–2002).

Paulina del Carmen Ramírez Jacinto v Mexico, Case No. 161–02, Report No. 21/07, Inter-Am. C.H.R., OEA/Ser.L/V/II.130 Doc. 22, rev. 1 (2007).

Prosecutor v Akayesu, ICTR, Case No. ICTR-96-4-1, Trial Chamber, Amended Indictment Counts 1, 2, 13–15 (June 1997).

——. ICTR, Case No. ICTR-96-4-A, Appeal Chamber, Appeal Judgment (1 June 2001).

——. ICTR, Case No. ICTR-96-4-T, Trial Chamber I, Judgment (2 September 1998).

Prosecutor v Anto Furundžija, ICTY, Case No. IT-95-17/1-T, Trial Chamber II, Judgment (10 December 1998).

Prosecutor v Brima, et al. ("AFRC Case"), SCSL, SCSL-2004-16-A, Appeals Chamber, Appeal Judgment (22 Feb. 2008).

Prosecutor v Delalic, ICTY, Case No. IT-96-21-T, Trial Chamber, Judgment (16 November 1998).

Prosecutor v Dragoljub Kunarac, et al., ICTY, Case No. IT-96-23-T & IT-96-23/1-T, Trial Chamber II, Judgment (22 February 2001).

——. ICTY, Case No. IT-96-23 & IT-96-23/1-A, Appeals Chambers, Appeal Judgment (12 June 2002).

Prosecutor v Duško Tadić, ICTY, Case No. IT-94-1-A, Appeals Chamber, Appeal Judgment (15 July 1999).

——. ICTY, Case No. IT-94-1-T, Trial Chamber II, Opinion and Judgment (7 May 1997).

——. ICTY, Case No. IT-95-17/1-A, Appeals Chambers, Appeal Judgment (21 July 2000).

Prosecutor v Radislav Krstic, ICTY, Case No. IT-98-33-T, Trial Chamber, Trial Judgment (2 August 2001).

Prosecutor v Sylvestre Gacumbitsi, ICTR, Case No. ICTR-2001-64-T, Trial Chamber III, Judgment (17 June 2004).

R v Bourne [1939] 1 KB 687 (1938).

R v R [1992] 1 A.C. 599 (1991).

Şahide Goekce (deceased) v Austria, Communication No. 5/2005, CEDAW Comm., CEDAW/C/39/D/6/2005 (2007).

Sandra Lovelace v Canada, Communication No. R.6/24, UN GAOR, 36th Ses., Supp. No. 40 A/36/40 p.166 (1981).

Sylvestre Gacumbitsi v The Prosecutor, ICTR, Case No. ICTR-2001-64-A, Appeal Chamber, Appeal Judgment (7 July 2006).

Toonen v Australia, United Nations Human Rights Committee, Communication CCPR/C/50/D/488/1992 (4 April 1994).

Uganda Association of Women Lawyers and others v the Attorney General, Constitutional Petition No. 2/2003 [2004] UGCC 1 (10 March 2004).

Velez and others v Novartis Pharmaceuticals, Novartis Corporation, and Ebeling, No. 04, Civ. 9194, S.D.N.Y. (31 July 2007).

References

Vertido v The Philippines, Communication No. 18/2008, CEDAW Comm., CEDAW/C/46/D/18/2008 (2010).

Vishaka and others v State of Rajasthan and others, A.I.R. 1997 S.C. 3011 (1997).

White v White [2000] 2 FLR 981 (2000).

Wilson and others v North Cumbria Acute NHS Trust (Settled December 2005).

Legislation

Arbitration Act. The United Kingdom of Great Britain and Northern Ireland. 1996.

Bill C-31: An Act to Amend the Indian Act. Canada. 17 April 1985.

Criminal Law Amendment Act. The Republic of Austria. 2006.

Decree No. 4444 on the Regulation of Certain Reproductive Health Services. The Republic of Colombia. 13 December 2006.

Domestic Violence (Crime Punishment) Act 2066. The Federal Democratic Republic of Nepal. 2009.

Homicide Act. Chapter 11, regional 5 & 6, Eliz. 2. The United Kingdom of Great Britain and Northern Ireland. 21 March 1957.

The Labour Code of The Socialist Republic Of Viet Nam and Implementation Documents. The Socialist Republic of Viet Nam. 1994.

Law Number 23 of Year 2004 Regarding Elimination of Violence in Household. The Republic of Indonesia. 2004.

Maria da Penha Law, No. 11.340. The Federative Republic of Brazil. 7 August 2006.

Organic Act 1/2004 of 28 December on Integrated Protection Measures Against Gender Violence. The Kingdom of Spain. 29 December 2004.

Promulgation of Combating of Domestic Violence Act, Act No. 4 of 2003. The Republic of Namibia. 24 June 2003.

Protection Against Domestic Violence Act, No. 27 of 2005. The Republic of Bulgaria. 29 March 2005.

The Protection of Women Against Sexual Harassment at Workplace Bill. The Republic of India. 2007.

Sexual Offences Act, No. 3 of 2003. The Kingdom of Lesotho. 22 April 2003.

Technical Norms on Care for Voluntary Termination of Pregnancy. The Republic of Colombia. December 2006.